# PAPER SOLDIERS

# PAPER SOLDIERS

## The American Press and the Vietnam War

★

C L A R E N C E   R.   W Y A T T

W·W·NORTON & COMPANY
*New York* · *London*

Printed in the United States of America

First Edition

The text of this book is composed in Sabon,
with the display set in Sabon
Composition and Manufacturing by
The Haddon Craftsmen, Inc.
Book design by Jacques Chazaud

Library of Congress Cataloging-in-Publication Data

Wyatt, Clarence.
Paper soldiers: the American press and the Vietnam War / by Clarence Wyatt.
p.   cm.
Includes bibliographical references and index.
1. Vietnamese Conflict, 1961–1975—Press coverage. 2. Vietnamese Conflict,
1961–1975—United States. 3. Press and politics—United States. 4. United
States—Politics and government—1963–1969. I. Title.
DS559.46.W93   1993
959.704'38—dc20        92-31577

ISBN 0-393-03061-X

W. W. Norton & Company, Inc., 500 Fifth Avenue, New York, N.Y. 10110
W. W. Norton & Company Ltd., 10 Coptic Street, London WC1A 1PU

1 2 3 4 5 6 7 8 9 0

# Contents

# Preface

Seventeen years after the collapse of the United States' effort in Vietnam, the American press's role in the war and its outcome remains an open and controversial subject.

For over twenty years, all have agreed on one point—the press was a major factor in the United States' failure in Vietnam. On the one hand, the press has been regarded by some as a savior that, through its aggressive and adversarial relationship toward the governments and militaries of the United States and South Vietnam, pulled aside the veil of official deception, making it possible for the American people in righteous wrath to bring the war to an end. Conversely, the press has been called a villain, one inspired by political and ideological biases to misrepresent the nature and the progress of the war, thus leading the American people to turn their backs on a "noble cause."

Is either of these two views accurate? Both are based on a belief that the press was a powerful adversary of the government and the military. However, research over the past few years has indicated that such a belief is misplaced. Content analyses of newspaper and television coverage show that, more often than not, the press reported official information, statements, and views with relatively little dissent.

Although this research weakens previous explanations for the press's role, it offers no other means for explaining what the press did or did not do. There is a need not merely to take a look at the coverage, but also to make a thorough analysis of how that coverage came to be, of the way the American press worked in Vietnam.

Such an understanding is important for a variety of reasons. First, we need to know how the press functioned if we are to understand fully what happened in Vietnam, and why. Second, this experience has much to tell us about American foreign and military policy. What effect, if any, does the press have on these policies? How can the press act responsibly in such matters? Should it be concerned with questions of "responsibility" for the conduct of American diplomacy? How does the press relate to the government and the military? Where does the American public fit?

Finally, and most importantly, the role of the press during the Vietnam War has significance for our political culture. Since the end of World War II, nuclear weapons and the Cold War have concentrated power over American foreign affairs and national security in the hands of the Executive Branch. An important element in the exercise of that power has been official control of information. Over the last forty years or so, the inclination and the ability of the Executive Branch to exercise such control have grown mightily. The Vietnam War is a prime case study of this development. How has the press reacted? What effect does this have on the American system of government? How will all this change now that the Cold War is over?

This book doesn't pretend to answer all of these and other important, related questions. But it at least hopes to provide a beginning point from which others may lead us to a better understanding of the role of the press in Vietnam and, through that, to a better understanding of American journalism, politics, and diplomacy.

# PAPER SOLDIERS

CHINA

Mekong

Lao Cai

Lai Chau

• Dienbienphu

Hong (Red)

Da (Black)

Viet Tri

HANOI

Hoa Binh

Nam Dinh

Haiphong

N O R T H   V I E T N A M

Luang Prabang

*Plain of Jars*

Thanh Hoa

*Gulf*

*of*

*Tonkin*

HAINAN

L A O S

Mekong

VIENTIANE

Vinh

Dong Hoi

T H A I L A N D

Savannakhét

Xé  *Banghiang*

Quang Tri

Khe Sanh

Hue

Danang (Tourane)

Mun

Saravan •

Pakse

*Tonle Kong*

• Ban Chavan

Dac To

Kontum

• Pleiku

S O U T H   V I E T N A M

BANGKOK

C A M B O D I A

*Tonle San*

Lomphat

*Tonle Srepok*

*Central Highlands*

Song Ba

Qui Nhon

Battambang •

*Tonle Sap*

Senmonorom

Krong

Ban Me Thuot

Nha Trang

Cam Ranh

*Gulf*

*of*

*Thailand*

Kompong Cham

Snuol

Mimot

Suong •

PHNOM PENH

Takeo •

Banam

Svay Rieng

Da Lat

Gia Dinh

Cholon

Bien Hoa

SAIGON

Rac Gia

*Mekong*

Vung Tau

*Mekong River  Delta*

S O U T H   C H I N A   S E A

VIETNAM

Con Son

0                           300 km

0                           300 miles

Chazaud

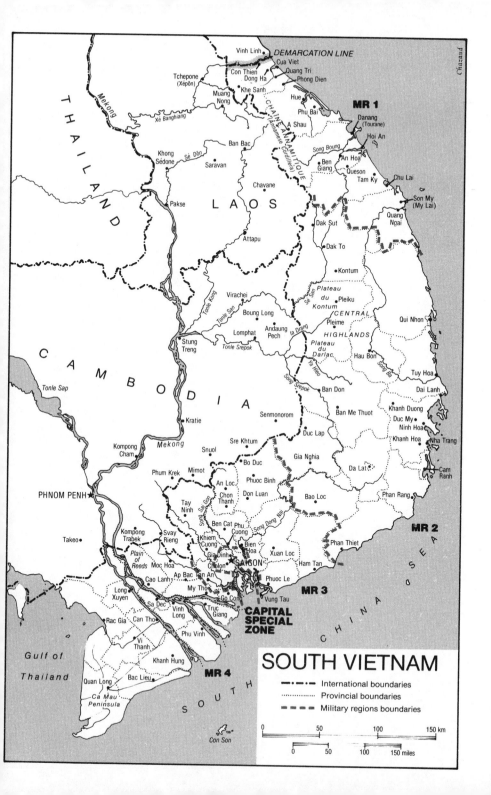

SOUTH VIETNAM

# 1

# A Different Kind of World

## The Cold War and Secret Government

THE RUBBLE NEAR ground zero was still hot, the radioactive dust still drifted in the summer winds of the North Pacific, when the United States government began figuring out how to live with the atomic genie uncorked at Hiroshima and Nagasaki. Over the succeeding months, the first chill breezes of the Cold War blew across these deliberations, adding urgency to the need to control the atomic "secret."

In September 1945, less than three weeks after the bombings, bills were introduced in Congress to establish a system of controls over atomic energy and weapons. On August 1, 1946, legislation sponsored by Connecticut Senator Brien McMahon, chairman of the Senate's Special Atomic Energy Committee, was signed into law. The McMahon Act, among other steps, mandated a strict secrecy over atomic research, at the time "the most rigorous control ever attempted in a democracy."[1]

In the very week when American leaders began debating the future of the weapon that had ended the Japanese war, a revolutionary movement in Vietnam acted to seize independence from the ashes of Japan's defeat.

Ho Chi Minh and other veterans of the Viet Nam Doc Lap Dong Minh Hoi, or Vietminh, had since 1941 struggled first against the French and then, through 1945, against the Japanese. When the Japanese Empire collapsed in August 1945, returning Vietnam to the control of a vastly weakened France, the Vietminh proclaimed the Democratic Republic of Vietnam on September 2, 1945. Few paid much attention to their proclamation. While the U.S. looked on in beneficent neutrality, the French reasserted their colonial hegemony in Indochina. By the end of 1946, a full-fledged war for Vietnamese independence was under way.[2]

They are curious bedfellows, these two—the Bomb and Vietnam—and yet together they symbolize the dawn of a different kind of world. For the first time, the very existence of American society was felt to be in imminent danger. To ensure the survival of the nation, the government took on vast new powers, including the power to declare secret large bodies of information and to punish severely violations of that secrecy. The McMahon Act marked the beginning of a new attitude on the part of the United States government toward information and the public's right to it.

For its part, the war in Vietnam signaled the beginning of the end of the colonial era, a tremendous realignment of power and interests in the world that would become a major theatre in the Cold War. Moved first by a need to hold France in an anti-Soviet front and later by a desire to support an anticommunist regime in the South, the United States would be drawn deeper and deeper into the Vietnam War.

Over the following years, these two developments—the American government's hardening attitude toward what it would and would not tell its own people, and its equally solid resolve to oppose the spread of communism in Indochina—would combine to create a crisis of confidence in the American system of government more severe than any since the Civil War.

## The New Secrecy

The federal government has been keeping secrets since the early days of the Republic, when Congress passed, in 1789, a "housekeeping statute," authorizing the head of each department to "prescribe regulations, not inconsistent with the law, for the custody, use, and preservation of records, papers, and property."[3] For most of the nation's history, however, the withholding of information was not a great concern, because the activity of the government was so limited.

But as the power of the federal government grew during the 1930s and 1940s, so did the perceived need and the power to limit the circulation of various types of information. An obvious concern was military information during World War II. There was relatively little dispute between the press and the United States military over such information. In the field, relations between the press and the military were fairly good. The reporters believed in the cause for which the nation was fighting and commanders took reporters into their confidence and accommodated their professional needs. A system of battlefield censorship restricted the release of information from the front. In Washington, senior members of the government and the military routinely held off-the-record briefings, their integrity rarely violated. General George C. Marshall, army chief of staff during World War II, held such briefings regularly for Washington bureau chiefs. Speaking of the press, Marshall said, "They gave me a very straight deal. I had no complaint to make at all. I knew who the people were and I had the feeling that I could trust them. They controlled themselves."[4]

The entire nature of secrecy within the federal government, and particularly in the Executive Branch, underwent a fundamental change with the advent of the Atomic Age and the Cold War. As fears intensified with Soviet rumblings in Eastern Europe and Berlin, Mao's triumph in China, war in Korea, and spy scares, loyalty oaths, and McCarthyism at home, so too did the perceived need for a secrecy never before seen in American government. Under Presidents Truman and Eisenhower, the federal government's ability and inclination to restrict information grew astronomically.

The McMahon Act, "an unprecedented attempt at statutory definition of one entire area of information made subject to stronger government control," had already become law.[5] President Truman enlarged the reach of government secrecy even further in September 1951 through Executive Order 10-290, which extended to hundreds of Executive Branch employees the authority to restrict any document by declaring it "confidential," "secret," or "top secret," and forbade disclosure of any such information by a federal employee.[6] The order, one commentator said, "gave just about everybody in Washington, including janitors, the right to withhold news in the sacred name of national security."[7]

The McMahon Act and especially Executive Order 10-290 represented in scope and philosophy a radical change from pre–Cold War information policies. The press quickly and loudly pointed out the dangers of such policies, citing their potential misuse to cover up political embarrassments rather than true national-security matters. The Associated Press Managing Editors Association called Truman's order "censorship at the source," and *U.S. News and World Report* editor David Lawrence, who called the order "our own 'iron curtain,'" forecast the chilling effect such a policy would have on public discourse. "Government employees will choose to remain silent," Lawrence said. "About the only information that the public may get officially will be that which the President and his political advisers deem good for the Administration's political fortunes."[8]

The issue continued to grow under the Eisenhower Administration. In November 1953, Eisenhower signed Executive Order 10-501, which was, with various modifications, to form the basis of Executive Branch information policy for the rest of the decade. The order attempted to soften the Truman policy by removing the authority to classify from a handful of agencies and, for several other agencies, limited that power to the department head. The order was intended, at least in part, to shore up the administration's already sagging relations with the press, but it left the broad sweep of the Truman order basically intact.

In reality, Executive Order 10-501 expanded the opportunities for the withholding of information. The order eliminated the "confidential" classification, the lowest of the three existing categories, but also created some thirty new labels, including NOT FOR PUBLIC INSPECTION, FOR AIR FORCE EYES ONLY, and ADMINISTRATIVELY CONFIDENTIAL." As V. M. Newton, chairman of the national journalism fraternity Sigma Delta Chi's Freedom of Information Committee, said, "the Department of Defense [has] started stamping 'For official use only' on almost everything in the Pentagon except the toilet tissue."[9]

This trend continued for the duration of the Eisenhower Administration. Restrictions on information increased, and criticism of them grew apace, creating an atmosphere of bitterness and distrust among the Eisenhower Administration, the Congress, and the press. Representative John Moss, Democrat from California and chair of the Government Information Subcommittee of the House Government

Operations Committee, declared that Eisenhower's information policies would "inevitably destroy the very keystone of American government—the principle that the operation of government must endure the crucible of public debate." Sigma Delta Chi declared that
"The imposition of secrecy on the broad and undefined ground of
'Executive privilege' reached a new peak . . . posing the most serious
threat to the theory of open government so far in the United States'
history." Even publications normally supportive of Eisenhower became critical on this issue. A *Saturday Evening Post* editorial
bemoaned the "paper curtain . . . drawn around increasing areas of
federal activity."[10]

The Eisenhower years had, thus far, seen a federal government
increasing both its concern for secrecy and its aggressiveness in maintaining that secrecy. These developments alarmed Congress and the
press. As Eisenhower entered his last full year as president, the stage
was set for one more scene which would dramatically illuminate this
complex issue.

## The U-2 Incident

May 1, 1960, promised to be like many another day Francis Gary
Powers had spent over the last four years. Powers, a thirty-year-old
Kentuckian, ostensibly flew weather-research missions for Lockheed
under contract to the National Aeronautics and Space Administration and the Air Force. But the actual mission of Powers and his
plane, a Lockheed U-2, was to conduct photoreconnaissance of the
Soviet Union for his real employer, the Central Intelligence Agency,
which had been carrying out missions like Powers' since 1956.

But May 1, 1960, was not routine. High over the city of Sverdlovsk, some twelve hundred miles inside the Soviet Union, something
exploded near Powers. The explosion damaged, but didn't destroy,
his plane and forced him to bail out without setting off the U-2's
self-destruct mechanism. Powers and his plane were soon in the
midst of some confused Russian farmers, and the governments of the
Soviet Union and the United States were in the midst of a serious
crisis.[11]

Officials at NASA and the CIA had previously devised a cover
story for the loss of a U-2. When it became clear that Powers and his

plane were missing, NASA, in consultation with the CIA and with Eisenhower's personal approval, announced on May 3 that "A NASA U-2 research airplane, being flown in Turkey on a joint NASA-USAF Air Weather Service mission, apparently went down in the Lake Van, Turkey, area at about 9:00 A.M. (3:00 A.M. E.D.T.), Sunday, May 1."[12]

The report drew little public attention until May 5, when Soviet Premier Nikita Khrushchev startled his audience at the opening session of the Supreme Soviet with the news that an American plane had been shot down over "the interior of the Soviet land." He charged the United States with "aggressive provocations aimed at wrecking" the Big Four summit conference scheduled for less than two weeks hence in Paris.[13]

Khrushchev did not disclose that the plane and the pilot had survived, or that Soviet technicians were busy developing the film from the U-2's sophisticated 70mm cameras.[14] Eisenhower "voiced serious doubts" about an immediate response, believing that "we should now remain silent until we knew what Khrushchev's follow-up was to be." But his advisers believed that a failure to make an immediate response would be taken as a tacit admission of the truth of the Soviet claims. Swayed by their reasoning and, more important, believing that there was no chance that pilot or plane had survived as evidence, Eisenhower instructed the State Department to release a statement consistent with that original NASA-CIA story.[15]

Deputy Secretary of State Douglas Dillon later recalled that the CIA and the State Department were "trying to draft a statement as to what we were going to say about this damn thing. We were having a *hell* of a time."[16] On May 7, both NASA and the State Department publicly stuck to the "weather-flight" story.

From the beginning of the crisis, American officials had two goals: to maintain the U-2 program's cover and to shelter Eisenhower from the incident's fallout. The first goal quickly went up in smoke. Immediately after the announcements by NASA and State, Khrushchev deftly sprung the trap into which the Eisenhower Administration had so obligingly jumped. Again speaking before the Supreme Soviet, an immensely pleased premier reported that the plane had been brought down deep in the Soviet Union and that "we have parts of the plane and we also have the pilot, who is quite alive and kicking." Khrushchev, waving photographs he claimed were taken by the U-2's cameras, also stated that Powers had admitted the purpose of his mission.[17] On the same day in which a New York Times editorial accused the leader of the Soviet Union of having "misrepresented the facts" of the incident, the leaders of the United States were caught, clearly and unequivocally, lying to the American people.[18]

Secretary of State Christian Herter realized that the first goal was now impossible, but still hoped to protect the president. Herter proposed releasing a statement denying "authorization for any such flights as those described by Mr. Khrushchev," but conceding "that in endeavoring to obtain information now concealed behind the Iron Curtain a flight over Soviet territory was probably undertaken by an unarmed civilian U-2 plane."[19]

Eisenhower had been reluctant to release such a statement, fearing that it would reinforce a public perception that he was removed from the management of even important details of his administration. Once again, his instincts were correct. Harry Truman said that "the President of the United States ought not to admit that he doesn't know what is going on." Senator Mike Mansfield asked, "Can any agency without the authority of the responsible political leaders assume the right to probe along a dangerous border and thus endanger the policies of the President?" Bothered by the implication that he did not have control of the presidency, Eisenhower decided that he must break tradition and assume public responsibility for his nation's spying. In a May 9 statement, he acknowledged that flights such as Powers' took place as part of a presidential directive "to gather by every possible means the information required to protect the United States and the free world from surprise attack. . . ." But even this *mea culpa* did not reveal the full truth, for Eisenhower did not want it known that he had been personally involved in the planning and approval of each flight almost since the program's inception.[20]

Criticism of the incident, however, tended to deal not with the fact that the government had lied to most of the Congress, to the press, and to the American people, but that it had not lied skillfully and convincingly enough.

Such was the major focus of the two congressional inquiries into the affair. Washington Democratic Senator Henry M. Jackson's Subcommittee on National Policy Machinery and the Senate Foreign Relations Committee not only failed to criticize the act of lying, they actually chided Eisenhower for eventually coming clean. Jackson's report concluded that "The golden word of intelligence is silence. Public revelation of sensitive intelligence is never a harmless act. It jeopardizes the normal conduct of foreign relations and compromises the sources of vital intelligence." The Foreign Relations Committee's chairman, Democrat J. William Fulbright of Arkansas, stated the point even more forcefully. The gravest mistake, Fulbright felt, "was made when the President assumed responsibility for the flight." It would have been better for Eisenhower to claim that the plane had been "stolen by the Russians," Fulbright said on an earlier occasion, than to admit the nature of the flight and his own responsibility.[21]

Editorial opinion on the incident covered the spectrum,[22] but, like Congress, the press focused most of its criticism on the incident's effect on the summit and on the lack of presidential control rather than on government dissembling. A *Baltimore Sun* editorial summed up the reaction fairly well when it contended that "To take exceptional chances of getting caught at the wrong time, and thus to be found out in flimsy fiction—to take exceptional chances, that is, without having determined in advance what to say if the essay should fail—is not good intelligence operation." Again, it seemed that what disturbed editors the most was not lying, but inept lying.[23]

This reaction by the press is even more interesting when one understands that a number of the nation's most important journalists and news organizations had been aware for years of the existence and the true mission of the U-2 flights. In the summer of 1958, *New York Times* military affairs correspondent Hanson Baldwin told Robert Amory, the CIA official in charge of the U-2 program, that he had discovered the U-2's real mission and was going to publish the story. "*Jesus, Hanson, No!*," exclaimed Amory. Allen Dulles appealed successfully to *Times* publisher Arthur Hays Sulzberger to hold Baldwin's story. By the spring of 1960, several more journalists had learned of the U-2 but did not reveal it, "because," as Chalmers Roberts of the *Washington Post* said, "we knew the United States very much needed to discover the secrets of Soviet missilery."[24]

To be sure, there was some protest from the press concerning the administration's deception. *The New Republic* complained of how "The President taxes our credulity" and blasted White House Press Secretary James Hagerty for saying that the main lesson of the U-2 affair was "Don't get caught." "What a canon for public conduct!" *The New Republic* cried. "What a standard for an Administration addicted to discourse about morality!" *The Nation* criticized the mainstream press for its collective conclusion that "It was just too bad that we got caught." If this reflected public opinion, *The Nation* said, "we must conclude that fifteen years of the cold war have indeed conditioned us to . . . a 'peculiar moral climate.' "[25]

## A Different Kind of World

Though relatively brief, the U-2 crisis both embodied many of the developments during the Truman and Eisenhower years and served as a point of departure for subsequent administrations concerning national-security information and press relations.

First, the incident illustrated dramatically the breadth and power of the national-security mentality and the new secrecy which sprang from it. In his first public statement on the U-2, President Eisenhower justified the flights by pointing to a Soviet "fetish for secrecy" which shielded preparations for war.[26]

Yet a legitimate American concern for security born in the chaos of the late 1940s had grown, feeding on a diet of fear and arrogance, into an obsession which threatened to consume the very rights and privileges it was devised to preserve. From whom was the cover story about the U-2 designed to keep the truth? Key members of Congress, the leaders of allied nations providing bases for the U-2, important news organizations, and even the Soviets had known about the flights from their beginning on July 4, 1956.[27]

No, once the plane was down, the attempt to maintain the fiction surrounding it had only one target—the American people—and only one purpose—to shield the Eisenhower Administration and the Republican Party from political embarrassment. This confusion of true national interest and mere political expediency would become one of the central social and political issues of the next three decades.

Second, the government's success in withstanding that embarrassment showed just how deeply American society had bought into the national-security mentality and the new secrecy. The opposition party, the Congress, the press, and the public instinctively rallied to the commander-in-chief in a time of crisis. Once again, criticism, when it came, pointed more at the ineptness of the deception than at the deception itself.[28]

And, third, the U-2 incident offered some clear lessons concerning government information and press relations in the age of the new secrecy. As the legitimate security concerns of the postwar era hardened into the national-security mentality, that policy began to change. A fear that the disclosure of vital information could provide material assistance to an enemy cast an ever broader and heavier shroud over the activities of the government. A sort of arrogance soon followed, based on the belief that the value of protection, of secrecy, automatically took precedence over everything else.

Together, this fear and this arrogance pulled the shroud over more and more remote corners of what had formerly been considered the public's business. Now the old policy of inclusion was being replaced by one based on exclusion of the press and the people. The government did not take the press into its confidence, but regarded it as another antagonist, to be treated with denial and deception. But so powerful was the national-security mentality that journalists, though they might protest, generally did not balk. The times, not the *Times,* had set the rules, and by those rules the game would be played.

And, finally, comes the question of the process by which information was released. The major lesson of the whole affair, in the eyes of Senate investigators and press commentators, was the need for greater coordination and control over the issuance of statements on such matters to the press and public. This notion of confusion and lack of coordination and control should not, however, be carried too far. The Eisenhower Administration's success in centralizing the control of national-security information was evident in the U-2 incident. *Every* statement during the crisis, from NASA's first release on May 3 to the "confession" on May 9 was *personally* approved by Eisenhower. Eisenhower himself was closer to recognizing the administration's major mistake. "The biggest error we made was, of course, in the issuance of a premature and erroneous cover story. Allowing myself to be persuaded on this score is my principal personal regret—except for the U-2 failure itself—regarding the whole affair."[29]

But for both the government and the people, the problem was more than one of a failed process. For the government, the problem was one of basing its actions on faulty and arrogant assumptions about what the Soviet Union could and would do about the U-2. For the American people, the problem was that its government chose to deceive—not accidentally, but calculatedly and deliberately.

As the development of the new secrecy during the 1950s was illustrated in the U-2 affair, other events were also moving toward turning points. In the week during which Eisenhower muddled out of the U-2 crisis, John Kennedy beat Hubert Humphrey in the West Virginia Democratic presidential primary, establishing himself as a national candidate and moving significantly closer to his eventual nomination and narrow victory over Richard Nixon. Just days before the Senate Foreign Relations Committee's hearings on the U-2, a National Security Council meeting worried about how to react to the sharp increase in communist activity in South Vietnam. How would John Kennedy, with his promise of youth and a New Frontier, handle the legacy left to him by his predecessors?

# 2

# Managing the News

*The Press, Public Information,
and Foreign Policy in
the Kennedy Years*

A LITTLE AFTER 6:00 P.M., Eastern Standard Time, on the evening of
January 25, 1961, he stepped onto the stage and into the view of
twenty million Americans watching on live television. Squinting just
for a moment as his eyes adjusted to the bright lights, "a study in
bronze skin and sandy hair" worthy of the cover of *Esquire* or *Sports
Illustrated*, he smoothed his tie, smiled his disarming smile, and
began answering questions.[1] For the next half-hour or so, he informed them, he amused them, but most of all he charmed them.
Who was he? A star performer meeting his fans? A celebrity promot-
ing some new product?

Yes and no. He was indeed a star, and some of his most loyal fans
were in the room that evening. And without doubt he was selling a
new product. But the man in the spotlight was not a Hollywood
matinee idol or an all-star athlete. He was John Fitzgerald Kennedy,
thirty-fifth president of the United States.

John Kennedy's first formal press conference as president was
more than a just a showcase for himself and his brand-new administration, however. This gathering embodied the increasing ability of
the federal government, and particularly the White House, to control
information and manipulate the press. During his thousand days in
office, Kennedy would raise that control and manipulation to an art
form.

The presidential press conference had evolved from a fairly closed process at its beginning under Woodrow Wilson to a more open affair during the Eisenhower Administration. Wilson and his successor, Warren G. Harding, responded to oral questions but allowed themselves to be quoted directly only by special permission. Calvin Coolidge and Herbert Hoover required reporters to submit questions in writing and in advance.[2]

Under Franklin Roosevelt, Harry Truman, and Dwight Eisenhower, the news conference became much less formal and, generally, more cordial. Roosevelt gathered the fifty or so reporters covering the White House around his desk, whereas Truman took them along on brisk walks around or near the White House grounds. Eisenhower was the first president to allow himself to be quoted directly on a routine basis. He also provided verbatim transcripts of the sessions and, by the end of his second term, allowed them to be recorded and filmed for later broadcast.[3]

The new Kennedy Administration understood the critical importance of its first appearance before the press. *Candidate* Kennedy's relative youth and inexperience dogged him throughout the campaign, as many Americans wondered if he was ready for the fearful responsibilities of being president in the nuclear age. It was imperative to establish himself quickly in the American mind as *President* Kennedy, but without sacrificing the aura of youth and "vigah" that had allowed him to squeak past the Eisenhower gerontocracy and its heir apparent, Richard Nixon. The new president and his advisers astutely looked to the still-young medium of television. A televised press conference would, they hoped, show him as the man with the facts, the man in control—*as the president*—while also highlighting the wit, the charm, and the looks that had always been among his strongest assets in the public arena of politics.

To ensure the desired results, President Kennedy and his press secretary, Pierre Salinger, made three crucial changes from the Eisenhower-model press conference. First, the gathering would be moved from the Indian Treaty Room in the Executive Office Building, where reporters could see the president's every grimace and flinch, to the comparatively cavernous auditorium in the new State Department building, a venue much more suited to the requirements of television. Second, Salinger instructed the ladies and gentlemen of the press that they no longer need identify themselves and their employers when asking a question.[4] This was, ostensibly, intended to save time by cutting down on reporters' urge to grandstand, but its larger purpose was to keep attention focused on the one real star of the show.

But the third and by far the most important change was to schedule a *live* telecast in the early evening. This would allow a charismatic, handsome president to exploit television's drama and immediacy and to avoid the filter of the press. Here he was, Daniel in the lions' den, ready to stand or fall under the questioning of the press and the judgment of the people. President Kennedy took the press conference "all the way. . . . [E]veryone hears him say everything." Indeed, some knowledgeable commentators, fresh from eight years of fractured Eisenhower syntax, feared a slip of the presidential tongue on live television; James Reston called a live news conference "the goofiest idea since the hula hoop."[5]

Despite Reston's misgivings, the new forum was almost universally applauded. Some observers focused on the new sense of openness and accessibility the live broadcasts engendered. *New York Times* television critic Jack Gould wrote: "Any procedure that permits a closer liaison between the average citizen and Washington is surely desirable, and last night in the living room there was a feeling of participation that had not existed before."[6]

Others talked about the favorable impression made by Kennedy himself. "The first Presidential press conference has turned out to be a success," said the Louisville *Courier Journal*. "Mr. Kennedy was in perfect command of himself and the information with which a President's mind has to be stocked." "Steady, resolute . . . bold, unswerving," the *Philadelphia Inquirer* said of the president. Kennedy's style also won the blessing of the Congress's chief information watchdog, as Representative John Moss emerged from a meeting with Salinger hailing the prospect of a freer flow of government information under Kennedy.[7]

It was a virtuoso performance by Kennedy. The secrecy, the antagonism between press and president under Eisenhower had seemingly been left behind.

Yet other characteristics sat side by side with these qualities that won such praise, characteristics that, taken together, reveal more completely the Kennedy Administration's attitudes and policies toward public information and the press. Knowledge of and sensitivity to the demands of journalism also brought the ability to manipulate the press. A willingness to be available, to be subjected repeatedly to the seemingly sharp questioning of reporters, also marked the desire to make the candidate/president the central source of information and to make his impression of events and issues the defining one in the minds of the press and the public. Within the appearance of spontaneity and candor was a reality of carefully rehearsed contacts with reporters that could be used to distract or mislead the press from unpleasant facts.[8] The fresh hope for a new openness and honesty could very well give way to disappointment over a continued obsession with control of information. And because of the Kennedy Administration's sophistication and aggressiveness, that obsession was even more dangerous than before.

## "A Former Newspaperman Now in Politics"

The promise, symbolized by the first news conference, of a departure from the information policies of the Eisenhower years was the product of a determined and skillful effort. This promise was based in part on the new president's carefully cultivated image as a man of letters, an image especially compelling in contrast to the perception of President Eisenhower as something of an intellectual lightweight. Kennedy not only read books, "he wrote them," as one White House observer marveled. His Harvard undergraduate thesis, a study of pre–World War II Britain, was published as *Why England Slept,* and he won a Pulitzer Prize for *Profiles in Courage.*[9] And, as he and his aides often noted, President Kennedy had worked as a reporter in the Hearst organization for a brief period after the war. The National Press Club, in fact, made Kennedy a member shortly after his inauguration. "John F. Kennedy, a former newspaperman now in politics, was approved for membership" read the notice posted on the NPC's bulletin board.[10]

Kennedy's kinship with the press also sprang from his genuine respect for journalists, especially for the best among them. They were smart, literate, tough, practical men (and for the most part they *were* men), men used to life at the center of the action, kindred spirits to the men of the New Frontier. Kennedy developed particularly close relationships with several journalists:

- Arthur Krock, *New York Times* columnist who had covered every president since Wilson, was a longtime friend of Joseph P. Kennedy and was the person enlisted by the elder Kennedy in his effort to publish his son's Harvard thesis.
- Benjamin C. Bradlee, in 1960 the assistant manager of *Newsweek*'s Washington bureau and later editor of the *Washington Post*, and his wife, Tony, became fast friends with their new P Street neighbors upon returning to Washington in 1957.[11]
- Joseph Alsop, Washington-based Jeremiah of the syndicated columnists, had known Kennedy for several years. In the late 1940s, when he was stricken by Addison's disease, Kennedy found "a welcome retreat from problems" in Alsop's Dumbarton Road home, a place he continued to visit for private dinners and conversations even after becoming president. Indeed, the last stop in the new president's Inaugural Night celebration was for a nightcap at the Alsop home. Alsop revealed something of his feelings for the new president in a letter to Ted Sorensen, Kennedy's chief aide and speechwriter, just days after the election. Alsop wrote, "I can not recall any episode in my close to thirty years as a political observer that has ever stirred and excited me so much as this one. No other choice that our people have had to make in my time has ever seemed to me so absolutely decisive. . . . The truth is," Alsop concluded, "that as a newspaperman I have not congratulated more than three victors in all my years on the fringe of politics."[12]
- Probably no journalist was closer on a personal level to John Kennedy than Charles Bartlett, Washington correspondent for the *Chattanooga Times*. Bartlett and Kennedy had met before the latter's 1946 campaign for the House of Representatives, and Bartlett introduced the new congressman to a George Washington University student of proper background, Jacqueline Bouvier. Bartlett was closer to the president's inner circle of family and staff than any other journalist. "Charlie is a tomb of secrets," reflected a fellow White House reporter. "He knows so much more than he can ever tell."[13]

Kennedy's natural interest in and affinity for members of the press was not without calculation. A careful courting of the press played a major part in his rapid rise from a junior senator with a playboy image to a political figure of national consequence. Kennedy knew that, in a more literate, more mobile, less centralized political culture, the powers of machine politics and party identification, while still significant, were beginning to wane, and that new influences were rising to take their places. As David Halberstam explains, Kennedy "was, above all else, a marvelously contemporary politician with a shrewd sense of the sources of power . . . and by nature Kennedy had a grasp of the new balance. He knew television and print were becoming more important all the time and that was a source of strength for him: he could always sell himself to the media."[14] Thus, after he emerged from the Democratic debris of 1956 as one of the party's new lights, Kennedy and his staff began to raise press relations to the level of art. For Kennedy, reporters were an integral part of the political process, and he included planning for the press in both the strategy and tactics of his political ascent.

Kennedy's approach to Time-Life, Inc., illustrates much about his attitudes and policies toward the press during this run for the White House. Kennedy regarded *Time* and *Life,* ruled by the conservative, staunchly anticommunist and pro-Republican Henry Luce, as the most important news outlets in the country, the key to the nation's vast political center. So, in a campaign where "all reporters were equal . . . most equal of all was Hugh Sidey of *Time,"* who had nearly unlimited access to Kennedy and his staff. This was not without effect. *Time* supported Nixon, though less than enthusiastically, and Luce himself, on a personal level, preferred Kennedy to Nixon. "He seduces me," Luce said of Kennedy. "When I'm with him I feel like a whore."[15]

The candidate cultivated other reporters and news organizations in the same manner, if not with the same intensity. He and his staff knew the reporters, their backgrounds, their interests, and were sensitive to the imperatives of their jobs, the most fundamental of which was to get out of a story. The governing principle for Pierre Salinger was "to make the campaign as easy for the press to cover as possible." The campaign furnished the press with transportation, food, and lodging. Journalists were also given new conveniences, such as a two-way phone in the car immediately behind Kennedy's so that wire-service reporters could file running accounts of any outdoor appearance, and instant transcripts of the candidate's speeches furnished by an around-the-clock stenographic service.

But, above all, reporters were given access and information. The candidate and his advisers not only made themselves available to the press—"Kennedy would as soon have dismissed his copilot as have dismissed the rotating trio of pool reporters who rode his personal plane everywhere," wrote campaign chronicler Teddy White—but they did so cheerily and enthusiastically. By Election Day, the reporters covering the Kennedy campaign "had become his friends and, some of them, his most devoted admirers. When the bus or plane rolled or flew through the night, they sang songs of their own composition about Mr. Nixon and the Republicans in chorus with the Kennedy staff and felt that they, too, were marching like soldiers of the Lord to the New Frontier."[16]

But even as the new administration and much of the national news media basked in the warmth of mutual admiration, signs began to appear that little of fundamental consequence concerning the Executive's attitude toward information and press policies had changed. The primary goal of Kennedy's press and information policies was to establish a high degree of White House control over federal-government information, especially that involving national-security matters. As Salinger stated it, "one of the central issues of our time [is] how a democracy, constituted with the freedom of the United States, defends itself in a cold war situation against an enemy which can operate in secret."[17]

For Salinger, this problem was first brought to a head by the U-2 incident of May 1960. Determined not to suffer a similarly embarrassing episode, Kennedy's men moved quickly to draw the reins of Executive information tightly to themselves. Within a week of taking office, Salinger created an information-coordinating committee, consisting of the top public-affairs officials from key Executive departments and agencies, including State, Defense, Treasury, the CIA, and NASA.[18] The very next evening, at the press conference so widely praised as a breath of fresh air, Kennedy stated firmly that, although "I do not believe that the stamp national security should be put on mistakes of the Administration which do not involve the national security . . . I must say I do not hold the view that all matters and all information which is available to the Executive should be made available at all times."[19]

The true nature of Kennedy's information policies quickly became clear. On January 27, 1961, two American fliers, held by the Soviets since their RB-47 surveillance plane was shot down over the Barents Sea on July 1, 1960, returned to the United States but were prohibited from granting any interviews. On the same day, the White House began a campaign to control public statements by senior members of the armed forces. A speech by Air Force Chief of Staff General Thomas D. White was held up when the White House questioned two paragraphs. Chief of naval operations Admiral Arleigh A. Burke "appalled" the White House with a proposed speech critical of the Soviet Union. Burke was ordered to rewrite the speech almost completely. Official but unidentified sources said that both actions were part of a White House plan "to control severely all statements affecting foreign policy and security intelligence." Whereas some observers saw the restrictions as characteristic of any transition period, others noted that "the demands for even the most routine news information were more stringent than any they could recall."[20] The Kennedy White House also tried to clamp down on unauthorized (as opposed to authorized) leaks.[21] Investigative services within the Pentagon— and even, reporters claimed, the FBI—were used in attempts to chase down and chastise leakers.[22]

The administration also admitted a desire to use the press to spread false information. Defense Secretary Robert McNamara told a largely sympathetic Senate Armed Services Committee that he had already clamped down on the flow of military information "of bene-fit to our potential enemies," and would continue to do so. Referring to a particular weapon program, the secretary then went on to ask the committee: "Why should we tell the Russians that the Zeus developments may not be satisfactory? What we ought to be saying is that we have the most perfect anti-ICBM system that the human mind will ever devise." McNamara's information chief, Assistant Secretary of Defense for Public Affairs Arthur Sylvester, described the administration's efforts as an attempt to "wed the pen and the sword."[23]

Such a union caused alarm among many of the president's foes and friends. The Republican Party quickly and predictably fell upon information policy as a way to bash Kennedy. *Battle Line,* a GOP National Committee publication, set the tone in the first week of the administration by calling Salinger the "czar and mastermind" of a "papa-knows-best" news policy and claiming that Kennedy subordinates and Democratic officials could not speak "at least until the events in which they participated had been Salingerized."[24]

Though more restrained in their criticism, many journalists observed the same tendencies. Early in the spring of 1961, the American Society of Newspaper Editors (ASNE) Freedom of Information Committee, chaired by Eugene Pulliam of the *Indianapolis News,* criticized the president for failing to live up to his promise of greater freedom of information and cited the State and Defense departments as particular culprits. However, Pulliam, along with many other journalists, acknowledged the unprecedented accessibility of the president and senior administration officials to reporters. "No corner of the building seemed to be off limits," remembered Hugh Sidey. "On some days more reporters went into the White House offices to talk with staff members than did government workers who had come on federal matters."[25]

But in exchange for this access reporters opened themselves up to manipulation. Veteran reporters warned that such intimacy, particularly with the president, would dull their aggressiveness. James Reston said, "It is hard to go into that House . . . and not be impressed with it and the terrible burden that the President has to carry. How could you help but be sympathetic?" But "once you become sympathetic," Reston warned, "it becomes increasingly difficult to employ the critical faculties."[26] Such access also bred an increasing dependence on these sources. Before Kennedy, reporters "could count on guidance 'at the highest level' only on the rarest occasion"; under Kennedy, reporters "count on it almost weekly." This allowed the White House to control to a significant extent the amount and type of information that went out. For example, by giving a reporter a mass of information, much more than he or she could verify independently under deadline pressures, the administration could put its particular "spin" on stories. This access to the top also tended to make lower-level sources reluctant to talk, especially when what they had to say differed from the official line.[27]

The administration also used control of access to affect journalistic behavior. As one correspondent said, President Kennedy "had this marvelous gift of being absolutely frank, giving you the impression that he's telling you more than he should—and he very often did— and that you sometimes sort of looked over your shoulder whether anybody's listening and you said to yourself, 'My God, I can't tell anybody about this.' " Such information was heady stuff for reporters, editors, and readers, and journalists positioned themselves favorably. Otherwise, they could be treated to a dressing down by the president or one of his aides or, worse, frozen out altogether. Even the all-important Sidey fell victim to "a truly monumental display of Presidential anger" in 1961, when his article in *Time*'s June 30 issue criticized the appointment of General Maxwell Taylor as special presidential military adviser. "Shortly after the article appeared, *Time*'s White House man found himself suddenly friendless. Telephone calls would be placed and not returned; trusted sources would be 'out' or 'busy.' "[28]

So quickly and forcefully did the full nature of the new administration's press and information policies emerge that even administration friends expressed concern. Representative John Moss in early March publicly asked Kennedy to hold to his campaign promise of a freer flow of information. A month later, Moss warned the president that "The subcommittee will follow the same procedures we employed with the Republican Administration in an effort to win acceptance of the critical need for a fully informed people." Joe Alsop reminded Ted Sorensen that both Franklin Roosevelt and Harry Truman had rallied the country to great initiatives through their handling of information. "In both cases," Alsop said, "the secret was total accessibility of officials with action responsibility. They briefed the press. The press briefed the country. And then the needed climate of action was first created, and then maintained." Arthur M. Schlesinger, Jr., Pulitzer Prize–winning historian and special assistant to the president, warned his boss in March 1961 that "There is increasing concern among our friends in the press about the alleged failure of the administration to do an effective job of public information and instruction as it should and must." Schlesinger pressed for more contacts between reporters and top officials. "Obviously this is a difficult matter. One can't just open up the government to make Joe Alsop happy, but some kind of selective openness should be sought after."[29]

But "selective openness" was not the same as "total accessibility." Nor was the "climate of action" of the Kennedy era based on the same public awareness and understanding that were, according to Alsop, the product of FDR's and Truman's information practices. Instead, the Kennedy Administration attempted to create a façade of openness behind which it could pursue its national-security goals beyond the reach of the public. And while the new administration was still educating itself about Vietnam, it brought these attitudes to what would become its most vexing and dangerous foreign policy and public-information problem—Cuba.

## Cuba Libre—The Bay of Pigs and the Missile Crisis

When, after six and a half years of struggle, Fidel Castro and his guerrilla army displaced the decayed regime of Cuban dictator Fulgencio Batista in the first days of 1959, the people and government of the United States were not sure how to react. Batista was corrupt and brutally indifferent to the welfare of the Cuban people; Castro promised sweeping reform in the political, economic, and social structure of the country. Castro's support among the populace was strong, and his own ideological leanings were unclear even to American intelligence sources.[30] Journalists, scholars, and political figures—including former President Truman and Senator John Kennedy—praised Castro's triumph as, in Kennedy's words, a "part of the legacy of Bolivar."[31] But during the remainder of 1959 and on into 1960, the true nature of Castro's ideas and plans emerged. His top leadership was clearly communist; private businesses were being nationalized; the Soviet Union and the People's Republic of China extended moral and material support; and Castro began to express sympathy for "liberation movements" elsewhere in the hemisphere. "By early 1960," Eisenhower wrote, "there was no longer any doubt in the administration that 'something would have to be done'—the questions were what, when, and under what circumstances?"[32] Eisenhower approved a plan under which the CIA would secretly recruit, train, arm, and provide logistical support to anti-Castro Cuban exiles for an invasion of Cuba, the purpose of which was to inspire a popular uprising against the Castro regime. By the time of the 1960 elections, the Cuban exile army had been training for several months in the jungles of Guatemala. Once the new administration had taken office, a young president eager to solidify his anticommunist credentials and persuaded by the zeal of top intelligence and military advisers decided to go ahead with the operation on April 17, 1961.[33]

The invasion was an unmitigated failure. Within two days, all but a handful of the rebels were dead or captured, and a roundup of suspected dissidents within Cuba had begun.[34] Kennedy disavowed any American involvement. He began a speech to the ASNE on April 20 by stating that "The President of a great democracy such as ours and the editors of great newspapers such as yours owe a common obligation to the people—an obligation to present the facts, to present them with candor and to present them in perspective." "I have emphasized before," he continued, "that this was a struggle of Cuban patriots against a Cuban dictator. While we could not be expected to hide our sympathies, we made it repeatedly clear that the armed forces of this country would not intervene in any way."[35] Though this was true in a technical sense—American troops did not land on the beach at the Bay of Pigs—Kennedy clearly failed to fulfill his self-stated obligation to the American people.

Such denials did little for Kennedy's credibility, for, as *Time* publisher Bernhard M. Auer said of the planning for the operation, "rarely have supposedly secret preparations received so much advance notice."[36] The planning for the invasion and the CIA's involvement had been an open secret in Guatemala, where it was taking place, and in the Cuban exile community in Miami, since it began in the spring of 1960. As time passed, the operation became known to more than a few journalists and news organizations in the United States.

Not until activity leading up to the invasion increased in early 1961 did a handful of journalists pursue the story. Richard Dudman of the *St. Louis Post-Dispatch* and Paul Kennedy of *The New York Times* went to Guatemala, but their resulting stories failed to highlight American involvement and downplayed the potential for an actual military operation against Cuba. By this time, the *Washington Post,* the *Miami Herald, The Wall Street Journal, U.S. News and World Report,* and *Time* were running pieces on the coming invasion, and other reporters were working on the story.

Chalmers Roberts of the *Post,* Karl Meyer of *The New Republic,* and, especially, Tad Szulc of *The New York Times* began to dig further. Meyer had put together a comprehensive story on the CIA's involvement. Roberts had been briefed by President Kennedy himself. And Szulc, one of the country's top investigative reporters, with excellent contacts in Miami, Latin America, and the American intelligence community, had learned even fine details of the operation by the first week in April 1961.

But this work did not affect the invasion. Meyer's story, a draft of which had been shown to Arthur Schlesinger by *The New Republic*'s editor Gilbert Harrison, was killed at the president's request. *Post* publisher Philip Graham held back on Roberts' reports without such urging. Nor, despite the myth of urgent phone calls from the White House to the Times Building, did *Times* publisher Orville Dryfoos, editor Turner Catledge, and Washington bureau chief James Reston need presidential entreaties to water down the Szulc story that eventually ran on April 7.[37]

Kennedy's statement to Turner Catledge not long after the incident that everyone, including the president, would have been spared much grief if the *Times* had run Szulc's full story is often quoted as evidence of Kennedy's growing political maturity, of his grudging acknowledgment of the press's role as a check in the political and governmental process.[38] But much more indicative of the administration's true feelings are other statements and actions.

The Bay of Pigs episode illustrates a number of disturbing elements concerning the Kennedy Administration's conception of government information, the role of the press in foreign policy, and the public's right to know. Most disturbing is the conscious decision to shield the planning of the operation from the public's view. Kennedy justified the secrecy by claiming that to disclose the planning would have put the lives of the rebels in jeopardy. This ignored the fact that Castro had long before placed spies in the training camps in Guatemala and probably knew as many details of the invasion as did the CIA. Such justification makes sense only if one accepts the premise that the government had the right to plan and carry out such activities without the knowledge of the public—only if one thinks strictly within the closed circle of national-security logic. The Kennedy team knew that such an ill-conceived idea, one in clear violation of American treaty commitments, could not survive the light of day. This was— no more, no less—a conscious decision to circumvent the constitutional and political process designed to direct and limit the activity of the government.

Not only did the administration lie; Kennedy and his subordinates tried to make such deception and hypocrisy acceptable, even commendable and patriotic. This effort began just days after the invasion, with a speech by Kennedy to the American Newspaper Publishers Association (ANPA) in New York City.

"I want to talk to you about our common responsibilities in the face of a common danger," Kennedy began. "In time of war, the government and the press have customarily joined in an effort, based largely on self-discipline, to prevent unauthorized disclosures to the enemy. In times of clear and present danger, the courts have held that even the privileged rights of the First Amendment must yield to the public's need for national security."

Kennedy went on to describe his perception of the world. "Today no war has been declared—and however fierce the struggle may be, it may never be declared in the traditional fashion." Nevertheless, Kennedy pointed out, "our way of life is under attack. . . . We are opposed around the world by a monolithic and ruthless conspiracy that relies primarily on covert means for expanding its sphere of influence." Such a world "requires a change in outlook, a change in tactics, a change in mission by the government, by the people, by every businessman or labor leader and by every newspaper." "I am asking the members of the newspaper profession and the industry in this country to reexamine their own responsibilities—to consider the degree and nature of the present danger—and to heed the duty of self-restraint which that danger imposes on us all." He concluded, "Every newspaper now asks itself, with respect to every story: 'Is it news?' All I suggest is that you add the question: 'Is it in the interest of national security?' "[39]

The press responded with dismay and not a little defensiveness. Although many journalists and news organizations acknowledged that the Cold War presented special challenges to the press, most also pointed out the great ambiguity in the term "national security." Frank J. Starzel, general manager of the Associated Press, agreed that responsible publications would not knowingly release information damaging to the national interest, but pointed out that "the problem centers in distinguishing between that which might damage or jeopardize and that which does not." Journalists also called upon the government to fulfill its own obligation to handle information judiciously. "The real culprit," wrote the editors of the *Detroit Free Press,* "is the hodgepodge of Government in Washington, the thousands of bureaucrats who know a little portion of a secret and who clamor for the limelight by telling it. Other culprits are the higher officials who clamp censorship on stories which the public has a right to know, and thereby force good reporters to go behind their backs to get the news." Some papers also asserted the press's role as a check on the Government. The *St. Louis Post-Dispatch* believed that the voluntary restraint called for by Kennedy "would undermine the essential mission of the press, which is to inform, interpret, and criticize." The *Minneapolis Tribune* stated that, "If our Government acts foolishly, slothfully, or otherwise unwisely, we may find ourselves propelled into a global, nuclear war. The only way our citizens can keep an eye on their officials in this life-and-death issue is through alert, responsible news reporting."[40]

Two weeks after his speech, Kennedy met with a group of press leaders in the Oval Office. He began the meeting by asking the journalists if they agreed with the view that the United States was now "in the most critical period of its history." According to one of the participants, the group answered in unison: "No." "From there on," this participant said, "the discussion was academic." The group felt that no additional restraints concerning national-security matters were needed. Felix McKnight, editor of the *Dallas Times-Herald* and ASNE president, said, "Any responsible editor makes that news judgment every day." McKnight went on to say that only "a declaration of national emergency or something like that" would necessitate such additional controls or guidelines.[41]

James Reston embodied the response of the press as a group. Even before Kennedy's speech to the ANPA, Reston pointed out that an essential question posed by what he called "the Cuban fiasco" was "How can the United States compete effectively against the Communists in the black arts of subversion when it has to put up with a lot of nosey reporters who snoop out and publish every dirty trick they discover?" Reston admitted that in a Cold War world some covert "maneuvers are not always fit to print" and that government and press needed to think through "where the press' responsibility to speak begins in this kind of subversive warfare and where it ends."

But Reston also refuted attempts to blame the press for the failure at the Bay of Pigs. "Even if all the reporters had been drowned at dawn three weeks before the inglorious landings, the bearded legions in Havana and their Russian accomplices would not have been denied much information," for Castro had agents in the training camps themselves, and Cuba Radio was broadcasting stories about an imminent invasion. Though this was a supposedly hush-hush operation, said Reston, "it was about as secret as opening day at Yankee Stadium. In fact the only people who knew very little about what was happening . . . were the American people who were unknowingly picking up the tab and may yet have to redeem the promises to chase the bearded bully boy into the Caribbean."

In a later column, Reston turned his anger upon the news media. "The trouble with the press during the Cuban crisis was not that it said too much, but that it said too little. It knew what was going on about the landings. It knew that the U.S. Government was breaking its treaty commitments and placing the reputation of the United States in the hands of a poorly trained and squabbling band of refugees. The same press roared with indignation when Britain and France broke their treaty commitments to invade Suez, but it had very little to say about the morality, legality or practicality of the Cuban adventure when there was till time to stop it."[42]

The Bay of Pigs crisis revealed as much about the press's attitudes toward military- and foreign-policy information and the public's right to know as it did about the government's. First, the press's response throughout the incident showed the power that the Cold War/national-security mentality had over mainstream journalism. Even though the planning of the operation and the United States government's role in it were an open secret almost from the beginning, American journalism failed to pursue the story with any aggressiveness until the weeks immediately before the plan's execution. Even then the most detailed stories, those that had some potential to derail the operation, were either killed completely or watered down. In one case this was done at the behest of the White House. More troublesome were at least two instances when the publishers of the nation's most influential newspapers *on their own initiative* pulled or altered stories on the invasion.

There was also very little self-criticism on the part of the press. It pursued an important story too late with too little. It was deceived and made a party to deception. It consciously withheld, on its own and under government pressure, information to which the people had a right. Yet this at least questionable performance came in for almost no analysis. One of the rare instances was Reston's May 10, 1961, column, in which he said that the press should have done more, perhaps as much as anything a personal *mea culpa* for his role in diluting Szulc's story. Most often the press simply threw the issue back at the government and acknowledged no responsibility for either shielding or divulging information.

At the center of all this is a confusion, an uncertainty, on the part of the press concerning its relationship to the government and the public, in essence a confusion over its conception of itself. On the one hand, the press agreed with at least the core of Kennedy's assertion concerning Cold War circumstances. But, on the other hand, had these circumstances not been used repeatedly, first by Eisenhower, now by Kennedy, as excuses to lie to the press, in turn to use the press to lie to the American people, for purposes concerned at least as often with political power and self-preservation as true national security? The press wanted to be a responsible actor with the government in trying times, but was it to be treated responsibly as a fellow participant or was it to be manipulated as a tool? Could the press assist the president in a time of crisis and at the same time serve the right of the people to know of the activity of their government? How could the press determine when it should pursue and publish and when it should not? These are the questions that the Bay of Pigs brought to the forefront; these were the questions that still hung in the air unresolved months later, when Cuba would once again provide the arena for another crisis involving the government and the press.

The capture of the remnants of the CIA-trained expeditionary force on the beach of the Bay of Pigs was not the end of Cuba as a trouble spot for John Kennedy. The collapse of the operation left Kennedy embarrassed and defensive, both domestically and internationally. The continued existence of a communist regime just off the Florida coast was a particularly large stone in the craw of the Kennedy inner circle. Beginning late in the fall of 1961, the administration secretly launched Operation Mongoose, a series of covert and subversive actions designed at least to embarrass and weaken the Castro government and, if possible, to eliminate Castro through assassination.[43] These actions did not go unnoticed by Castro's chief patron. Whether to safeguard Cuba against the perceived threat of an American invasion, to redress, at least symbolically, the Soviet Union's disadvantage in nuclear weaponry, to bolster himself against hard-liners in the Soviet leadership, or because of some combination of these and other concerns, Khrushchev decided in the late spring or early summer of 1962 to place eighty launchers for medium- and intermediate-range missiles in Cuba. These weapons were able to reach most of the major urban, industrial, and military sites in the Eastern United States.[44]

Even though Khrushchev and his colleagues were attempting to place the facilities secretly so as to present Kennedy with a *fait accompli,* by September rumors were rife in the United States of a Soviet military buildup, including some sort of missile capability, in Cuba.[45] Kennedy deflected these stories, for not until October 15 did he have conclusive evidence that offensive missiles capable of delivering nuclear warheads to the United States were being installed in Cuba.[46]

The events following October 15 are familiar. The next morning, the president decided to keep knowledge of the evidence in the fewest possible hands and to maintain the appearance of normal routine. Later that morning, ExCom, the so-called Executive Committee of the National Security Council, met for the first time. This group would spend the remainder of the week, with and without Kennedy, judging new intelligence and formulating a response. By Friday, October 19, the group had settled on two options to present to the president: (1) begin with a blockade of Cuba to prevent shipment of additional weapons, attempt to convince Khrushchev to remove existing weapons and launchers, and pursue other military action only if necessary; (2) remove the missile sites through immediate air strikes, to be followed if need be by a full-scale invasion.

Early the next morning, Kennedy, campaigning in Chicago, canceled his remaining stops and returned to Washington. At a 2:30 meeting that afternoon, the decision was made to implement the first option and, at 7:00 P.M. the following Monday, the president informed the American people of the existence of the missile sites and of the planned American response. By Sunday the 28th, after tense encounters between Soviet freighters and American warships at sea and even tenser communications between Soviet and American officials, an agreement was reached by which the missiles and launchers would be dismantled and returned to the Soviet Union.[47]

Just as Khrushchev had hoped to complete the installation of the equipment in secret, Kennedy and his advisers hoped to maintain a wall of secrecy around their knowledge of Khrushchev's actions at least until a response had been decided upon and was being implemented. But just as Khrushchev was found out by American intelligence, Kennedy, despite Schlesinger's claim that "the secret had been superbly kept," was found out by the American press. By Saturday, October 20, despite the effort to maintain normal schedules, veteran watchers of the White House, State Department, and Pentagon knew that something was up. The next night, James Reston, by leading National Security Adviser McGeorge Bundy to believe he already had the full story, pieced together the main elements of the crisis, including the fact that it involved Soviet nuclear weapons. As Under-secretary of State George Ball said, "This town being what it is, I marveled that it should have taken Scotty Reston, of all people, four days to discover what was going on."[48]

In another sense, though, Schlesinger was right about a "superbly kept" secret, for, even though reporters were digging the story out, only the barest evidence of the speculation appeared in print. For example, Reston, almost immediately after talking with Bundy, received a call from Kennedy, who told him that he was going to address the nation the next evening and that he needed another day of secrecy in which to complete preparations for his response to the Soviet action. Kennedy then asked Reston to sit on the story for a day. Reston responded that he was sympathetic to the president's request but that he had to file his story and that his superiors in New York would decide on publication. Kennedy then called *Times* publisher Dryfoos, who agreed to hold Reston's copy.[49] Reston himself later said, "I have no doubt at all about that one. I think this was a case where military security was paramount, and I think we were right not to print it."[50]

Instead, it was other actions of the government before and after the president's announcement that once again stirred the embers of the press–public-information controversy. This latest flap between the news media and the Executive Branch fell into three main issues.

*The Right to Lie.*  The government made calculated use of the press as a conduit for false and misleading statements—"disinforma-tion," as it would later be known. This was to keep the Soviets guessing—guessing about just how far Kennedy would push the con-frontation.

Several such instances occurred before and after the president's speech on the 22nd, according to a chronology of "news-manage-ment control" compiled by the ASNE's Freedom of Information Committee. Kennedy's sudden "cold" is a well-known, and relatively harmless, example.[51] More troublesome was the Pentagon's October 20 denial of any knowledge of offensive weapons in Cuba or of the fact that any American military forces were on alert. The government's statements were clearly designed to mislead, for photographs of missile sites had been developed and analyzed on the 15th, and various military units, including the bombers of the Strategic Air Command, were being readied for action as early as Wednesday the 17th.

The government also dissembled in describing the naval quarantine. In a briefing immediately following Kennedy's speech, McNamara, according to the ASNE's chronology, "said that any ships that failed to observe the blockade would be shot out of the water." However, what was portrayed as an "airtight" blockade was in fact a "selective" one. Numerous ships were allowed to travel unimpeded to Cuba, not all the contacts made between United States Navy ships and Soviet and third-country vessels were reported, and at least some interceptions "apparently were staged, although the public was led to believe they were real."[52]

*"One Voice."*   During the emergency's first week, the president sought to keep information in the fewest possible hands. In the weeks that followed, he attempted to control as tightly as possible what information would be made public and who would release and comment upon it—"to have the Government speak with one voice," as he put it.[53]

He took several steps toward this end. First, the ExCom moved to make the news media as dependent upon official sources as possible by denying reporters access to ships implementing the quarantine or to the base at Guantánamo. The group also decided that, after the public announcement of the crisis, any information to be released about the situation would be coordinated by the Office of the Assistant Secretary of Defense for Public Affairs, headed by former *Newark News* correspondent Arthur Sylvester. Sylvester's office took control, holding at least two briefings a day, more during the height of the crisis, making a variety of Executive Branch and military personnel available to the press, and feeding to reporters a steady diet of carefully selected information.[54]

The president also centralized the release of information by trying to restrict unauthorized leaks from within State and Defense. (Authorized leaks, however, would continue to spring forth when they suited Kennedy's purposes.) New Pentagon rules required Defense personnel in Washington to report on the time and substance of

conversations with journalists by the end of the day when the encounter took place. This requirement was waived if a representative
of the public-affairs office was present during the interview. State
Department instructions were a little less specific, asking that the
name and employer of the journalist be reported along with the subject, but not a summary, of the discussion.[55]

Kennedy also tried to limit *what* information could be released.
On October 24, a White House statement listed twelve broad categories of information relating to intelligence data and methods and to
the disposition and capabilities of United States military forces. The
memo stated that "publication of such information is contrary to the
public interest," and concluded by urging editors and news directors
to seek the advice of the Pentagon when questions arose. "Such advice will be on an advisory basis and not considered finally bind-
ing. . . ."[56]

*"News as a Weapon."*    Not only did the president and his advisers work to control the flow of information during the missile crisis,
they also assertively defended that effort. During his first news conference following the emergency, Kennedy said he had "no apolo-
gies" for the secrecy maintained in the eight days between October 15
and October 22. "I don't think that there is any doubt that it would
have been a great mistake, and possibly a disaster, if this news had
been dribbled out" before the extent of the buildup was fully evaluated and a response had been determined. Nor did he apologize for
the efforts to coordinate all government statements after his speech,
noting the need to make sure that a consistent message was being
presented to the Soviets. Pierre Salinger, in a speech to the Women's
National Press Club, not only denied that the Kennedy Administration had manipulated information, but then accused the press of
being the manipulators. "Let me say we in Government are neither
stupid enough to believe we can fool you nor clever enough to do it if
we wanted to." In fact, it was only "at the desk of our newspapers'
city editors and managing editors and at the desks of our radio and
television news directors" that such manipulation could occur, said
Salinger, who then called for a "fundamental study" to determine if
journalists were acting in the public interest.[57]

Though a variety of officials defended information policies during
the missile crisis, Pentagon spokesman Arthur Sylvester attracted the

most attention. In the flush of relief and satisfaction following the crisis, Sylvester made two statements describing and defending the administration's use of news. To a group of Air Force public-affairs officers meeting in Las Vegas, Sylvester attributed much of the British Empire's former world dominance to its ability to control and manipulate information, and noted that the French and the Soviets had followed suit. But, said Sylvester, "I think we as a people have been slow to realize this. . . . But today in a cold war, the whole problem of information, how it is used and when it is used, when it is released becomes a very vital weapon," one that must be at the disposal of the president, and "must be in line with what he and his top advisors are doing." The next day, Sylvester repeated this view and defended its application during the missile crisis. "The results, in my opinion, justify the methods we used." Some weeks later, Sylvester stoked the controversy even more when, in response to a question, he told members of the New York chapter of Sigma Delta Chi that in such an emergency as the missile crisis the government had an inherent right "to lie to save itself."[58]

The boldness with which the administration defended its missile-crisis policies concerned journalists very nearly as much as the policies themselves and brought forward from the press a barrage of criticism.[59] So, in defense of its own legitimacy, the press responded loudly, accusing the administration of "news management."[60] "There is," editorialized *The New York Times*, ". . . no doubt that in time of crisis a sense of responsibility and restraint on the part of all public information media is imperative. . . . But to attempt to manage the news so that a free press should speak (in Sylvester's words) 'in one voice to your adversary' could be far more dangerous to the cause of freedom than the free play of dissent, than the fullest possible publication of the facts." *Commonweal* called administration policy as expressed by Sylvester "cynical and dangerous" and said that "It is one thing to remain silent in a crisis; it is quite another to justify a deliberate misleading or deception of the public." *The Nation* offered Sylvester "a kindly piece of advice . . . : 'If your job requires you to lie, go ahead, but don't talk about it so much. And don't lecture the press, because it knows quite as much about this moral dilemma as you do.' "[61]

Longtime Kennedy friend Joe Alsop, particularly concerned about the State and Defense directives regulating contacts between officials and reporters, communicated his fears directly to the president. In late November 1962, Alsop, in a private letter to Kennedy, pointed to the threat to open government such rules, enforced by "Arthur Sylvester's bun-faced minions," contained. Alsop believed that such openness was "the chief safeguard of the public interest," protecting the nation from what he saw as the danger of an increasingly passive government. The pressure to be "more active and bold . . . can only be created by national debate, and this is only possible, in turn, if the government is frustrated in its attempt to shove the great problems under the rug."[62]

Some journalists, though agreeing that problems did exist, cited other considerations. Many again looked to the Cold War. Walter Lippmann contended that deception was "a necessary part of the unpretty business of preparing for and carrying on wars, both hot and cold." Lester Markel, Sunday editor of *The New York Times,* felt strongly the urgency presented by Cold War conditions: "The question of how much [national-security] news . . . shall be released and when, must be left largely in the hands of the government." Other journalists blamed the press for not being more aggressive. Richard Horchler of the Cowles news organization saw in American society a "drift toward conformity, orthodoxy, the surrender of individual judgment, the valuation of security over freedom" as an "apparently inevitable consequence of war, cold or hot," that was manifesting itself in the press in tendencies to rely too heavily on government information and a willingness to be used by public officials. Karl E. Meyer, writing in *The New Statesman,* said that "one sometimes has the despairing feeling that no country has more freedom of the press and uses it less."[63]

Congress for the most part held its collective tongue during the crisis itself. After the emergency was resolved, however, the affair quickly entered the realm of domestic politics and was fair game. As *Newsweek* described it, "The Republicans pounced on Cuba and laid bare every flaw in the Administration's handling of the crisis and its aftermath." The GOP leadership did not refrain from making news, or at least Kennedy's policies toward it during the missile crisis, a weapon in its own arsenal, releasing in March 1963 a detailed statement accusing the administration of "scores of deceptions" concerning Cuba and other national-security matters.[64]

The most thorough scrutiny of news policies was, however, directed by Democrat John Moss, chairman of the House Subcommittee on Foreign Operations and Government Information. Moss's growing uneasiness about the general direction of Kennedy information policies bloomed in the hothouse of the missile crisis. During the crisis, Moss ordered a preliminary staff inquiry into information procedures to be implemented. Soon after Sylvester's "news as a weapon" statement, Moss announced plans for a broad investigation of government information policies.[65]

The hearings, which ran intermittently from March 19 through June 5, 1963,[66] revealed a government more and more willing and able to hide more and more of its activity from the American people and the constitutional process, a press that was becoming more and more concerned and confused about what the government was doing in the name of national security and what that activity was doing to its own status, and a public that was becoming more and more confused and unsure about whom to believe. The whole news-management controversy, sparked by early actions of the administration and fanned by Kennedy's attempt to control information, particularly that concerning foreign and military policy, spread cynicism, even bitterness, throughout the relationship between the Executive Branch and the press for the remainder of Kennedy's presidency. The promise of a government and a public brought closer together through the medium of the press, held out so tantalizingly by President Kennedy's first news conference, had been crushed by the pressures on both the government and journalism. A joke making the rounds of Washington captured the feeling. "When Arthur Sylvester says the government is lying, he's telling the truth," the joke went. "When Pierre Salinger says the government is telling the truth, he's lying."[67]

## Conclusion—Managing the News

First Vietnam. Then Watergate. Together these twin traumas marked the great and dramatic divide between an era of relatively blissful government-press cooperation, everyone on the same team, and a time of always bitter, sometimes hysterical and self-destructive distrust and antagonism between journalists and public officials that, in the end, diminished both professions in the eyes of the people.

So goes the popular conception. But the reality, as opposed to the myth, is not nearly so simple and neat, not some sudden awakening of villainy in the government and of moral vision and courage in the press. In most supposed watershed events, conditions simmer before the seemingly sudden and visible eruption. So it was with the relationship between the United States government and the American press. Their relationship developed in an environment that was set and strong well before many people in this country paid much attention to or cared what was going on in an obscure corner of Southeast Asia.

That environment was determined in large part by the status of the two institutions. Both were paradoxes of certitude and ambiguity. The United States government, particularly the presidency, was at once feeling its oats and feeling its way. The United States emerged from World War II as the globe's pre-eminent power, charged—if only by itself—with restoring order and prosperity and protecting its own and its allies' interests against the supposedly ruthless and monolithic threat of communism. To counter this threat, to maintain its ability to do so, and to avoid the internal division caused both by the effort and by possible failure, the government and particularly the presidency, felt increasingly compelled to act secretly.

The press was at a similar point. Journalism was completing its development from a craft into a profession.[68] Gone, or nearly so, were the days when reporters were only slightly more respectable than the criminals and corrupt businessmen and politicians they covered. College-, even graduate-school-trained, reporters were better paid, and were, especially at the top levels of the profession, people of national influence, the professional and social peers of judges, senators, even presidents. American journalism was also flush with wealth. The expanding population, its increasing prosperity and literacy, made newspaper and magazine publishers rich. Even television news, the poor stepchild, was coming into its own. And, finally, the press was, in Tom Wicker's description, shifting from "objective" reporting to "interpretive" reporting. Instead of a strictly "who, what, when, and where" type of reporting, journalists were increasingly willing to ask "why" and "how" and "what if." Especially in the domestic realm, the press was at the height of its power, as would soon be symbolized by the *Sullivan* v. *The New York Times* case then making its way to the United States Supreme Court, which gave the press almost unlimited protection as it investigated and commented upon public figures.[69]

But in foreign affairs the press was by no means so confident. First, foreign coverage was expensive and, in most papers, had little market appeal. For most of the senior journalists, the men and few women who were running news organizations or were its most respected reporters and commentators, World War II was the formative experience. The relationship between the press and the government reflected the public consensus on the war. The issues were simple (or at least were made to seem so); the rules on what could and could not be reported were few, uncomplicated, and enforced with some measure of consistency; where everyone stood was clear. With relatively few exceptions, the press and the government worked cooperatively to achieve total victory. The Cold War, another conflict where the threat and the United States' moral and political position were evident, another conflict that made anything passing for dissent at the best unfashionable, at the worst traitorous, reinforced this relationship.

And, finally, despite its venom and exaggeration, Salinger's comment about journalists and news management bore some truth. Journalism's very purpose could be defined as news management, "because," as Walter Lippmann said, "the raw facts are indigestible."[70] Every decision, every action or inaction by a reporter or an editor, is a form of "news management" as real as that of the government.

The question then becomes what drives these decisions, what interests, values, and pressures guide the press's shaping of the news. In the early 1960s, in the area of national security, these interests, values, and pressures were unclear, shifting, and often at odds. Thus the press was achieving unprecedented legitimacy and power just at the moment when the challenges to that legitimacy and power, and the consequent and often contradictory responsibilities, were also reaching new levels.

The two Cuban crises made this paradox especially clear, and were especially revealing previews of what was to come in Vietnam. First, on the part of the administration, was the almost reflexive desire, bred by fifteen years of the national-security mentality, to conduct foreign policy in the shadows. Next came the implementation of specific steps to make this possible. Centralizing the control of information in the White House, denying reporters access to the scene of action and alternate sources, either shutting journalists off from information entirely or making them dependent on an overwhelming diet of official information, using the police power of the government to intimidate both the sources and the recipients of leaks—all these were practiced by Kennedy, and Eisenhower before him, long before Vietnam was more than a funny word to more than a handful of Americans.

The press just as instinctively sought to protect its credibility. But, for all its bravado, for all its near-religious invocation of the First Amendment, the public's right to know, and the democratic process, the press could not or did not challenge the government when it might have made a difference. For good or ill, responsibly or irresponsibly, willingly or unwillingly, during the Bay of Pigs, during the missile crisis, and during the U-2 incident before them, the press first went along with the government, then complained about it afterward.

These incidents were very short in duration. Though controversy and recrimination remained, the actual time for decision and action, for both the government and the press, passed quickly. But what would they do during a longer crisis, one in which the United States was more deeply and extensively involved, and the need for public support and sacrifice was greater? What would they do when the threat and the nation's commitment were less dramatic and certain than they were in World War II or the early days of the Cold War? What would they do when "the line is so thin these days between war and peace"? As Reston warned during the Moss hearings, such questions were not hypothetical, for "We are engaged in quite a war [in Southeast Asia] . . . and this country hasn't the vaguest idea that it is in a war."[71] Just what, then, would the government, the press, and the public do with Vietnam?

# 3

# Dramatize the Truth

## Coverage of Vietnam, 1955–60

THE FIRST STORY *The New York Times* ran about Vietnam in 1955 was a January 1 dispatch from Hanoi describing a five-hour-long parade held that day in the city to demonstrate against "United States imperialism." The United States was accused of attempting to wreck the Geneva Accords, and South Vietnamese Premier Ngo Dinh Diem was dismissed as an American "lackey." In details large and small, the unidentified reporter drew a picture of the close kinship between Soviet and Chinese communism and the new regime in North Vietnam. The North Vietnamese troops wore uniforms resembling those of the Chinese People's Liberation Army, and they marched "Soviet style . . . in parade step with tommy guns strapped across their chests and bayonets pointing forward." "Again in the Soviet tradition . . . the military parade was followed by a cortege of 300,000 persons [carrying] large portraits of Ho Chi Minh, the members of the Government, Mao Tse-tung, Stalin, Lenin, Engels and Marx."

Another dispatch, this one from Haiphong, ran in the *Times* a few days later. "The Vietminh authorities are laying the foundation for a tightly regimented police state," the report began, noting that "the whole Vietminh system, like that of other Communist nations, is based on a system of propaganda agents" whose "job it is to spread the word among the people and inform the authorities of popular spirit and of individual dissidence."[1]

Later in the month, the *Times'* Dana Adams Schmidt reported from Washington on the impending visit and report of General J. Lawton Collins, President Eisenhower's special envoy to South Vietnam. Schmidt wrote that "intelligence reports" and "Washington officials" indicated growing strength on the part of Diem and greater progress against communist subversion. "He [Diem] appears to be gaining popularity and at the same time self-confidence and some political skill. If present trends continue there is hope that the free world can beat the Communists in the political struggle for South Vietnam." These same sources admitted to a good deal of pessimism concerning the country during the previous year, but felt that "now the optimists are gaining the upper hand" and that "press and magazine reports from the field have not caught up to the new drift of affairs."[2]

The *Times'* first editorial on Vietnam in 1955 appeared January 5. In it the paper's editors warned of complacency in the face of "falsehood and chicanery" emanating from the "supposedly 'sovereign and autonomous' " state of North Vietnam, now run by the "Communist-controlled Vietminh." "We are up against a campaign of lies," the editors declared. "Obviously we have to dramatize the truth."[3]

These articles and editorials from January 1955 together embody the elements of the coverage of Vietnam by the mainstream American press—the national, mass-circulation news organizations—from 1955 at least through 1960.

First, the dispatches and editorials looked at Vietnam mainly as another thrust and parry in the United States' fencing match with a monolithic communist conspiracy. Vietnam was reported not so much as a *Vietnam* story but as a Washington or Moscow or Paris story. Second, the articles and editorials, which already simplified the story by setting it in a Cold War framework, reduced it to an even more elemental level by focusing on Ngo Dinh Diem as the barometer of success or failure for the American effort there. Third, one of the editorials cautioned Americans not to become "complacent about the situation in Indochina," yet the press itself was to fall victim to just such complacency, at least if concern can be measured by the amount of coverage. After a brief flurry of attention in the first few months of 1955, dispatches from or about Vietnam appeared in the pages of *The New York Times, Time, Newsweek,* and *U.S. News and World Report* as rarely as a cold day hit Saigon.[4]

The *Times'* coverage of Vietnam in January 1955 reveals one more characteristic of the American news media's relationship to the Vietnam story during the period. The Dana Schmidt story was based on and reflected information and conjecture furnished by American officials. And though datelined Hanoi and Haiphong, the dispatches from Vietnam were *not* written by reporters based there. Reporters were there only on a visit—an extended one perhaps, but a visit nonetheless. No major American news organization would establish a bureau staffed by a correspondent with full-time responsibility for covering Vietnam until the AP sent Malcolm Browne to Saigon in November 1961.

In short, the press did not devote significant resources to the Vietnam story. This characteristic is actually the most important of all, the one that links the others and that shaped Vietnam coverage in the last half of the 1950s and into the early 1960s. Much of the power of the press supposedly derives from its "agenda-setting" and "gate-keeping" functions, the ability to exercise a significant, even decisive, control over the information that reaches various segments of American society. Through this capability, supposedly, the press can play a large part in determining what issues are important and how they are to be discussed—in a sense, can dramatize the truth. Not so in Vietnam. Because the press largely ignored the early stages of American involvement in Vietnam, this power rested in other hands, which used it to mold what the American public knew about the obscure little country with the odd name somewhere in Southeast Asia. The press's function and role during the whole period of American involvement in Vietnam, all the way to 1975, began to be set well before any but a handful of Americans knew Vietnam existed.

## "How to Be a War Correspondent"

American reporters had ventured into Vietnam even before World War II. When the war between the French, attempting to retake the jewel of their colonial empire, and the Vietminh, a communist-led nationalist movement, began in late 1946, Vietnam became a more regular though still-infrequent stop on the itinerary of Far East correspondents.

American interest in the Indochina war increased somewhat after 1949 and 1950. The triumph of Mao's communists in October 1949 was followed the next June by the North Korean invasion of South Korea. Both confirmed a growing perception that Asia was fast becoming the most important arena of the Cold War. The goal of containing communism, now globalized, became the foundation stone of American postwar foreign policy. In late 1950, the United States established a small Military Assistance and Advisory Group (MAAG) in Saigon and joined France and the three "Associated States of Indochina"—Laos, Cambodia, and Vietnam—in a mutual security agreement. At the same time, the Truman Administration began providing direct economic and technical assistance to Vietnam. By 1952, the United States had provided over $50 million in such aid and was shouldering a third of the cost of the war itself.[5]

Despite this support and a string of commanders filled with élan, France's position in Vietnam had, by early 1954, become extremely precarious. The French people grew impatient with the war's cost and put increasing pressure on French leaders, in the words of General Collins, "to get off their fannies" and end the conflict. But by the spring of 1954, General Henri Navarre's plan to lure the Vietminh into open battle had been turned against him, and the French bastion at Dienbienphu was under siege.

In the meantime, Indochina had emerged as the major topic of the conference on the Far East being held at Geneva. As the shadow of death lengthened across the valley at Dienbienphu, the pressure on the French government to end the fighting increased. The French asked for American air strikes, using small atomic weapons if necessary, against the Vietminh, but Eisenhower refused after failing to secure British support. A month later, on May 7, Dienbienphu fell, and with it the French Empire in Asia. Not long after, a new government was formed in France with the promise to reach a settlement within a month or resign. On July 21, his self-imposed deadline, Premier Pierre Mendès-France signed the Geneva Accords with the Vietminh, the Soviet Union, and the People's Republic of China, agreeing to the temporary partition of Vietnam at the 17th parallel and to the eventual withdrawal of all foreign military forces from Indochina.[6]

Covering the First Indochina War was not particularly onerous duty for American reporters. Peggy Durdin, a free-lance writer for

*The New Yorker* and other publications and wife of *New York Times* Far East correspondent Tillman Durdin, described Hanoi as "a delightful mixture of home-grown raffishness and imported elegance." Her husband concurred that "war coverage out of Hanoi has its compensations. You can jeep to the front, 25 miles away, of a morning and return in the evening to a dinner of onion soup, grilled pigeon, chocolate soufflé and champagne."[7]

Coverage of the war did face some limitations. First, the French attempted to control the flow of information out of Vietnam. The French Army practiced battlefield censorship. As Tillman Durdin told his colleagues at the *Times,* "French censors in Indochina are charming and accomplished if, occasionally, a little rough on copy." Durdin told the story of the Associated Press stringer who was not allowed to make a reference to the hills of northern Vietnam "resembling peaks in a Chinese landscape painting" because the French command was then particularly concerned about possible Chinese intervention in the border area. To make matters worse, the censors had little or no ability to speak or read English.[8]

The censors were fairly easily circumvented, however, by shipping stories to Singapore, Hong Kong, or Tokyo to be filed. The support system that the French developed for correspondents provided a more subtle and effective means of directing the press. The French Expeditionary Corps furnished transportation, food, lodging, and, most important, regular briefings and communiqués on the action.[9] By feeding reporters the information they needed on a timely basis, the French were able to go a long way toward hiding unfavorable developments and emphasizing positive ones. Information provided by the French command was notoriously self-serving and often downright false. As a French Foreign Office public-affairs officer said in an apparently fleeting moment of candor, the rule of the official spokesman was *"mentir et démentir*—to lie and to deny."[10]

Reporters readily acknowledged that such manipulation and distortion went virtually unchallenged. Why?

The explanation for the coverage of the First Indochina War lies in the state of foreign coverage in the American press of the 1950s. The walls of American isolationism had supposedly tumbled amid the din of World War II and the Cold War. Even so, there was still relatively little interest in foreign news in the United States. Even the major news organizations—the wire services, *The New York Times, Time,*

*Newsweek, U.S. News and World Report,* CBS, and NBC—maintained foreign staffs small in relation to the vital role that the United States now played in the world's affairs and that those affairs played in the life of the United States.[11]

Otto Friedrich, now a senior writer for *Time* but in 1953–54 a reporter for the Paris bureau of United Press, wrote "How to Be a War Correspondent," a scathing indictment of foreign coverage by American news organizations. "In New York, where the budgets were made out, and where the executives made speeches about a free and responsible press, only a certain amount of money could be allotted for foreign coverage, if there was to be any foreign coverage at all. It was an utterly inadequate amount, in terms of what could or should have been done. . . . But the money had to be extracted from editors and publishers, who all basically wanted something for very nearly nothing."[12]

If news executives wanted foreign coverage in general for "very nearly nothing," they wanted coverage of Asia for less than nothing, as the already meager resources were directed almost entirely to Europe. For example, of *Time*'s fourteen overseas bureaus, Hong Kong and Tokyo, and their three reporters, were responsible for all the Pacific and Asia. *Newsweek* covered Asia with two reporters working out of Tokyo, and *U.S. News* had one "regional editor" working out of the same city. Of *The New York Times'* twenty-eight foreign offices, only three—Hong Kong, Tokyo, and Melbourne—were in Asia or the Pacific.[13]

Friedrich illustrated in bitter detail the effect this had on coverage of the First Indochina War. When the UP bureau manager in Paris tried to get his superior to station a reporter in Vietnam, Friedrich recalled, "the executive couldn't see any need for it because 'we always got the play' "—in other words, because enough client newspapers and broadcast outlets were picking up United Press material to keep it competitive with the Associated Press on the story. The wire services "had one basic source of news, the French Army communiqués. And since Agence France-Presse (AFP) relayed the communiqués to Paris very soon after they were issued in Hanoi, it was very economical for an American agency to depend on its Paris bureau, rather than a Hanoi correspondent, to write the three or four daily war stories that were needed in New York or Chicago. We had stringers in Hanoi, of course," continued Friedrich, "but such part-time correspondents are rarely worth even the pittance they get. . . . [T]heir chief function was to provide a certain legitimacy to our use of their byline and the magic dateline: Hanoi."[14]

When he was transferred to the Paris bureau, Friedrich said, he assumed that writing about the war was essentially a matter of re-writing the French Army's communiqués. But he was soon told that "There was no point in even writing a story that just reported what was happening . . . because such things usually ended on some edi-tor's dead-spike. That verdict, I soon learned, was perfectly right. The story that got into the paper—and getting into the paper was our reason for existence—was the one that showed 'enthusiasm,' " which consisted of "writing about something as though it were excit-ing, even though you knew nothing about it, even though you are thousands of miles away, even though it is not exciting at all." For example, the army communiqué reports simply that "airplanes bombed the Communists." "We are not told how many planes, what type, what they dropped, or even where, but enthusiasm translates this into 'Waves of American-built Bearcat fighter-bombers zoomed low over cleverly camouflaged Red positions and rained down bombs and fiery napalm. . . .' " "I assume the executives knew noth-ing of the fakery that went on—they didn't want to know." Thus, said Friedrich, "we war correspondents strapped on our helmets, consulted our maps and our day-old French newspapers and our lurid imaginations, and aimed our typewriters at the front page."[15]

Even if the "enthusiasm" described by Friedrich was unique to UP, the same conditions and pressures that created it were at work in other news organizations as they attempted to cover the war. As Friedrich concluded, "From both ends of the news cycle . . . came pressure for fiction rather than facts." On the one hand, the French attempted to manipulate and restrict information in a variety of ways. On the other hand, news organizations forced their reporters to rely on suspect information provided by French sources or, as Friedrich described, on their own creative spark.

Of the two conditions, the latter is by far the more important. Without a greater investment of journalistic resources, there was no chance to resist the French public-affairs machine. "The basic fact," said Friedrich, "is that it would have cost a lot of money to support one of those red-blooded American reporters in Indo-China. Figure at least $100 a week in salary and at least $50 a week in expenses, and is it worth it? It might be, if an American newspaper really wanted to find out what was going on in Indo-China. But that would involve finding out the answers to complicated and embarrassing questions. . . . But that was not what American editors wanted. They wanted stories of good guys fighting Reds, and that was what they got."[16]

Trends concerning the press's role in the war were already coming into focus. A government and a military determined to put the best face on their activities attempted to control the flow of information about the war. This manipulation was made easier because of the pressures, inclinations, and mechanics of journalism as practiced in the United States. Together these resulted in coverage that was not the precursor of the aggressive and independent American journalism commonly attributed to the Vietnam War of the 1960s. Instead, that coverage, what there was of it, followed official sources and fit the story into a simple and convenient context.

## "Ngo Dinh Diem, 10,000 Years"

A look at the early years of the relationship of the Republic of Vietnam and the United States provides a needed background to understanding the functioning of the American press during the later years of the war.

By the fall of 1954, the Vietminh defeat of the French, the Geneva Accords, and continued Soviet and Chinese encouragement of communist insurgencies lent a defensive and uncertain cast to the discussion of American policy and prospects in Asia. A National Security Council study conducted in the late summer of that year proposed a number of steps to turn the situation around. First, the United States led the establishment of the Southeast Asia Treaty Organization in September 1954, providing a legal and diplomatic cover for American activity in Vietnam. Next, the study called for action, overt and covert, to embarrass, harass, and weaken the Vietminh as it attempted to create a government north of the 17th parallel. Finally, and most portentously, the NSC identified "a friendly non-Communist South Vietnam" as the linchpin to which the United States' hopes in Southeast Asia were tied.[17]

"Had it looked all over the world," George C. Herring wrote in his study of American involvement in Vietnam, "the United States could not have chosen a less promising place for an experiment in nation-building." "[I]n southern Vietnam, chaos reigned." The economy was a shambles. Nearly a million refugees flooded into the country from the North. Institutions of government and administration were weak or nonexistent. Criminal organizations and quasi-religious sects, each with its own private army, fought one another and the government. A strong, unified, confident army was poised in the North while ten thousand or more agents of the Vietminh, trained to weaken the government and prepare the way for reunification under Northern leadership, remained in the South after partition.[18]

Into this bleak picture stepped the Americans. By midyear 1955, the Eisenhower Administration had sent over a thousand American experts and over $400 million in military and economic aid to the fledgling country. As the decade proceeded, the United States became involved in almost every aspect of South Vietnamese life. The South Vietnamese armed forces were completely reorganized. Agricultural experts worked to increase rice yields, to restore the rubber industry, and to introduce new products and methods. Physicians and nurses went to South Vietnam to improve the quality and accessibility of medical care. Economists attempted to stabilize the South Vietnamese economy. Police and administrative experts came from Michigan State University. American Protestant and Catholic missionaries ran a variety of relief efforts. From 1955 to 1960, the United States government invested over $1 billion in the country.[19]

American news organizations did not follow suit. As the story of "good guys fighting Reds" faded with the French from Vietnam, so too did the interest of the press. Even if the dispatches coming out of the country during the First Indochina War could be characterized as a torrent, the coverage of Vietnam from 1955 through the rest of the decade slowed to a barely perceptible trickle.

The story during the period was the viability of South Vietnam and of the United States' effort to turn it into a bulwark against communism in Southeast Asia. Nation-building lacked the visceral human drama of combat. Editors could not sell papers and satisfy business managers and publishers with screaming banner headlines such as "NEW MIRACLE RICE SEED USED IN LONG AN PROVINCE" or "NEW SCHOOL BUILT IN TAN THOI." Reporters did not win Pulitzer Prizes and Nieman Fellowships, syndicated columns and big salaries, by writing of the intricacies of land reform or the thoughts of the average South Vietnamese villager. Nor did the story lend itself to the relatively simple spot news—the who, what, when, where, how many—of war reporting. And if even war reporting strained journalistic resources devoted to Vietnam, a story as deep, long-running, and dull as that of nation-building was certainly beyond the reach of mainstream American journalism in the 1950s.

The Cold War was, of course, the dominant interpretive framework. *Times* foreign policy columnist C. L. Sulzberger, on a tour of Vietnam, declared that "A political battle more significant than Dienbienphu is now being fought in Vietnam. The United States, with all its prestige, is actively engaged . . . on behalf of the existing Government in the south. Therefore, should it fail to achieve stability and should communism eventually win this area, it would be a direct slap on America's 'face' in Asia."[20] *U.S. News* asked, "With Northern Vietnam already given up to the Communists, what are the chances of saving the rest of Indo-China? And if Southern Vietnam is lost, will all of Southeast Asia fall to the Communists?" And columnist Joseph Alsop warned that, if South Vietnam fell, so would Laos and Cambodia. "Laos and Cambodia are the keys to Thailand. Thailand is the key to India and Japan. And the loss of South Asia will surely produce grim repercussions further afield, in the Middle East, North Africa and even Europe."[21]

But if the Cold War was the frame that American journalism used to fix the Vietnam scene of the 1950s in place, the focus of the picture was surely that of a short, pudgy little man in a white tropical suit, sometimes smiling but more often with jaw set resolutely or lips pursed and brow furrowed in a slight frown. This little man, Ngo Dinh Diem, quickly emerged for the American government and press as the embodiment of South Vietnam and the United States' involvement there.

The French were not gracious losers. The desire to maintain some sort of political and economic position in Vietnam combined with Gallic pride to make French behavior in the year after Geneva less than helpful. France openly made overtures to Hanoi and conspired with the factions in South Vietnam opposing the government. This intrigue was still more frustrating to the Americans because of the apparent vacuum of leadership in South Vietnam. Even those suspicious of Ho's Marxist-Leninist ideology acknowledged the powerful pull exercised by his leadership of the successful nationalist struggle against France; no one in the South, it seemed, could rival Ho's appeal on that score.[22]

Into this vacuum stepped Ngo Dinh Diem. Diem was born in 1901 in central Vietnam, near the imperial capital of Hue, where his father was chief counselor to Emperor Thanh Thai. After the emperor's removal by the French in 1907, the Ngo Dinh family made a modest living from a few acres of rice land. Diem's father "scraped together the money to educate his six sons." After studying briefly for the priesthood, Diem was selected to attend the School of Law and Administration, the French-run training institute for the native civil service.

Like his father, Diem would see his life disrupted by the French. He proved to be an able administrator and, by age twenty-five, had become a district chief. Three years later, he was promoted to provincial governor. In these two jobs he developed his passionate, enduring hatred of communism as he encountered the work of the nascent Indochina Communist Party. Diem waged a countercampaign against communist propaganda and also ferreted out and arrested communist agents, sending them off for "re-education." So successful was Diem that Emperor Bao Dai named him interior minister—the most important post in the native government—at the tender age of thirty-two. However, he had accepted the job only after French assurances that he would be given free rein to institute reforms. When, after only three months, those assurances proved hollow, Diem resigned.

For almost the next twenty years, Diem tried to position himself as an alternative to the French puppet Emperor Bao Dai and Ho Chi Minh. Before and during World War II, he rejected the overtures of the French, the Japanese, and the Vietminh. By 1950, Diem was in the United States, trying position himself for leadership in Vietnam from there and from Europe. During nearly two years in the United States, he lived at a Catholic seminary in New Jersey operated by the Maryknoll order. Living "like any novice," engaged in household labor and prayer, Diem also used his proximity to New York and Washington to develop an important network of influential friends, including Francis Cardinal Spellman, Supreme Court Justice William O. Douglas, and Senators John Kennedy and Mike Mansfield. By the summer of 1954, events finally caught up with his ambitions. Bao Dai summoned Diem home. On June 18, as one era of his country's history ended and another began, Diem became premier of South Vietnam.[23]

Diem was *not* the United States' handpicked appointment. Many Americans, especially those observing the situation day to day in Saigon, agreed with Chargé d'Affaires Robert McClintock, who called Diem a "messiah without a message." General Collins doubted Diem's ability to pull the country together and suggested that the United States threaten to withdraw its aid if the situation did not improve perceptibly in the near future.[24]

The doubters seemed to have their concerns verified during the so-called sect crisis of March through May 1955. Among the most powerful of the forces arrayed against Diem in his first year were three groups: the Hoa Hao, the Cao Dai, and the Binh Xuyen.

The first two groups were religious sects. The Hoa Hao was a Buddhist splinter group whose appeal was based on its asceticism and on the legendary charisma of its founder, Huynh Phu So. Its current leaders were no less colorful. Tran Van Soai had made a fortune from "taxes" levied by the sect. Military leader Ba Cut bragged of his sexual proclivities—he practiced homosexuality openly and, according to him, with great vigor and frequency—and of his fanatic opposition to the French and Diem. The Cao Dai was described as "a mixture of Christianity, Buddhism, Confucianism, and Taoism," with its own pope and College of Cardinals. Among the saints of the Cao Dai pantheon were former French Prime Minister Georges Clemenceau, Victor Hugo, Joan of Arc, Charles Chaplin, and, pending his death, Sir Winston Churchill. The Binh Xuyen had no religious pretensions but was, instead, an organized-crime syndicate whose leader, Bay Vien, made Al Capone look, according to Robert "Pepper" Martin of *U.S. News,* like "a piker. Bay Vien didn't buy police protection. He just took over the police."[25] Each group enjoyed significant popular appeal and had sizable, well-armed military forces hardened by combat with a variety of foes.

Almost from the moment he took office, Diem worked to control the sects.[26] The crisis came to a head during the last week of April 1955. On Tuesday the 26th, Diem fired the Binh Xuyen police chief, established a new police headquarters outside the French security zone, and declared that the Binh Xuyen would not be allowed outside the French section of the city. Government troops and Binh Xuyen soldiers fought with tanks and artillery, often firing at point-blank range.[27]

On Friday the 29th, just past 1:00 P.M., the unmistakable "thump" of mortar shells landing on the grounds outside was heard through the open windows of Freedom Palace, Diem's home and administrative center, signaling the beginning of a final Binh Xuyen assault. To the surprise of everyone, the premier and his troops showed unexpected decisiveness and bravery. As the shelling started, Diem ordered the army to push the Binh Xuyen out of Saigon once and for all. Within a few days, the government troops had routed the Binh Xuyen forces.

American officials in Washington, heartened by Diem's performance, moved forcefully to bolster him. By midsummer, government troops had dispersed the Hoa Hao forces and the Cao Dai army was in the process of surrender. Through the summer and fall, Diem's strength and American enthusiasm for him grew apace, until both were cemented by Diem's overwhelming victory over Bao Dai in an October referendum. From this point on, the United States' commitment to Diem became one of its strongest.[28]

In the early months of 1955, the American press locked in on Diem just as quickly. His struggle to retain power became an easily comprehended symbol for his country's much more complicated struggle for survival and also supplied at least some portion of drama and conflict, missing since the end of the First Indochina War.

As the sect crisis began to unfold, coverage had not been so sanguine about Diem's prospects. A *Times* background piece acknowledged some of the criticisms of Diem circulating in Saigon. "Irascible over minor annoyances, he lives a solitary life, relying for help mainly on his four brothers, a fact his foes cite in charges that he is trying to establish a patriarchy." Earlier, a *Times* editorial had noted the difficulty of Diem's task and his "unimpeachable integrity," but lamented that "South Vietnam does not have a chief of state with sufficient political following to insure a government of real 'leadership' in crisis."[30]

Joe Alsop, always ready to foresee disaster, questioned Diem's staying power. Writing from Saigon during April, Alsop conceded that Diem "is wholly honest and an undoubted patriot," but went on to add that he was also "narrow, obstinate, and petty," so suspicious that he was "unwilling to delegate [even] the issuance of passport visas," and, "above all, completely out of contact with the broad mass of his people and the political realities of his country."[30]

The weekly news magazines present an interesting contrast. *U.S.*

*News* had little coverage, compared with its competitors, and what there was took a largely neutral tone. *Time*'s coverage, however, was supportive of the premier. The cover of *Time*'s April 4 issue was a portrait of a wise, determined Diem, the tropical paradise behind him about to be engulfed in the flames of war, and the South Vietnamese flag flying behind him being ripped asunder by the communist sickle. The lengthy article inside, reported by *Time*'s Hong Kong correspondent, John Mecklin, painted a similarly admiring picture. "A resilient, deeply religious Vietnamese nationalist," *Time* called Diem, "who is hindered with the terrible but challenging task of leading the 10.5 million people of South Viet Nam from the brink of Communism into their long-sought state of sovereign independence." After listing a number of accomplishments, the article judged that "the progress, slow but clearly discernible, represents an almost personal triumph for single-minded nationalist Diem." The closest *Time* came to any negative characterization of Diem was the acknowledgment that he was "a man with his share of imperfections."[31]

*Newsweek,* however, went significantly further in cataloguing Diem's drawbacks and in projecting his imminent downfall. "Diem has no real backing, no political machine of his own. . . . Even the Army is not uniformly behind him," the magazine reported in its April 11 issue. Two weeks later, Newsweek noted growing American doubts about Diem's leadership and also concluded that his two principal assets, "his scrupulous honesty and his reputation as anti-French," had been wasted. By early May, *Newsweek* had virtually written Diem off. After listing other Diem weaknesses, *Newsweek* concluded that now "How to replace Diem was the problem."[32]

Diem's stirring triumph over the sects and his subsequent consolidation of power changed the press's tune. The volume of coverage decreased from 1955 to 1960, but what reporting there was from South Vietnam lavished praise on Diem. As South Vietnam prospered, Diem and his country became the shining star in the constellation of United States foreign policy. This chorus reached something of a crescendo in 1957. In February, Diem narrowly escaped injury during an attempt against his life. A *Times* editorial reviewed South Vietnam's progress and concluded that "Behind many of the gains has been . . . the strong and faithful figure and presence of President Diem. We rejoice that his life has been spared. His country will need him for a long time to come."

The hosannas rang even higher as Diem visited the United States in

May. Foster Hailey, who was present at the assassination attempt, wrote in a *New York Times Magazine* preview of Diem's visit that the February attack "was not the first time Mr. Diem had shown that high degree of courage that Ernest Hemingway once defined as 'grace under pressure.' And not just physical courage, but spiritual and moral courage as well." In 1945, Ho Chi Minh was Vietnam's "one great symbol of independence." Today, Hailey declared, "President Diem is that symbol, the undisputed leader of one of the most promising old-young countries in Southeast Asia." *Time* praised Diem, who, "slowly and almost unnoticed by the outside world, has brought to South Viet Nam a peace and stability few would have dared predict when his country was dismembered at Geneva three years ago," and thanked "proud, doughty little Ngo Dinh Diem" for reminding Americans of the "deep meaning of this high-minded, unprecedented, costly U.S. experiment" of foreign aid. By 1960, even Joe Alsop credited "the strong personality of President Diem" for having "brought temporary order to South Viet-Nam."[33]

The only significant note of discord in the 1950s came in the summer of 1959, as Albert M. Colegrove, a reporter for the Scripps-Howard chain, outlined in a series of articles what he called "an outrageous scandal" in the American aid program to South Vietnam. Colegrove cited missing property and money, sloppy accounting procedures, and inefficient direction among his charges. The charges drew sharp responses from the Eisenhower Administration, the Congress, and even other segments of the press. Ambassador to Saigon Elbridge Durbrow called the charges "distorted and false," and aid administrator Arthur Z. Gardiner and MAAG chief Lieutenant General Samuel T. Williams denied any discrepancies in the accounting of funds or property. When asked why he had not checked the allegations with these senior officials, Colegrove replied, "I was given the word by many people . . . that if I tipped my mitt, doors would be closed to me."[34]

Despite its quick burial, Colegrove's series foreshadowed the beginning of a change in the amount and tone of coverage of Vietnam. Vietcong guerrilla and terrorist activity had commenced two years before but was virtually invisible amid the flood of optimism and self-congratulation. With Hanoi's spring-1959 decision to resume armed conflict, however, the combat became too frequent and intense to ignore.[35]

Criticism of Diem began to appear during 1960. On April 18, sev-

eral prominent South Vietnamese signed the so-called Caravelle
Manifesto charging Diem with "denying elementary civil liberties,
carrying on 'one-party' rule and copying 'dictatorial Communist
methods.' " Both Tillman Durdin of the *Times* and Pepper Martin of
*U.S. News* acknowledged the validity of some of the charges in May
articles. Durdin detailed the influence of Diem's brothers over the
government, suppression of free expression, vote rigging, and favoritism in government appointments. But, concluded Durdin, none of
Diem's critics had a sufficient political base to challenge him, nor
could they deny the security and prosperity that had been achieved.
Martin also noted Diem's accomplishments but added that "The
manifesto issued in Saigon is the first open warning that a strong man
apparently must be more than anti-Communist to win full support
against the Reds."[36]

Both of these issues—the increasingly aggressive military activity
by the communists and the increasingly vocal political activity by
Diem's opponents—erupted into the headlines in November 1960. In
the wee hours of November 11, five battalions of elite troops attacked
Diem's palace headquarters in an attempt to overthrow the government. For nearly a day, Diem maneuvered, buying time to bring loyal
forces to Saigon. By the 13th, the rebellion—inspired, according to its
leaders, by Diem's authoritarian rule and his failure to deal aggressively enough with the insurgency—was crushed, and most of its
leaders were in jail.

Though most coverage of the attempted coup was supportive of
Diem, it also found some truth in the rebels' grievances. A *New York
Times* editorial said, "We are happy that President Ngo Diem has
survived this major test of his power. . . . But it would be unwise for
the President or his friends here to ignore this warning of discontent
which have been heard in South Vietnam for months now, long
before this coup." *Newsweek* called on Diem to heed the revolt as a
"grim signal of the extent of opposition to his authoritarian regime."
But the article left considerable doubt as to whether its advice would
be taken. "When the one-day coup was over, rebel leaders were in
jail, some 100 soldiers were dead, and Radio Saigon was chanting its
familiar paean: 'President Ngo Dinh Diem, 10,000 years.' "[37]

So the story of Diem—and of the way the American press covered
him and his country—had come full circle. In early 1955, Diem was
battling opponents in the streets of Saigon while the American press

questioned whether he could or should remain in power. In the years that followed, Diem and South Vietnam could do no wrong as they became inseparable in the American mind, beacon stars in the dark night of the Cold War. By late 1960, though, Diem once again faced an armed rebellion and, again, the American press was questioning his role.

What accounts for this swing in press opinion on Diem? Was the press out to "get" Diem one moment and boost him the next? Those who later blamed a supposedly adversarial press for the U.S. defeat in Vietnam would say yes.

Such an explanation simply does not fit the facts. First consider the pattern of coverage. In the years 1955 to 1960, Vietnam received the most attention when Diem was under attack and the future of his country was uncertain—in other words, when the story was most dramatic and exciting. The desire for a good story, not the desire to bring Diem down, accounted for this.

Also, if Vietnam had been important enough to the press for them to shape the story to some preconceived notion, news organizations would surely have invested more resources in the country. But even the major American news organizations attempted to cover all Asia with a mere handful of people. The fundamental fact is that the American press simply was not very interested in Vietnam, certainly not interested enough to pursue its own "mission" there.

Instead, other forces set the agenda for the Vietnam story. Extremely conscious of the need to present a positive image to the world, Diem exercised strict controls, including censorship, over the domestic press. Diem preferred to win over foreign reporters, but he did occasionally bring negative pressure to bear, including arresting them or expelling them from the country.[38]

Diem also tried to influence the press in the United States. The South Vietnamese government employed an executive of the Harold Oram public-relations firm at an annual fee of $38,000.[39] Diem also received a great deal of free public-relations help from an influential "Vietnam Lobby," similar to the China Lobby that generated support for Chiang Kai-shek. This lobby was led by the American Friends of Vietnam, founded in December 1955 "to enlighten American opinion" on South Vietnam's importance as "a bulwark of freedom in Southeast Asia." The group sponsored fund-raising events, staged seminars, testified to Congress, and commissioned books and magazine articles, employing such writers as Sol Sanders, a journalist who later covered South Vietnam for such publications as *Newsweek* and *U.S. News*.[40]

But by far the most powerful and important influence on the coverage of Vietnam was the United States government. Developing a truly independent network of knowledge and sources in Vietnam, even during the relatively tranquil years of the late 1950s, would have been extremely difficult even if the press had wanted to. So the press, on the occasions when it did cover the country, relied on the largest and most influential purveyor of information, one not without a vested interest in the situation and how it was reported.

The United States, with a significant amount of money and prestige riding on Diem, wanted to make its investment look good. First, the Eisenhower Administration portrayed the commitment to Diem and South Vietnam as an important part of the effort to contain the worldwide advance of communism. This effectively removed the relationship from political discussion, so powerful was the foreign-policy consensus imposed by the Cold War. The Eisenhower Administration also sought to create a positive image for Diem, even when doubts existed. "While classified policy papers through 1959 thus deal with risks," wrote the authors of the Pentagon Papers, "public statements of U.S. officials did not refer to the jeopardy. To the contrary, the picture presented to the public and Congress . . . was of continuing progress, virtually miraculous improvement, year-in and year-out."[41]

The press's reliance on the government for information caused another problem. During the 1950s and well into the 1960s, the United States had no independent information-gathering system in Vietnam, and was forced to rely on intelligence and data supplied by a regime that, as the Pentagon Papers put it blandly, "discouraged realism."[42] Thus, in many ways, the relationship between the American press and the United States government in Vietnam during this crucial period was one of the blind leading the blind.

The risks and problems of such a relationship were not unknown, even at the time. A 1960 survey of public-relations work in the United States in behalf of foreign governments maintained that "the economics of U.S. news coverage" resulted in "[h]ordes of reporters" following the American president's every move while "the ranks of American journalists covering the rest of the world are remarkably thin," making the press—and the American people—vulnerable. "The facts we need to know are often concealed from us or get to us too late. All of a sudden there may be a blow-up in a country with which we have been deeply involved." *The New Republic* lamented "the failure of most experts on Vietnam to publish an accurate, honest appraisal of the economic, social, and political facts of life in the country and the flooding of American newspapers and magazines with false praise." Even Joe Alsop believed that, in the case of Vietnam, "public relations and foreign policy do not mix well."[43]

But these were voices crying in the wilderness. The supposed power of the press to set agendas, to keep the gate of information, did not exist, at least in this case at this time. Instead, the press settled for a meager investment of its resources in the area. Because of this, it settled for shallow coverage, based on simple contexts. The press also relied on a government that was increasingly determined and able to carry out its national-security policy in secret and that was, to make matters worse still, itself forced to rely on inadequate or inaccurate information.

For these reasons, the American public had little choice but to accept coverage that at best failed to present the whole story, and at worst distorted and misrepresented what was happening in Vietnam. In short, because of an American press unequipped to deal with the story and an American government willing and able to shield or manipulate the story, the early scenes of the tragedy in Vietnam were played out in whispers and asides, behind drawn curtains or offstage altogether, beyond the comprehension of the American people.

## "A Difficult Balance to Strike"— The President, the Press, and Vietnam in 1961

If the world John Kennedy inherited on January 20, 1961, could be characterized as a circus, surely he would be its ringmaster—young, strong, confidently directing far-flung events in the full and pitiless view of an attentive public. Such was the image he developed during his drive for the White House. Such is the image that has survived him.

American journalism emerged in a similar role in the early 1960s.

Major news organizations generated unprecedented revenues, and their owners and chief executives were counted among the nation's leading business figures. Editors, columnists, and reporters were now educated at the best colleges and professional schools, and were the peers of the influential people they covered. The American press built an image as a director, not merely a chronicler, of issues and events in American society, an image that has survived to this day.

Both images owe much to the Vietnam War. In life, Kennedy was the resolute young president creatively and energetically meeting the challenge of communism in Southeast Asia. The press, for its part, remains in the popular mythology of the war an important, perhaps the decisive, influence on how the effort there eventually ended.

Both images are more the stuff of legend than fact. John Kennedy was buffeted by hundreds of crises, domestic and foreign. More than ringmaster, Kennedy was a juggler, attempting to keep the world from crashing around him. And, like all performers, he did not care to be publicly embarrassed. He tried to highlight situations that were to his advantage and shield from view those that could prove inconvenient. Nor was the press, despite its new status, in control of its own direction, particularly in foreign and national security matters. The government was increasingly prone and able to manipulate, or withhold altogether, important information in these areas, while the press would not or could not make an allocation of its own resources sufficient to challenge the government's control.

These conditions held especially true for both Kennedy's and the press's approach to Vietnam during most of 1961. Both president and press were increasingly aware of the problems in Vietnam, but for both it was one of many demands on limited stocks of time, talent, and money. For most of 1961, both president and press chose to make only modest investments in Vietnam, essentially continuing the course set during the Eisenhower years. Consequently, both found themselves at the mercy of other forces until, as the year drew to a close, the stage was set for significant changes in the relationship of president and press to the Vietnam story.

The pull of other events was the first force to shape Kennedy's approach to Vietnam during 1961. Following the attempted coup the previous November, the situation in South Vietnam continued to worsen. Diem retreated deeper into Freedom Palace and the self-serving irrationality of his family, the Vietcong grew more aggressive, and American civilian and military officials in Saigon split over how much to pressure Diem to institute political and administrative reforms.[44]

Despite all this, Vietnam remained a "peripheral crisis" for Kennedy during most of his first year in office. "We've got twenty Vietnams a day," snapped Attorney General Robert Kennedy when Stanley Karnow tried to discuss the issue with him.[45] The Bay of Pigs, the civil war in the Congo, the failed summit in Vienna, and Berlin all were arenas in which the overriding contest with the Soviet Union was being played more urgently, it seemed, than in Vietnam. Even in Southeast Asia, Vietnam could not get top billing: the crisis in Laos dominated the stage.[46]

Thus, for most of 1961, Kennedy sought to prevent further deterioration in Vietnam without jeopardizing other security or political interests. In January, he approved a modest $41 million in additional military aid and began general discussions on reforming the South Vietnamese government and economy. Even after a series of foreign-policy embarrassments increased the symbolic importance of Vietnam, Kennedy sought to maintain the status quo through limited actions: a few hundred more Special Forces trainers; a new ambassador; the formation of an interagency "Vietnam Task Force"; and a good-will tour by Vice-President Lyndon B. Johnson.[47]

At least in part because of what the Pentagon Papers called "near-minimal response" from Kennedy, other influences took charge of the situation for most of 1961. For one, the Vietcong seized the initiative as it stepped up the volume of its activity steadily through the year. In a June letter to Kennedy, Diem himself acknowledged that "the military situation at present is to the advantage of the communists. . . ." By September, a State Department summary reported that since the first of the year Vietcong strength had more than doubled, the number of attacks the guerrillas initiated each month had tripled, and they were shifting from small- to large-unit actions. One such attack, in which the Vietcong seized and held temporarily the provincial capital of Phuoc Thanh, had "a shattering effect" on Saigon, only fifty-five miles away. At September's end, Diem was ready to welcome an increase in the number of combat troops working as advisers and was asking the United States for a formal bilateral defense pact.[48]

Finally, the United States placed itself in the hands of Ngo Dinh

Diem. If, as he entered office, Kennedy was willing to continue the pressure against Diem, he soon questioned the strategy's worth. In an Oval Office meeting on Vietnam in late January, Secretary of State Dean Rusk told the president that Americans "were caught between pressing Diem to do things he did not wish to do and the need to convey to him American support. It was a difficult balance to strike; and Diem was extremely sensitive to criticism." "The U.S. thought it vital that Diem do better," said the Pentagon Papers, "but increasing his confidence in the U.S. had top priority." But by backing off from negative pressure, such as threatening to withhold aid funds, and relying instead on positive encouragement, the United States diminished its minimal leverage even more, and the situation in South Vietnam continued to go from bad to worse.[49]

The same sorts of influences affected the American press's relationship to the Vietnam story during 1961. Like the president, the press did not devote significant attention or resources to Vietnam. The area was still being covered by the same small number of regional correspondents that had been assigned to the Far East in 1955. Even in Southeast Asia, Laos, not Vietnam, was the big story. As the Pentagon Papers noted, *The New York Times Index* for 1961 had eight columns of citations for Vietnam (North and South), and twenty-six for Laos. For most of 1961, Vietnam was, literally and figuratively, a sidebar.[50]

The United States government continued to be the major influence on coverage of Vietnam. Only some major change in the story—a sharp increase in military activity or a sudden shift in American policy—would change the level of the press's interest. The Kennedy Administration, through its own approach to Vietnam, encouraged the perception that Vietnam was more or less stable. By avoiding such developments for most of the year, through its own actions and with the cooperation of the Vietcong, Kennedy avoided giving the press any reason to change the way it covered Vietnam.

The government also took more active steps to shape Vietnam reporting. The psychological section of the Vietnam Task Force's initial report, encompassing information and propaganda issues, made a number of recommendations. It called for the development of "agricultural 'show-places' throughout the country, with a view toward exploiting their beneficial psychological effects." The report also suggested that steps be taken to "compile and declassify for use of media representatives in South Vietnam and throughout the world, documented facts concerning Communist infiltrations and terrorists' activities," and to "increase the flow of information to media representatives of the unsatisfactory living conditions in North Vietnam."[51]

If a sampling of coverage from 1961 is any indication, the government met with at least some success in steering press coverage in these directions. Kien Hoa Province was a model "agricultural showplace," with Lieutenant Colonel Pham Ngoc Thao as its chief. Thao, a former Vietminh guerrilla, was seemingly meeting with encouraging results in countering Vietcong activity in his area. Kien Hoa, described by U.S. Ambassador to South Vietnam Durbrow as the "showcase province [that] most foreign correspondents [were] directed to," became the highlight of Joe Alsop's spring-1961 trip to Southeast Asia. Alsop cut short his visit to other parts of South Vietnam in order to spend more time with Thao, because, "when a Western reporter finds a corner of the world which particularly inspires hope, the impulse to linger there is all but irresistible."

North Vietnamese support of the Vietcong also became a consistent theme in news reports. *Time* described the rush of activity along the Ho Chi Minh Trail "as the Communists pushed supplies and reinforcements to the jungle fighters who are battling to take over South Viet Nam." And the bleak conditions in North Vietnam were also noted with some regularity. Joe Alsop described the North Vietnamese people as "bitter, disillusioned, and hostile to their Communist regime," and the country as a "state of hostile wretchedness . . . a ripe target for precisely the kind of underground assault now being made in South Viet-Nam." *Time* referred to South Vietnam as the "richer prize," an "even more tempting target for the Reds—and a standing contrast to the poverty-stricken Communist North."[52]

The press's approach to Vietnam, like that of President Kennedy, was also shaped by the Diem regime. There was a brief respite in this process in the weeks leading up to the April 1961 presidential elections in South Vietnam. Diem adopted a more enlightened attitude toward the press, domestic and foreign. He allowed reporters to attend National Assembly committee hearings at which his subordinates were testifying. He also made himself and his Cabinet ministers more accessible to the press, holding more news conferences and issuing blanket invitations for them to accompany him on campaign trips around the country.[53]

Some of these positive steps continued after the election, but for the most part Diem's suspicions of a variety of real and imagined opponents, including foreign reporters, began to deepen. As the new U.S. ambassador to South Vietnam, Frederick Nolting, reported not long after he arrived in South Vietnam, Diem was vigorously complaining "about his difficulties at home which he believes arise in part from the bad press which he gets abroad. I myself," Nolting added in a hint of problems to come, "have not found any substantial evidence for the extreme allegations frequently made concerning this regime."[54]

Nolting's attitude was a sign of the general shift away from the pressure tactics that the Kennedy Administration feared would aggravate further the existing tension within the American official community in South Vietnam and between the Americans and Diem. With that shift, the positive steps toward opening the regime to the foreign press began to fall by the wayside. For example, the South Vietnamese government tried to downplay the extent of the VC assault in Phuoc Thanh, in direct opposition, a State Department cable protested, "to intent [of] joint US-GVN [Government of Vietnam] action program of increasing flow of free information about VC insurgency. GVN will eventually be caught out on this by commercial correspondents and credibility which [is] still not good will be depressed further." Indicative of the Diem retreat from the press and from American advice was the following lament of the United States Information Service (USIS) chief in Saigon: "In bi-weekly US/GVN psyops [psychological-operations] meeting, USIS offered Civic Action minister technical assistance and advisory resources to better expedite and exploit GVN military, domestic news. GVN countered with typical evasion of offers relating to sensitive material by inviting USIS submit suggestions 'for consideration and study.' "[55]

Reflecting the increasingly strained relationship between Diem and the American team, the press began to report on the significant problems Diem faced. Reports during the spring and summer pointed out that his regime had "so far failed to win the active support of South Vietnam's population," that he was personally isolated from his people, that his methods mirrored those of the communists in their authoritarianism, their constant suspicion and surveillance, and their implied threats, and that his administration was riddled with gross inefficiency, nepotism, and corruption. But he was also, it was written, the only real alternative to the Vietcong. The "rub of the U.S.

problem in Vietnam," said *Newsweek,* is that "the only available leader with the strength and the courage to resist the Communists is also a dictator."[56]

The relationship between Diem and the press, like that between Diem and the United States government, darkened further in the fall, as Diem became even more isolated. *Time* referred to Diem's "clique-ridden, narrowly based government"; *Newsweek*'s Far East correspondent Robert S. Elegant painted a bleak picture of a South Vietnam rotting from within and wondered if the United States might not "have to reconcile itself to political changes at the top." Diem responded to such statements by drawing even further away and by lashing out at particular news organizations. For example, the South Vietnamese had long accused Cambodia of allowing the Vietcong to use the border area of the two countries as a base area. In November, *New York Times* reporter Robert Trumbull, with the assistance of the Cambodian military, spent four days traveling through the area by jeep and helicopter, and reported that no evidence of such activity was found. For disputing Diem, the *Times* and Trumbull came "under special attack" in the government-controlled newspapers of Saigon.[57]

The tension between foreign correspondents and Diem, and the reporters' concerns about the situation in South Vietnam, were clear enough in the mainstream press. But in articles for other outlets and in private communications the picture was even more foreboding. Stanley Karnow, in *The Reporter* of January 19, 1961, catalogued the problems of the Diem regime, most of them caused, or at least aggravated substantially, by Diem's inability to offer positive leadership. "Diem seems to have paralyzed rather than inspired those around him," Karnow wrote. "The characteristics that made Diem a success in 1955 and 1956—obstinacy, single-mindedness, and guile—are his most obvious weaknesses today. If he is unable to change, there is not much hope that he, or perhaps even the country, can last." Jerry Rose, a photographer-correspondent working in the Far East for Time-Life, wrote in *The New Republic* that "the strength of South Vietnam is fading" because of the "fanatic devotion" of the Vietcong and because the mandarinism that formed the basis of Diem's rule had drained the soul from Vietnamese society. Even staunch Diem friend and supporter Sol Sanders, working for the Tokyo bureau of the McGraw-Hill World News Service, cried

"What a mess!" as he described to Joe Alsop the ability of the North Vietnamese to move with impunity through Laos and Cambodia as they turned up the pressure on Diem.[58]

Takashi Oka, the East Asia correspondent for *The Christian Science Monitor,* summed up the feelings and perceptions of many of his colleagues in a long, impassioned letter to his editor back in Boston. "President Diem appears to have lost all touch with reality," Oka wrote. "His sole concern appears to be the survival of his regime, which he literally equates with himself." Oka ended with the prediction that "the next few weeks are likely to be climactic for South Vietnam. . . . There is a climate, an atmosphere, a feeling of expectation tinged with apprehension, which cannot go on at this pitch forever."[59]

For most of 1961, the Kennedy Administration and the mainstream American press continued the basic approach to Vietnam set during the Eisenhower years. Since mid-1955, both the United States government and the American press had been satisfied to maintain the status quo in South Vietnam. Because it assessed the situation in South Vietnam in only a surface way, the United States government never successfully addressed the fundamental problems of the country. And because the press paid only the most cursory attention to the Vietnam story, it was controlled by a variety of forces, not least of which was an American government that sought to conduct foreign and military policy in the shadows.

As a consequence, neither the Executive Branch nor the press—one charged by the Constitution with the responsible conduct of the people's foreign policy, the other protected by the Constitution so that it could responsibly inform the people of that conduct—fulfilled its responsibility. Over those years, the situation in South Vietnam had gradually deteriorated, until it reached a crisis point at which it would have to be decided, as Lyndon Johnson told President Kennedy, whether the United States was to make "a major effort in support of the forces of freedom" in South Vietnam "or throw in the towel."[60]

Oka was right. The next weeks and months were to be a watershed in the relationship between Vietnam and the American people, government, and press, as what had been called "the quiet war" was about to become a lot noisier.

# 4

# In Country

## The Press Comes to Vietnam, 1961–62

"The competing noises of the big helicopter's rotors and engine are deafening, deadening, downright painful. . . . The sense of being trapped in an aerial cement mixer is just beginning to be a bit oppressive when suddenly the little delta town of Rac Gia comes into sight, lying on a river among palm gardens, with an airport on its flank. Swiftly the helicopter descends. Swiftly 12 wiry little Vietnamese rangers clamber aboard. . . . To surprise, to envelop, to catch the communist leader and his troops are now the missions of the 57th Transportation Squadron and the two companies of Vietnamese soldiers they are carrying. . . . For one passenger at least, it is a new way of going into a fight. What will it be like? one asks oneself. And then, quite suddenly, a patch of brighter green shows up ahead. The soldiers fan out rapidly, running hunched over, through a dry rice field. And our helicopter and all the others take to the air again, looking for all the world like a convey of giant mantises."[1]

Joseph Alsop

"Alsop NYK [New York] Tribune gets to ride on helicopter mission after two days in Saigon superseding correspondents who have been waiting their turn for weeks stop If NYK Times cannot safeguard its correspondents against this kind of favoritism eye [I] want to quit."[2]

Homer Bigart

ONE REPORTER GETS to take a helicopter ride. Another doesn't. One journalist takes advantage of position and influence. Another, without the same leverage, reacts angrily, almost petulantly. One insignificant incident in an already long war.

Perhaps. But if all wars have their telling moments, small occurrences that throw larger issues into sharp relief, Vietnam overflowed with them. And in the early, critical pages of the story of the American press and the Vietnam War, the Alsop-Bigart episode is just such a moment.

Joseph Alsop, one of the nation's most widely read newspaper columnists, wrote from Washington for the *New York Herald Tribune*. Having served in China during World War II, first as chief of the Lend-Lease mission and then as a captain in General Claire Chennault's staff, he was considered something of an expert on the Far East. Regarding himself still more as a reporter than as a commentator, Alsop went overseas several times a year to observe firsthand the situations and issues he wrote about. Alsop was extremely well connected in the Washington power circuit, particularly during the Kennedy years. He was an intimate of congressmen, ambassadors, Cabinet officials, even the president himself. On just about any national political figure's short list of journalists to be wooed, or at least neutralized, Alsop's name was prominent.

At age fifty-five, Homer Bigart was three years older than Alsop. Like Alsop, he began his career with the *Herald Tribune* and had become one of the most respected figures in American journalism. But, unlike Alsop, Bigart had chosen to spend his career as a foreign correspondent. He gained particular fame for his coverage of war, winning Pulitzer Prizes for his dispatches from the Pacific in 1945 and Korea in 1950. He went to work for the *Times* in 1955, covering flare-ups around the world. From January to July 1962, he had been assigned to Saigon, to work exclusively on South Vietnam. Bigart's influence came from his status as the most respected foreign correspondent for the nation's most respected newspaper.

By mid-1962, events had convinced both Alsop and Bigart of the need to oppose the advance of communism in Southeast Asia, particularly in South Vietnam. Alsop saw "intelligent, united, and energetic top-level leadership" and "a corresponding lift of Vietnamese morale and fighting spirit" adding up to "solid progress." Bigart instead saw a doomed policy, led by unimaginative and deceitful men. These "leaders" attempted to save a regime more concerned with its own preservation than with the welfare of its people.[3]

These contrasting judgments symbolize the conflict between the press corps in South Vietnam and U.S. and South Vietnamese officials.

The root of the conflict, the story went, lay in the youth and politics of a small group of reporters based in South Vietnam. Depending on one's point of view, these reporters were either (1) free of the old political attitudes of World War II and the early Cold War and thus able to question the U.S. cause in South Vietnam and the wisdom and credibility of Vietnamese and American officials; or (2) ignorant of the threat that the United States faced in South Vietnam and equally determined to discredit the American effort and to bring down Diem. Both portrayals assume that the press possessed a significant inclination and ability to take on government and military officials.

This adversarial, even obstructionist, image of the press originated during the Kennedy years and remains strong today because of one fundamental flaw—the failure to understand *how* the war was covered.

The twenty months or so between April 1961 and December 1962 were perhaps the most critical time in the long story of the American press and the Vietnam War. This period raised almost all the important questions concerning the press's relationship to the Vietnam story for the rest of the war. Answers to the questions surrounding the press and the war in 1962—and in the years to follow—lie in the press itself. The answers, in short, lie in why Joe Alsop got to take a helicopter ride and Homer Bigart did not.

## Need for Commitment

By the fall of 1961, Vietnam had moved to the forefront of administration concerns. Through the summer, various agencies had drawn up different plans for countering the Vietcong advance. Most of them involved the introduction, in some shape or form, of American combat troops. During an October 11 meeting, the National Security Council decided to dispatch yet another fact-finding mission to the country, this one headed by special presidential adviser General Maxwell Taylor.[4]

Maxwell Taylor was, in Karnow's words, "Kennedy's kind of soldier": heroic battlefield commander, handsome, cultured, intellectual. In 1960, Taylor authored *The Uncertain Trumpet*, a sharp indictment of Eisenhower's "massive-retaliation" military strategy that confirmed candidate Kennedy's growing fascination with limited war and made "flexible response" a touchstone of President Kennedy's own national-security thinking. Taylor was so disturbed by his observations in Vietnam that he cabled his report to the president from Saigon and the Philippines rather than wait to deliver it by hand.[5]

Though the Taylor report encompassed a variety of views, it emphasized that "South Vietnam is in serious trouble; major interests of the United States are at stake; but if the U.S. promptly and energetically takes up the challenge, a victory can be had without a U.S. take-over of the war." Taylor recommended several steps, including increased training and material support. Taylor also suggested the dispatch of a six-to-eight-thousand-man force, ostensibly to aid the South Vietnamese in relief and recovery efforts following serious flooding in the Mekong Delta. Such moves would raise South Vietnamese morale and show the seriousness of the United States' commitment to Southeast Asia.[6]

"It *is* really now or never if we are to arrest the gains being made by the Viet Cong," Assistant Secretary of Defense William Bundy told the president. Even so, Kennedy was still reluctant to send combat ground forces to South Vietnam. The introduction of even a relatively small force would itself create the need for reinforcements, and the inevitable casualties would cause domestic political problems. Thus, Kennedy chose to forestall, but not foreclose, the sending of such forces by sharply enhancing the amount and extent of assistance.

This increased aid's most important element was the assignment of combat support units, such as helicopter companies, air-ground support squadrons, and intelligence and communications units. The U.S. would sharpen and expand its advisory effort, and would also provide increased economic support to the South Vietnamese military. Finally, changes would be made in the organization and number of personnel "as are required for increased United States participation in the direction and control of GVN military operations."

As it had for six and one-half years, the United States was still trying to do just enough to keep South Vietnam stable. But a stronger military and political threat from the Vietcong and an increasingly recalcitrant partner in Diem made "just enough" a great deal more. Both the level and the nature of the United States' investment in South Vietnam had begun to change.[7]

The extent of that change became visible within weeks. An array of military equipment, from rifles to radios to twin-rotored helicopters, poured into South Vietnam by the shipload. New facilities to support the increased effort were built across the country. American support troops and advisers flew ARVN (Army of the Republic of Vietnam) soldiers into battle, provided close air-support, taught counterinsurgency tactics, and sprayed the forests and rice paddles of Vietcong strongholds with defoliants. The old MAAG was upgraded and expanded into a new Military Assistance Command–Vietnam (MACV). The appointment of four-star General Paul D. Harkins as its commander signaled this new command's importance. Soon the French flavor of Saigon gave way to a decidedly American tang, as the streets, restaurants, bars, and brothels filled with American servicemen.[8]

The Vietnam situation had changed in two basic ways. First, combat activity increased dramatically. Second, American military personnel played an increasingly prominent role in that combat. These changes acted on two fundamental traits of American journalism.

First, Vietnam became much more of a war story. Combat reporting—simple, dramatic, and direct—had a traditional appeal for American editors and readers. The heightened tension of the time enhanced this attraction. The Cold War heated up as Khrushchev and Kennedy engaged in a battle of nerves across the globe. That South Vietnam was the primary place where this struggle, albeit through proxies, had become "a genuine war" made it even more newsworthy. The press had another "good guys shooting Reds" story.[9]

The second trait—American involvement—was the decisive factor. In *Deciding What's News,* his study of how news judgments are made, Herbert Gans cited "ethnocentrism" as the first of his eight "enduring values of the news," those basic assumptions and ideas that shape news coverage. And, Gans continued, "the clearest expression of ethnocentrism appears in war news." When Americans were shooting at Reds, the interest of American journalism was piqued significantly.[10]

Thus, over the next weeks and months, the mainstream American press changed the way it covered Vietnam. First, major American news organizations increased their investment in the Vietnam story. By January 1962, the Associated Press, United Press International, and *The New York Times* had established permanent bureaus in South Vietnam. Although it would be several months before the news magazines opened bureaus, they began to beef up their presence by adding stringers in Vietnam and by shuffling or adding reporters in their Far Eastern bureaus. The television networks, whose evening news broadcasts were still only fifteen minutes long, followed a pattern similar to the magazines'.[11]

The establishment of a resident press corps in South Vietnam both signaled and reinforced a second very important change. Before the Taylor mission and the subsequent shift in the American commitment, Vietnam was not at the center of either the government's or the press's interest, and not a story filled with dramatic, fast-paced action. Between the suppression of the sects in 1955 and the November 1960 coup attempt, the press covered the story as one of trends and conditions, depending on analysis, background, and context. Most coverage depended upon off-the-record and on-the-record briefings from high-level American and South Vietnamese officials who could give the kind of "big-picture" information that suited the press's level of interest and the way it had chosen to cover the story.

But with the increase in combat and American involvement in it, the Vietnam story became much more of a breaking story, composed of spot news, and demanding continuing, constantly updated coverage. Broad, interpretive information no longer sufficed for those reporters and those news organizations that had decided to cover the "new" Vietnam story. News executives increased their commitment of resources to Vietnam. This commitment created pressure to justify the sizable investment through a steady flow of usable, marketable coverage. Reporters and news organizations needed the stuff of spot news, especially American war news—who, what, when, where, how many.

This information was unavailable, however. The South Vietnamese government, motivated by Diem's long-standing suspicion of the foreign press and by his more recent desire to inflate his successes against the Vietcong, gave little hard information to the American press, and what it did give was suspect. Nor did the Kennedy Administration offer much help. Kennedy tried to emphasize South Vietnamese leadership and to downplay the U.S.'s own involvement in the war.

All this highlights one of the most important and fundamental problems plaguing the study of the press and the Vietnam War: the failure to understand the dynamics of American journalism, particularly the ways these dynamics determined how the Vietnam story would be covered over the years.

Soon, two different pictures of the war began to appear in the American news media, one increasingly critical of the way the war was being conducted and pessimistic about its prospects, the other supportive of those who led the effort and optimistic about its future course. Soon, these two pictures of the war and those who painted them would come into direct and bitter conflict, a conflict born not of differences in age or experience, politics or ideology, but of the dictates and demands of journalism as practiced in the United States in the early 1960s. And the same factors that created this conflict would also make these months a special—indeed, a golden—period for American journalism during the Vietnam War.

## "The Privileged Few"

The resident American press corps in South Vietnam was still small enough, as Karnow put it, to "sit around a small table in the Hotel Caravelle bar." A few names figure prominently. Malcolm Browne of the Associated Press came in November 1961, followed quickly by Homer Bigart of the *Times* and Ray Herndon of UPI. AP photographer Horst Faas soon arrived from Algiers, and in April 1962 Neil Sheehan joined the UPI staff. In July, David Halberstam replaced Bigart. Other news organizations that had not yet assigned correspondents were employing stringers, Merton Perry of *Time* and Francois Sully of *Newsweek* most prominent among them. Important regional correspondents included Stanley Karnow, Charles Mohr, and Jerry Rose of *Time*, Robert Elegant of *Newsweek*, Robert P. Martin of *U.S. News and World Report*, and Peter Kalischer of CBS. For these journalists and their colleagues—"the privileged few," Halberstam called them—it quickly became clear that, for reasons good and ill, Vietnam was a very special assignment.[12]

Before going to Vietnam after his assignment in the Congo, Halberstam was asked by Bernard Kalb if he had found any city in Africa appealing. "I allowed as how I hadn't," Halberstam said. "Bernie was horror-stricken; every correspondent, he insisted, should fall in love with at least one city. . . . Then I went to Saigon and found out what Bernie meant."

Much of what Halberstam and others found so alluring about Vietnam can be summed up in one word: Saigon. Fed by the waters of the Saigon and Bassac rivers, the city was a garden in which all the exotic sights, sounds, smells, and sensations of Southeast Asia bloomed. Saigon harbored many contrasts: abject poverty and helplessness living in the shadow of opulence and power; Christianity, Buddhism, Confucianism, Taoism, and spirit worship practiced within the same city block; people of Chinese, Cambodian, Indian, Indonesian, and other origins thrown into the already confused ethnic mix that made up the Vietnamese people; a playground in a state of war.

Physically untouched by the war, Saigon was in 1962 still the "Paris of the East" that American reporters had known since the 1940s. *The New Yorker*'s Robert Shaplen regarded it as "the loveliest of the Southeast Asian capitals"; he was pleased to find that it had "retained its sense of buoyancy and well-being." The restaurants offered excellent French, Chinese, and, for the adventurous, Vietnamese food. The nightlife was still vibrant. La Cigale, the favorite night spot of Halberstam and his roommate, Faas, had good food and "the best singers in town," including Miss Yen Hung, "who looked like a Vietnamese Joan Baez and sang French songs with the anguish of an Edith Piaf." Also prominent among the city's attractions were its women. "Saigon was a great city for girl watching," and many male reporters could wax poetic about the charms of Vietnamese women and their traditional clothing, the *ao dai*. A *Time* correspondent described Saigon's "beautiful fragile girls, like exotic moths in their flowing skirts split at the waist over trousers of silken gauze." For many American men, "there was an intensity about the Vietnamese women, from the little bar girls, who were ordered to wear uniforms but managed to look brazen anyway, to the First Lady herself."[13]

Even on a limited salary and expense account, a resident correspondent could live comfortably in Saigon, especially if he was willing to patronize the black-market currency exchange. They stayed at the best hotels—either the Continental, whose French imperial glory was becoming somewhat frayed, or the newer Caravelle, starker but more modern and efficient—or found places of their own. Faas and Halberstam, for example, rented a huge villa from a German Embassy official on home leave. Many correspondents, who were making several hundred dollars a month in salary and expenses, retained at least one servant, the best of whom made "\$20 a month or less to work seven days a week, doing all the washing, cleaning, cooking."[14]

This same buying power also brought the best of Saigon within reach. Halberstam described Saigon as "one of the great cities in the world for a gourmet." He and Faas went regularly to a restaurant in Cholon called The Diamond, "which specialized in cracked crab. We would order vast quantities of the shellfish. . . . Throwing the empty shells aside, we barely talked to each other in the scramble for choice pieces." An evening on the town, including the company of a young woman, was also inexpensive. Oriental art and antiques could be collected at bargain prices. On top of all this, the correspondents had access to American commissaries and post exchanges and the wealth of goods they stocked.[15]

Charming and exciting as Saigon was, the story itself brought these reporters to Vietnam, and the story made Vietnam "a reporter's dream."[16]

First, it was a war story. By February 1962, some forty to seventy "violent incidents," ranging from terrorist attacks to battalion-size engagements, took place every day. This action claimed twenty-four hundred or more ARVN, Vietcong, and, with increasing frequency, American casualties a month. By the spring of the year, more stories on combat action appeared in the mainstream press. *The New York Times* ran a summary of action several times a week and directed greater attention to more significant incidents. The wires provided a constant update on combat news to their print and broadcast clients. The weekly newsmagazines, though less committed to breaking news than the *Times* or the wire services, also included summaries of action or featured certain incidents with some regularity.[17]

For men like Bigart, combat action was nothing new. But the younger men, such as Halberstam, Sheehan, and Browne, had to learn to work in such situations. Each of these three men has described his first combat mission in Vietnam, and the similarities in their accounts foreshadow the frustrations that each would soon feel.

Malcolm Browne came to Vietnam in late 1961 and went on his first operation in December. He accompanied an ARVN unit working in Kien Hoa, south of Saigon in the Delta, the "showcase" province of Colonel Pham Ngoc Thao that so fascinated Joe Alsop. The operation was supposed to seize two hamlets along a canal and trap a

Vietcong battalion. But after several hours of slogging through muddy rice paddies, the ARVN troops had succeeded only in killing an unarmed farmer, leaving a widow and two frightened children, and tearing down a hut covered with antigovernment slogans. "It looks as though the Viet Cong got away again," the commander told Browne.[18]

In the summer of 1962, Neil Sheehan went on his first helicopter assault with a battalion of the ARVN Seventh Division and got a first powerful insight into the war. "In my mind," he wrote later, "as in the minds of other Americans recently come to Vietnam . . . the Viet Minh were a distinctly different generation of guerrillas from the Viet Cong. The Viet Minh of my thoughts had been patriots, by and large nationalists," whereas "the Viet Cong guerrillas were misguided peasants who had been gulled into following the wrong side by Communists who were the enemies of good men everywhere."[19]

But when his helicopter landed, he saw in the distance men wearing uniforms "like those I had seen Viet Minh guerrillas wearing in photographs of the French war." And when the ARVN commander questioned an old man, both he and the peasant kept referring to the Viet Minh. "Why?" Sheehan asked a Vietnamese reporter. "I thought we were after the Viet Cong." "The Americans and the government people in Saigon call them the Viet Cong," the reporter answered, "But out here everyone still calls them the Viet Minh." At that moment, Sheehan realized that "the Viet Minh were back, and that the South Vietnamese leadership realized it too. "Only the Americans knew neither the Vietnamese they were depending on to work their will, nor the Vietnamese enemy they faced."[20]

Halberstam's first operation was on October 3, 1962. Like Sheehan's, it was a helicopter assault with a unit of the Seventh Division. During his day in the field, Halberstam learned a number of simple things: how to walk in the muck of a rice paddy, how to cross a canal on a bamboo pole, what kind and how many pairs of footgear to bring. But he also learned that the ARVN he observed was not interested in engaging the Vietcong, and that the American advisers and support troops in the field were quite discouraged. "This was what the war was like," they told him, "hot and frustrating and unrewarding, days filled with violations of the most obvious kind of military sense, days spent hoping desperately for the break which would make the enemy fight."[21]

The Vietnam story also engaged the reporters because of its goals. Here was a war American in its ideals—helping a small nation throw off the legacy of colonialism and resist the threat of communism. These were ideals the reporters believed in. Browne said that, "as a citizen of the Free World, I hope the challenge represented by Vietnam is met." Halberstam agreed with the domino theory, which saw Vietnam as "the key to a large part of South Asia," and worried that, "if the Vietnamese, who are perhaps the toughest people in Southeast Asia, fell to the Communists, the pressure on the other shaky new nations would be intolerable."[22]

Vietnam also rapidly became an American war in a physical sense. Tons of additional war materiel flowed into the country's docks and airfields. Substantial numbers of new advisers, who would take a much more active hand in assisting the South Vietnamese armed forces, also arrived. "When commercial planes land at the Saigon airport," Pepper Martin of *U.S. News* reported, "the stewardesses announce: 'Will all American military personnel please remain aboard the aircraft until arrangements can be made for them to disembark?' From one half to two thirds of the well-dressed young men in civilian clothing stay in their seats." When Kennedy took office in January 1961, fewer than one thousand American soldiers were in South Vietnam. By the end of the year, that number had grown to over three thousand, and would reach nine thousand by the end of 1962.

The Americans made their presence felt everywhere in Saigon. "In the dining room of the plush Caravelle Hotel, junior officers in sport shirts sampled the excellent *lapin sauté chasseur;* and in the European-style sidewalk cafés, tall United States Army Rangers sipped beer, unsuccessfully trying to look inconspicuous." By February, thirteen Saigon hotels were filled with American troops, sleeping four or five to a room in some cases. And along the Rue Catinat—recently renamed Duong Tu Do, or Freedom Street—American-style watering holes were springing up and the bar girls were learning pidgin English.[23]

As this presence grew, the activities and prospects of the Americans in Vietnam became a focus of press reporting. Reporters described Americans in the field with South Vietnamese troops, flying helicopters and other aircraft, building bridges and radar towers, spraying crops and jungle areas with defoliants. "Americans are now fully, formally, and irrevocably committed to the defense of South Vietnam."[24]

As coverage of Vietnam gravitated toward the Americans, naturally enough, so did the press corps. "Friendships between Americans and Vietnamese were formed only slowly," remembered Halberstam; Americans and Vietnamese who associated too closely became suspect in the eyes of both governments. Instead, Americans tended to associate with other Americans. "Americans arrived in Saigon to find other Americans; they went to an American PX and American movies; they rode in buses with other Americans, and flew with other Americans in the field in American helicopters; often they slept in American quarters with fellow Americans, eating, more often than not, at American messes."[25]

The resident press reporters had been sent to cover this story, and they set out to do so with great energy in less-than-ideal conditions. The State Department rated Vietnamese as one of the world's most difficult languages to learn. None of the new resident press corps spoke Vietnamese, though most spoke at least a smattering of French, as did many of the South Vietnamese with whom they came in contact. The climate was also difficult. Average annual temperature hovered around eighty degrees Fahrenheit, with a humidity that could be overwhelming. Trips to the field were challenging. More bothersome than the obvious fear of being injured or captured were the physical conditions they faced. The terrain in the Delta was almost invariably wet and muddy. Halberstam described the conditions he found during his first trip there. As the helicopter landed, "the Vietnamese scrambled out into the water that came up to their shoulders. I decided it would come to my waist, jumped out and felt it seep over my shoulders too, which meant a soggy ham sandwich for lunch and the end of my Minox camera. But there is one good thing about landing in a rice paddy; the shock is so abrupt and complete that for the rest of the day you won't bother trying to stay comfortable or clean or dry." At the end of the day, Halberstam had "learned just how much of a tenderfoot I was. My neck was red, but my feet were a dismal pasty white; they were the feet of the dead."[26]

If the field wasn't tough enough, the resident press had working facilities in Saigon that were, at best, spartan. The *Times*, for example, shared the two-room office-apartment of UPI correspondent Neil Sheehan. The press corps depended on the South Vietnamese Post,

Telephone, and Telegraph services to get dispatches out of the country.[27]

The resident reporters worked very hard to satisfy their employers' demand for copy. When Peter Arnett arrived in Saigon in June 1962, he found Malcolm Browne "beating a two-finger tattoo on his old Remington . . . trying to complete the daily 700 words of copy we used to send then to Tokyo." The wire services, especially in those days, provided the vast majority of war coverage. The wires, serving a variety of clients and operating on morning and evening news cycles across four time zones in the United States, worked almost constantly to gather, check, write, and transmit breaking news. Bigart and Halberstam operated under only slightly less pressure, as they fed daily material to the *Times*. The regional correspondents and stringers for the newsmagazines didn't have such time constraints, but they also had less control over what they covered and how it was used. The home offices picked story ideas and dictated them to the reporters in the field. The reporters then wrote and dispatched to a writer in New York or Washington a weekly "file" of some fifteen hundred to two thousand words. None of this might actually appear in the magazine. The several days' lag time between when a story was filed and written and when the magazine appeared complicated the magazine correspondents' job even further. They had to give stories a longer shelf life by putting them into some sort of analytical framework and speculating on the future consequences of recent developments.[28]

These conditions were difficult, but the greatest challenge faced by the resident American press corps came from the policies and actions of the South Vietnamese and United States governments. At the moment that the American press chose to devote increased attention and resources to the Vietnam story, American and South Vietnamese officials tried to take the story away.

## "A Matter of Great Sensitivity"

During its first months in office, the Kennedy Administration took a fairly relaxed attitude toward the limited coverage of Vietnam, but certain stories and journalists did stir some interest. For example, in April 1961, Joe Alsop, a strong supporter of Diem, wrote a series of columns from Southeast Asia about the increased threat to South Vietnam, implying that Kennedy hadn't done enough to counter it. Alsop, while in Vietnam, told Ambassador Durbrow that Diem was "very bitter" toward the United States for not supporting him sufficiently, and Alsop added that he agreed. Durbrow complained to Rusk that "correspondents have finally been allowed to 'discover' [the] 18 months old war and Diem has found a new toy to badger us." But the episode was passed off fairly lightly. Counterinsurgency expert and Diem adviser Edward Lansdale told Kennedy aide Walt Rostow that "Joe is expert at using the needle on Ambassadors. . . . Probably Durbrow wrote the message too soon afterwards and was still somewhat in a state of shock."[29]

Several concerns moved the Kennedy Administration to pay much more attention to press coverage of Vietnam after the Taylor mission. Kennedy had to provide sufficient military and moral support to Diem to stop and reverse the Vietcong advance. This required unqualified public statements backing Diem, and a private policy that gave up any attempt to pressure him into political or social reforms.[30] It also meant that Kennedy had to identify South Vietnam as a foreign-policy priority. But talking too much about Vietnam would raise public fear of U.S. participation in another Asian war, with all the attendant domestic political risks. Thus, Kennedy had to bolster Diem but play down the degree of American involvement. To this end, the Kennedy Administration began to restrict and manipulate information about the war. It was, the president said in a press conference, "a matter of great sensitivity."[31]

Within weeks of the Taylor mission and the commencement of the American buildup in South Vietnam, the clampdown on information made itself felt. First, the United States government acquiesced to Diem's suspicion and hostility toward the American press. The root of the problem "was the Ngo Dinh family's unshakable belief in its own infallibility. . . . The palace seldom lied intentionally to the press," said John Mecklin, USIS chief in Saigon at the time. "It often tried to persuade reporters to accept absurdities, but it usually believed them itself—and regularly tried to sell the same absurdities to the U.S. Mission, often, unhappily, with greater success." The South Vietnamese government provided almost no facilities or assistance to newsmen, and when reporters found other sources, often sources in disagreement with Diem, "a dangerous vicious circle" developed. Diem believed that the United States government controlled the

American press as he controlled that of South Vietnam. When the press reported something he did not like, he blamed American officials, accused them of undermining him, and became more stubborn and withdrawn. American officials then blamed the press for hurting the war effort. "To put it another way," Mecklin said, "it became unpatriotic for a newsman to use an adjective that displeased Mme. Nhu."[32]

The Kennedy Administration also took steps of its own to shut the press away from the story. In late November 1961, a joint message of the State and Defense departments and the USIA was sent to Saigon, with White House approval, ordering all American personnel to give nothing more than "routine cooperation to correspondents on coverage [of] current military situation in Vietnam." In February 1962, the hold on information became even tighter. On the 6th, Admiral Harry Felt, the commander of United States forces in the Pacific, banned reporters for Western news agencies from American-piloted helicopter assault missions. At a news conference the next day, a reporter asked Kennedy "how deeply are we involved in what seems to be a growing war and what are the rights of the people to know what our forces are doing?" Kennedy explained the United States' limited role and South Vietnamese leadership, then denied any obligation to inform the American people by declaring that "this is an area where there is a good deal of danger and it's a matter of information. We don't want to have information which is of assistance to the enemy—and it's a matter that I think will have to be worked out with the Government of Vietnam, which bears the primary responsibility."[33]

These growing restrictions received a definitive statement later in February. On the 20th, another joint State-Defense-USIA message, Cable 1006, was transmitted to Nolting. The message, written by Deputy Assistant Secretary of State for Public Affairs Carl T. Rowan, was personally approved by Rusk, Pentagon chief McNamara, and Salinger, among others. Because Cable 1006 stated the fundamental—and controversial—press policy of the United States government well into 1963, it's worth looking at in some detail.

The message began positively enough. "US interests [can] best be protected through [a] policy of maximum feasible cooperation, guidance and appeal to good faith of correspondents," it said, and "speculative stories by hostile reporters [are] often more damaging than the facts they might report."

But the cable quickly turned to some "guidelines which we believe

[are] in our national interest" and that must be followed "if we [are] to avoid harmful press repercussions on both domestic and international scene." The first two of the cable's seven points urged American personnel not to "grant interviews or take other actions implying all-out US involvement." The third item stated that stories on civilian casualties "are clearly inimical to national interest." Items 5 and 6 emphasized the need to support Diem and "that articles that tear down Diem only make our task more difficult."

The remaining two guidelines were, however, the key to the whole memorandum and provided the muscle to hold or manipulate information about the war. First, "operations may be referred to in general terms, but specific numbers—particularly numbers of Americans involved—and details of material introduced are not to be provided. On tactical security matters, analyses [of] strengths and weaknesses and other operational details which might aid enemy should be avoided." Finally, "correspondents should not be taken on missions whose nature [is] such that undesirable dispatches would be highly probable." The first guideline essentially forbade release of casualty information or other information on American troops' involvement except that provided by official sources. The second decreed that American reporters be kept away from any but the most tightly controlled and favorably stage-managed situations.[34]

Cable 1006's message was refined and emphasized over the coming months. For example, the government worked out a plan to achieve "maximum discretion, minimum publicity" for United States air operations in South Vietnam. If an American-piloted plane shot down a hostile aircraft, American personnel were to remain silent unless questioned directly by the press. The South Vietnamese Air Force (VNAF) was then to "claim credit through GVN information channels. Plausibility will be reinforced by scheduling VNAF aircraft in air at time and in general area of action." If an American plane went down for any reason, officials were to explain "that accident occurred while aircraft engaged in routine orientation flight." Other guidelines instructed American personnel returning to the United States from Vietnam that "This is not a U.S. war and personnel being interviewed should not imply the U.S. is fighting this war."[35]

Despite Cable 1006, the government became "increasingly concerned over constant implications in press generally of U.S. participation and direction" of the war during 1962. In April, for example,

Assistant Secretary of State Averill Harriman asked Nolting to re-emphasize the importance "of minimizing US presence and reducing public impression US going beyond announced objectives." American officials went so far as to order ships carrying military equipment to unload at more isolated locations than the main Saigon waterfront. One day, while sitting at a sidewalk café overlooking the Saigon docks, Karnow pointed out the ferry ship *Core*, carrying forty-seven helicopters on its deck, to the army public-information officer with him. The officer made "a mock squint in the direction of the gigantic ship and replied, 'I don't see nothing.' "[36]

This policy did not achieve the desired result. The Kennedy Administration did not understand how the relationship of the press to the Vietnam story had changed. The administration believed that reporters based in Vietnam would be satisfied with the paltry information dispensed by South Vietnamese and American officials. But the war's "increasing ferocity" and the United States' deepening involvement had moved major news organizations to increase their investment in the story.[37] That investment had to be justified by a steady stream of coverage flowing from the cramped bureaus in Saigon to editorial offices in New York and Washington. To provide this coverage, the press needed dependable sources of information. Such information was not available from official sources. Seeking combat-related action stories and news of American involvement, the reporters in Saigon naturally looked to the men with the greatest firsthand knowledge of both: American troops in the field.

Halberstam described how he came to this point. "In these early days of my Vietnam assignment I was trying to decide how to evaluate this perplexing war. How do you add up thirty minor engagements each day, almost all of them in places you've never been to, and with no substantive information to cast light on the significance of the situation? It was very quickly obvious to me that the story could not be covered from Saigon briefing rooms, despite all the multicolored arrows on the maps." Halberstam consequently decided to make the ARVN Seventh Division, headquartered in My Tho, just south of Saigon in the Delta, his "litmus paper" for the war.[38]

Access to these sources was facilitated in two ways. First, the most significant action of the war was taking place in the Upper Mekong Delta, "forty miles south of Saigon on a good road," Halberstam said. Later, the war would spread throughout the country and the press would depend much more heavily upon the military for transportation, but for now the war—and the sources—were a cab ride away.

The fact that the reporters and the field advisers had much in common also eased access. Like most of the resident reporters, the captains and majors that advised ARVN battalions were young, in their late twenties to early thirties. Reporters and soldiers alike had been identified as comers, young men of exceptional ability and energy whose selection for service in Vietnam marked and tested them for further advancement. They had gone through the same life experiences. They had grown up certain of the rightness and the reach of American power and convinced that that power faced a severe test from communism. "In our lifetime the enemy had become clearly identifiable, and many of the officers and reporters felt strongly and instinctively that Vietnam was the place to draw the line," Halberstam wrote. The reporters came to respect and to identify with these men. "There was a sense of camaraderie in the bar that night," Halberstam continued, "for we were all participants in this private little war in Vietnam. We were all obsessed by it, and awed by the vast ignorance, even indifference, about it in the United States."[39]

The advisers and support troops quickly became the primary sources of consistent, credible information for the resident press corps and regional newsmagazine correspondents. Soon the reporters reflected the attitudes and concerns of these sources in their reporting.

America's increasing role in the conduct of the war became the theme of much of the coverage. "Sometimes the line between American assistance and American participation was blurred," reported *Newsweek*. "Gun-carrying U.S. field advisers have been told not to stay behind at headquarters but go with the Vietnamese troops into the swamps and jungle. The Americans are not supposed to shoot, unless they are in danger—but danger is everywhere outside the towns." "It's in the field," wrote Pepper Martin of *U.S. News*, "that you see how intimately involved Americans are in this war." He described Americans piloting helicopters, Americans accompanying operations and participating in combat, Americans patrolling the waters of the South China Sea. Bigart reported MACV's attempt to hush up the fact that the first American helicopter crewman to be wounded in Vietnam had been denied a Purple Heart—the government hadn't recognized Vietnam as a combat zone for Americans. "Eight of twenty planes of the United States Army Light Helicopter Company have holes from Communist bullets," wrote Bigart. "The crews cannot follow the subtlety of Washington thinking and are indignant." "How deeply is the United States committed here?" asked Halberstam. "Americans and Vietnamese live together, march together, fight together and die together, and it is hard to get much more involved than that."[40]

The frustration and pessimism of the men in the field also began to appear in the coverage. The timidity of South Vietnamese commanders, and the Vietcong's ability to strike and get away, were major concerns. *Newsweek*'s François Sully described a massive operation, using helicopters and armored personnel carriers, that, like many others, ended with "the familiar frustrating announcement: No contact with any major enemy force." Halberstam wrote that "Americans are bothered by the Vietnamese failure to patrol [and] the lack of a sense of urgency in the fight against a quick and elusive enemy. There is some feelfing on the part of the Americans in the field that, despite all the talk of counter-guerrilla tactics, the real battle has yet to be joined."[41]

The stubbornness, ineptitude, and isolation of the Diem regime— and how they interfered with the war effort—also disturbed Americans in the field. This too ended up in the coverage of the reporters to whom they talked. "The basic problem," said *Newsweek*, "is that the Vietnamese Government does not command respect in the rural areas," because of "a sickening atmosphere of insecurity, suspicion, and government clumsiness." Pepper Martin decried Diem's corruption of the military. "The President distrusts his own armed forces," Martin wrote, and "commanders, in turn, are unwilling to risk their careers by engaging in bold, imaginative operations that might risk the President's wrath." Bigart summed up his impressions at the end of his tour by stating that, despite the United States' "massive and unqualified support" of Diem, "victory is remote. The issue remains in doubt because the Vietnamese President seems incapable of winning the loyalty of his people."[42]

The advisers and other troops closest to the situation also resented optimistic statements by top-level officials. Jacques Nevard, in Saigon for the *Times* between Bigart's departure and Halberstam's arrival, wrote that the administration's "cautious optimism . . . is not widely reflected among Americans stationed here to help in that fight." Halberstam said that, in the rush to put the best face on developments, "there sometimes seems a tendency to describe results before they have been attained and a parallel tendency to discredit pessimistic reporting." "It should be reported," Halberstam continued, "that there is considerably less optimism out in the field than in Washington or in Saigon and that the closer one gets to the actual contact level of this war, the farther one gets from official optimism."[43]

Reports like these increasingly disturbed the South Vietnamese government and the Kennedy Administration, and both took steps to stop or counteract it. Both governments attempted to deny reporters access to combat operations. The South Vietnamese followed reporters, ransacked their rooms, and tapped their phones. They monitored dispatches and messages out of and into the country over the PTT (Post, Telephone, and Telegraph) cable system, and delayed or destroyed those found offensive. Diem rarely saw reporters, and when he did they were subjected to increasingly long and irrelevant monologues. Lower-level South Vietnamese officials were ordered to answer only written questions approved in advance. South Vietnamese information officials frequently chastised reporters. Expulsion from the country was the ultimate penalty. Bigart, ordered out in March 1962, was allowed to stay only after Nolting's intervention. *Newsweek*'s Sully was kicked out in September, after writing an article critical of the Nhus. NBC's James Robinson had been in the country only two weeks, and had yet to file a story, when he was expelled in October. His offense was supposedly failing to file for a visa, but he was actually paying the price for earlier NBC reports that had disturbed the South Vietnamese government.[44]

Though the United States government and military's main effort to shut out the American press involved acquiescing in these South Vietnamese actions, they also took steps of their own. Certain American facilities were off limits to American reporters. For example, military police detained Jerry Rose of Time-Life and Peter Kalischer of CBS when they tried to photograph the Bien Hoa air base, outside Saigon. Reporters' stories were monitored. Arthur Sylvester sought and obtained NBC's cooperation in withholding from further broadcast a two-minute report on rough treatment of VC prisoners by ARVN soldiers. The CIA was rolled out to check the accuracy of a Bigart dispatch describing a successful Vietcong ambush of an ARVN convoy. They concluded that the ambush showed official claims of diminished VC strength and increased peasant loyalty to be so much "wishful thinking." (The CIA agreed with Bigart.)[45]

American officials also encouraged visits by journalists based in the Unted States. These, they hoped, would produce positive reports. In late 1961, Rusk encouraged Nolting to assist Howard Sochurek, a Time-Life writer whom the administration considered "trustworthy and discreet." Sochurek had, not incidentally, agreed to submit his copy to the Vietnam Task Force for approval before publication. Richard Tregaskis, author of *Guadalcanal Diary*, received a great deal of assistance from MACV and embassy information personnel—including access to helicopter assault and fighter-bomber missions—while in Vietnam during late 1962 and early 1963 gathering material for his *Vietnam Diary*, a glowing account of the effort in South Vietnam.

Joe Alsop also got special treatment. By 1962, Alsop had become one of Diem's strongest supporters; Nolting told Aslop's wife that Diem "still thinks he [Alsop] is the only American who has exactly the right line on Viet-Nam (which is not far wrong)." While in Saigon, Alsop stayed in the ambassador's residence. He had instant access to the top ARVN commanders, the top American officials, and, to Bigart's anger, that prized place on a helicopter mission. The Kennedy Administration was amply rewarded for its attention. Alsop praised the American leadership in Vietnam and credited the new American commitment, as evidenced by the helicopters, for the beginnings of hope in a previously gloomy situation.[46]

It didn't take long for frustrations to rise to the surface. Kennedy's strategy of silence on Vietnam came under fire, as did his attempts to restrict other information. In Vietnam itself, conflict arose between a loose group of free spirits—the resident press corps and American advisers—and top American and South Vietnamese officials and journalists based in the United States.

The root of the conflict lay not in generational or ideological differences. To be sure, many among the American press corps working in Vietnam were young, but two of the toughest, most persistent questioners of official optimism were veteran correspondents Homer Bigart and Pepper Martin. And almost unanimously, the American press corps strongly supported the goal of resisting communism in Southeast Asia. The conflict lay, instead, in the needs of journalism itself. Reporters needed dependable and relevant information, but the South Vietnamese and American governments denied that need. Turning then to Americans in the field for information, journalists found that, as Halberstam said, the closer one got to where the war was actually going on, the farther one got from the official optimism of Washington and Saigon.

In many ways, this was the golden era of Vietnam journalism, when the press actually came close to fulfilling the role that legend has granted it. Having been shut off from all but the sketchiest official information, the press found—and were found by—other sources, who provided the reporters the information they needed to do their jobs. These reporters exhibited a high level of creativity, persistence, and bravery as they tried to overcome the obstacles placed in their paths. They also showed an aggressiveness and skepticism toward official information that their predecessors, and many of their successors, did not.

This period was only a way station, however, in the Vietnam story. The press's relationship to the story was growing and changing. The conflict with officialdom would grow worse before it got better.

# 5

# "Let Them Burn"

## The Buddhist Crisis of 1963

ON THE MORNING of June 11, 1963, David Halberstam was awakened by a phone call from Nguyen Ngoc Rao, a Vietnamese reporter for UPI. "His voice was almost out of control," Halberstam remembered. "All I could understand was that I should get to the corner of Le Van Duyet and Phan Dinh Phung streets as quickly as possible."

When Halberstam arrived, he thought it was just another demonstration. "But at that moment I looked into the center of the circle and saw a man burning himself to death." In the middle of the street sat seventy-three-year-old Thich (Venerable) Quang Duc, a picture of serenity and composure despite the now roaring flames. As he burned, young priests handed out his biography. Another priest, with a microphone, repeated over and over, in English and Vietnamese, "A Buddhist priest burns himself to death. A Buddhist priest becomes a martyr."[1]

Quang Duc's suicide symbolized the last year of the Diem regime. Fear and repression had built over the years. Now they were consuming Diem and his family as certainly as the flames consumed Quang Duc's body. This fear and repression spread to the American press corps—its relationship to the Vietnam story, to the U.S. and South Vietnamese military and government, and even to other journalists.

## "I Am Sick of It"

By the spring of 1962, things were bad between the president and the press. Vietnam had become yet another brick in the wall of secrecy being built by his administration. Kennedy's candor regarding Vietnam was questioned by a variety of sources.

Reporters and news organizations in South Vietnam complained the loudest. *The New York Times* was especially vocal. It didn't take long for Homer Bigart to go public with his feelings about the restrictions. "The United States information policy on Vietnam has not been marked by candor. Official secrecy has curbed reporting," he said. He gave examples of "the fiction that United States service men are keeping discreetly in the background." These included U.S. warships patrolling the South Vietnamese coast and planes with South Vietnamese markings manned by American crews.[2]

In May, Bigart and other American correspondents asked visiting Defense Secretary McNamara to ease the restrictions, especially on helicopter missions and American casualty reports. "Mr. McNamara listened sympathetically." But he made it clear that "the Administration believes the American correspondents . . . are magnifying incidents where American servicemen find themselves in combat situations and are writing too much about American casualties." "Mr. Secretary," Bigart complained during the meeting, "we're not getting enough news." McNamara countered that the reporters were getting "a great deal of news—a very great deal." "Yes," replied Bigart, "but I'm having to work too hard for it."[3]

When Halberstam arrived in South Vietnam, American officials tried to court him, feeding him selected bits of information and praising his coverage. But Halberstam had been warned. Bigart told him that Saigon "is full of American spooks trying to silence the few honest Americans who will level with correspondents." Jacques Nevard also cautioned him to beware of overly solicitous officials. "They're making a play for you," he told Halberstam, "and they're very, very glad Homer's gone."

Soon Halberstam was just as critical. "A stream of V.I.P.'s and local officials has breathed the official line of cautious optimism until it seems that each man, buoyed by the optimism of the last, is a bit more optimistic than his predecessors," he wrote. The result "was an outward rigidity and orthodoxy at the top that was unique among American missions overseas."[4]

The men of the *Times* were even more critical in private. James Reston, then the *Times'* Washington bureau chief, protested Bigart's threatened expulsion in late March. When State Department officials said that they would be glad to "assist" Bigart, Reston exploded. "Assist? At what? Packing his bags?" Bigart wrote to his editors, "This has not been a happy assignment. . . . Too often correspondents seem to be regarded by the American mission as tools of our foreign policy. I am sick of it. Each morning I take a pen and blot off another day on the Saigon calendar."[5]

Other news organizations joined in. *Newsweek* said that "The military won't say what's going on or where until its over. Vietnamese officials tend to regard newsmen as suspect propagandists." Pepper Martin told his editors that "restrictions imposed by the U.S. Embassy make it impossible to report fully on the extent of American participation in the war effort here. . . . The curtain of secrecy looks like a U.S. Embassy effort to confuse and disguise the situation." An AP dispatch said that "one of the battles being fought in South Vietnam involves the problem of finding out what is going on and reporting it to the people of the United States. Many correspondents here feel they are losing" that battle.[6]

The frustration, suspicion, and anger grew with each affront in 1962. Four Special Forces enlisted men were captured during a Vietcong attack on a South Vietnamese Civic Action Platoon in April near An Chou, 360 miles north of Saigon. Two of the Americans were wounded and eventually killed by their captors.[7]

The two remaining Americans turned up three weeks later, released voluntarily by the Vietcong. But the head of South Vietnam's Civic Action Program, a deft self-promoter named Ngo Trong Hieu, claimed they had been freed by his militia forces. Kennedy even sent Diem his "deep appreciation" for the rescue.

The fiction was soon revealed, and Hieu, in a fit of pique, refused to attend the news conference he himself had called. American officials went ahead with the questioning, hoping to salvage something from the mess. Within minutes, they regretted the decision. The two Green Berets had been ordered to deny that any conditions were attached to their release. But they had forgotten that they had seen

Peter Kalischer of CBS earlier in Danang. They had given him one of the propaganda leaflets the Vietcong forced them to carry. Kalischer, who was at the news conference, dramatically produced one of the leaflets. When reporters rushed to file stories on the deception, their dispatches were held at the cable office for up to twelve hours.[8]

The trouble didn't end there. First came the expulsion of François Sully of *Newsweek*. An article in the August 20 issue of *Newsweek* raised the ire of Madame Nhu, and an all-out campaign against him began. Surveillance tightened, and the Diem-controlled newspapers accused Sully of being "an opium smuggler, a Viet Cong spy, and a patron of sex orgies." Within days he was ordered out of the country.

The night the order came down, a group of reporters gathered in a room at the Caravelle, arguing over a response and questioning Sully until 3:00 A.M. Although Sully was neither the most respected nor the most popular correspondent in Saigon, they realized that an attack on him was an attack on all of them. The group split over what to do. Browne, Sheehan, and Nevard wrote a strong protest to Diem, calling his attitude toward the press "contrary to the interests of free people everywhere," and sent a copy to Kennedy. The other correspondents, deciding that Sully wasn't worth the risk, sent a milder protest. But the complaints only hardened Diem's position. Despite pleas from Ambassador Nolting, the order stood, and Sully left the country on September 9.[9]

The Sully affair made matters worse all the way around, and the conflict grew as the fall wore on. In mid-October, the South Vietnamese Joint General Staff ordered that all questions to South Vietnamese commanders be submitted in writing and all answers be cleared through the top levels of the government. Colonel Huynh Van Cao, commander of the Seventh Division, operating in the important northern Mekong Delta region, went even further. He banned reporters from visiting his area without special permission from Saigon.

A little over a month later, the order shut American reporters out of one of the biggest operations of the war to that time. On November 20, fifty helicopters carried eight hundred South Vietnamese troops and over two hundred American flyers and advisers into the heart of War Zone D, a Vietcong concentration northwest of Saigon, near the Cambodian border. The mission had been classified "secret." When the press attempted to find out more from MACV, chief public-information officer Colonel James Smith informed them that

"There is nothing we may report on this operation. We have been told this by the Government of Vietnam." When a reporter tried to tap a usually reliable source inside MACV, he was told that his friend "had been ordered not to talk by the South Vietnamese Joint General Staff."[10]

The situation bordered on the silly. MACV tried hard to find out who had leaked the number of helicopters participating in the operation. It dropped the effort when told that a reporter who lived near the air base had simply counted the helicopters from his bedroom window. An American adviser said that, "From the moment the 50 helicopters hit the target and unloaded, the Communists knew what was happening and the people up in Hanoi knew soon after. Apparently the only people who were not supposed to know were the American and Vietnamese people."

This absurdity angered American advisers and reporters. The advisers felt they were being "muzzled by the South Vietnamese Government with the support of the United States Government" and believed that "Americans at home have too little knowledge and understanding of what is going on in Vietnam." Halberstam gave public and private voice to the frustrations of the press. He told his readers that the U.S. and South Vietnamese governments were trying to shut reporters out. In private he was less restrained. "Halberstam stormed into my office," Mecklin remembered, "slammed a letter addressed to Ambassador Nolting on my desk, and sat shaking with rage while I read it." Halberstam had been converted from "a neutral bystander into an angry man." He criticized the attempt to hide the operation and, in particular, blasted the American command, "from General Harkins on down," for going along with it.[11]

By the end of 1962, relations were thoroughly poisoned. Madame Nhu declared that American reporters in South Vietnam were "intoxicated by communism." Reporters had no love for the Ngo Dinh family. At an embassy reception, Nolting offered the customary toast to the host country's head of state. One correspondent "clutched his glass to his chest and said in a voice that at least a dozen of the Ambassador's American and Vietnamese guests could hear: 'I'd never drink to that son of a bitch.'" Another reporter dismissed a chance to interview Diem, by then a rare thing for the resident press, saying that "Diem would just talk a lot of crap and we would have to print it."[12]

The split in the American community in South Vietnam was more disturbing. "Saigon was unique among overseas posts I had known," Mecklin said. "One day I took a poll of the country team members. Not one had ever been invited for lunch, or even a drink by a local reporter." Instead, "the newsmen preferred to spend their leisure hours with each other, or their secret sources, talking themselves into a persecution psychology that reached the state of Pavlov's dogs." Halberstam wrote, "It had become clear to me very soon after my arrival in Saigon that the relationship between the American mission and the American press in Vietnam was quite different from any other in the rest of the world." "In general," he continued, "a relationship of mutual respect exists between ambassadors and reporters in most underdeveloped countries. . . . But in Vietnam these relationships simply did not exist."[13]

The split had become bitter and personal. "A visitor from Mars admitted to the official inner circles in both Vietnam and Washington could have been excused if he got the impression that the newsmen, as well as the Viet Cong, were the enemy," Mecklin remembered. Upon hearing that a reporter had barely missed taking a Vietcong bullet in the foot, "a senior official snapped his fingers in disappointment, like a man who had missed a putt on the golf course. Everyone laughed." Halberstam told his editors that "John Mecklin, in an appalling drunken scene . . . told me that 'I've never seen anything to match the way they [American officials in Saigon] hate you.' "

Reporters felt the same way. A little song, sung to the tune of "Twinkle, Twinkle, Little Star," was popular with reporters and advisers: "We are winning; / This I know. / General Harkins told me so. / If you doubt me, / Who are you? / McNamara says so too."

"We all personalized the struggle," Neil Sheehan wrote, "but Halberstam personalized it more than anyone else," and General Paul Harkins was the particular bane of Halberstam's existence. Halberstam was "openly contemptuous" of Harkins. "At the annual Fourth of July reception at the Embassy residence, he refused to shake hands with the general, embarrassing Harkins, who was accustomed to a world where one concealed one's feelings." At dinner one night with several reporters and a newly arrived Foreign Service officer, Halberstam tore into Harkins. "As he talked he got angrier and his voice rose. He raised his big fist, banged it down on the table, and shouted his prosecutorial summation: 'Paul D. Harkins should be court-martialed and shot!' "[14]

In the first twelve months of the American buildup, the press conflict swelled like the storms that swept in from the South China Sea. The year 1963 would bring crises that, like a typhoon, would shatter the status quo.

## "A Miserable Damn Performance"

By 1963, strong relationships based on respect, common outlook, and—to no small degree—complementary self-interest developed between the press and its field sources. The most publicized and important was between the American press and Lieutenant Colonel John Paul Vann.

Vann was the senior adviser to the ARVN Seventh Division and its commander, Colonel Huynh Van Cao. Vann represented the best and the worst of the American effort in South Vietnam: a passionate commitment to helping a people resist armed coercion, combined with a similarly passionate arrogance in believing that the United States government knew what was right for South Vietnam.[15] He could not fathom the idea of failure in Vietnam. The French had been defeated because they were colonialists, and because they had never gotten over the humiliation of World War II. On the other hand, "history had not shown Americans to be fallible." Vann was, in Sheehan's phrase, "a guardian of the American empire."[16]

Vann had the most important job with the most important unit in the most important theatre of the war. Its population, material resources, and proximity to Saigon made the northern Mekong Delta, the Seventh Division's area, crucial. Vann resolved to make the Seventh a potent fighting force. This strategy included pumping up the aggressiveness and the ego of Colonel Cao, making the reluctant commander into the "Tiger of South Vietnam."

Through the summer of 1962, Cao became just that. The Seventh Division, aided by Vann's guidance and American helicopters, put the Vietcong on the defensive. Diem praised Cao lavishly, and Harkins was just as pleased with Vann. MACV cited Vann's area as a model and encouraged the press to talk to him. Vann also used the press to build up Cao. Vann hailed Cao's abilities to reporters; and, "the night before an operation," Sheehan said, "he would give the assembled correspondents a pep talk on 'emphasizing the positive' in our stories in order to encourage our ally."[17]

But Vann's tactics soon backfired. In Cao he had created a monster, one so enamored of his own prowess that he would no longer accept Vann's advice, but also restrained by his sense of self-preservation. In July 1962, Vann's intelligence sources pinpointed the position of a Vietcong Main Force battalion. Vann planned a predawn helicopter assault that would, for the first time in the war, trap and destroy a major Vietcong unit. But the whole operation fell apart when Cao failed to engage the Vietcong.[18]

Vann's efforts rapidly unraveled. Time after time, Vann and his men devised plans, only to see Cao fail to implement them. Time after time, sizable Vietcong forces could have been cornered, but Cao "would never spring the trap." At first Vann concealed his frustration even from his own men, but soon he was opening up to them and, on a very selective basis, to the press.

Correspondents had gravitated to the Seventh Division and its dynamic adviser even without Harkins' encouragement. "Reporters follow a story," Sheehan said, and "the story in 1962 . . . was the pivotal fighting in the northern half of the Delta." Vann became more candid as his concern increased. The bond between Vann and the reporters grew. "Once a reporter had demonstrated that he would endure discomfort and expose himself to danger by marching through the paddies and spending nights in the field . . . he was accepted by these amiable and sincere men, and frank discussions followed," said Sheehan.

Vann and the reporters shared a belief in the United States' effort in South Vietnam. By the beginning of 1963, they also shared mutually reinforcing self-interests. Vann's impatience with Cao and an unresponsive American military command grew, and he carefully used the press to air his concerns publicly. The equally frustrated reporters came to respect and protect jealously an invaluable source.[19] Soon the frustrations of Vann and the reporters exploded.

In late December 1962, U.S. Army intelligence detected a Vietcong radio transmitter operating near My Tho, the Seventh Division headquarters. Through the ARVN command, it ordered the division to move against it. But instead of the 120 or so Vietcong that Vann expected, ARVN troops ran into 350 Main Force guerrillas who had decided to stand and fight. The Vietcong, put on the defensive by American helicopters and armored personnel carriers, had learned to fight back. Near the village of Tan Thoi and the hamlet of Bac—Ap Bac in the local dialect—the Vietcong chose to test their new tactics in a major engagement.[20]

American and South Vietnamese military leaders had yearned for such a fight. This was the chance to bring the power of a modern army to bear on a bunch of "raggedy-ass little bastards." But the Battle of Ap Bac, January 2, 1963, made the problems of this particular war starkly evident. The Vietcong had once again been underestimated, and the effectiveness of American technology once again overestimated. Political and career concerns so distorted the ARVN that even commanders who wanted to fight were hamstrung. American advisers had a hard time pushing the South Vietnamese into action.[21]

The American command refused to acknowledge these problems. Moreover, the authorities tried to discredit those persons who brought them to light. The Vietcong had chosen to stand and fight. And they had done well, bringing down five helicopters and escaping still intact as a fighting force. The American and South Vietnamese leadership ignored this reality, attempting to portray the operation as a great victory. The morning after the battle, with the Vietcong long gone, Cao staged a fake assault on Bac. South Vietnamese artillery pounded the hamlet, killing or wounding sixteen ARVN soldiers, after which infantry troops and armored vehicles "liberated" the area. Soon after, General Harkins arrived and declared to a group of reporters, "We've got them [the Vietcong] in a trap and we're going to spring it in a half an hour."

The reporters knew better. They had seen the positions held by the Vietcong, the evidence of their orderly withdrawal, the damaged helicopters, and the South Vietnamese and American casualties. Sheehan and Nick Turner of Reuters had been caught in Cao's phony assault. They dived into the muck of a canal to avoid the shelling. They loaded the bodies of ARVN soldiers into helicopters when the other troops would not.

They and other reporters finally heard the full blast of Vann's anger. "It was a miserable damn performance," Vann said. "These people won't listen. They make the same goddamn mistakes over and over again in the same way." Sheehan remembered that "the level of indiscretion was commensurate with the level of disgust." Vann, his subordinates, and the helicopter pilots vented their frustration. The correspondents' anger built too. "There was something obscene about all of this to me and the other reporters," Sheehan wrote. "Amid this maiming and dying, a Vietnamese general who should have been serving in an opera company rather than an army was heaping macabre farce on macabre farce while an honor guard waited upon him. An American general with a swagger stick and a cigarette holder . . . who would not deign to soil his suntans and street shoes in a rice paddy to find out what was going on was prattling about having trapped the Viet Cong."[22]

Reporting of the battle reflected the intensification of the war and the conflict over its portrayal. Halberstam's January 3 dispatch conveyed Vann's bitterness. Halberstam portrayed Ap Bac as "particularly galling." Other reporters offered similar pictures. *Time* called Ap Bac "a brutal defeat of the government forces," as did *Newsweek*. Even the strongly pro-Diem Sol Sanders, now working for *U.S. News and World Report*, compared the atmosphere in Saigon to that he remembered in Hanoi in 1951. "Twelve years ago in a cruel, gray winter in Hanoi I saw the French begin to lose their war in Indo-China. . . . Now in South Vietnam . . . you get a feeling that the process is being repeated."[23]

Ap Bac stirred concern at the top of the American political and military leadership. "Prior to Ap Bac," Sheehan wrote, "the Kennedy Administration had succeeded in preventing the American public from being more than vaguely conscious" of the war. But now, in the early days of 1963, "Ap Bac was putting Vietnam on the front pages and on the television evening news shows with a drama that no other event had yet achieved." Part of the impact was the leadership's doing. For a long while, it had issued a steady stream of positive pronouncements. The contrast between assertion and reality was too great.

The White House and the Joint Chiefs tried to downplay the coverage. A secret assessment prepared for Kennedy became the basis for public statements by top officials. They insisted that only one helicopter was actually lost. (The other four had been repaired and flown out.) They claimed that Cao's staged action on the 3rd was an actual contact with the Vietcong. They also accused the press of having "distorted both the importance of the action and the damage suffered by the US/GVN forces."[24]

Just days after Ap Bac, the Joint Chiefs sent a fact-finding mission to South Vietnam. Its top-secret report included no small amount of attention to press relations. The discussion focused on what the reporters were doing wrong. The report criticized the press for raising doubts about "the courage, the training, the determination and the dedication of the Vietnamese armed forces." It also dismissed the reporters' information from Ap Bac as "ill-considered statements made at a time of high excitement and frustration by a few American officers." Admiral Felt told Dean Rusk that Sheehan's reporting was a particular example of the "bad news . . . filed immediately by young reporters without checking the facts."[25]

The reporters didn't take this criticism lying down. Sheehan wrote that they seized on Ap Bac "as if we had been waiting for it because, beleaguered as we felt, we *had* been waiting for it." Halberstam blasted "headquarters officers [who] became angry not with the system which produced the defeat, nor with the Vietnamese commanders who were responsible for it, but with the American advisers who observed and criticized it and with the American reporters who wrote about it." At an airport press conference in Saigon just two days after the battle, emotions on both sides were still running high. Felt turned on Neil Sheehan. "So you're Sheehan," he said. "You ought to talk to some of the people who've got the facts." "You're right," Sheehan shot back, "and that's why I went down there every day."[26]

Harkins immediately realized that Vann had leaked the Ap Bac reports, and wanted to dismiss him just as quickly. Cautioned that firing Vann so abruptly would be a public-relations disaster, Harkins relented, but continued to pressure Vann. Despite reporters' pleas that he protect himself, Vann and his men fed more information than ever to the press corps. "We decided," Sheehan said, "he was deliberately sacrificing his career in order to alert the nation to the danger of defeat in this war."

Truly, Vann and Ap Bac did even more. They deepened the split between the press corps and the American leadership. They gave a foretaste of the dangers of unrealistic optimism and self-delusion. Like the Cuban missile crisis, the Bay of Pigs, the U-2 affair, and dozens of smaller incidents before them, Vann and Ap Bac convinced reporters that the U.S. government could and would lie to its people, especially in affairs of state and security. Reporters learned that "the secrecy that in the 1940s had protected the nation was by the 1960s concealing the fact that the system was no longer rational."[27]

On April 3, 1963, Vann was at Tan Son Nhut airport on his way home. He had turned over his advisory post two days before, the post he had assumed a year before with such self-assurance and enthusiasm. Now he left, frustrated and disappointed. The reporters with whom he had shared so much respect were there too. As he boarded the plane, the reporters gave him a handcrafted silver cigarette box inscribed with their names and the message: "To Lt. Col. John Paul Vann / Good Soldier, Good Friend / From His Admirers in the American Press Corps." Vann was leaving, but the education he had given these reporters stayed with them.[28]

## "Let Them Burn,
## and We Shall Clap Our Hands"

A month after Vann had left South Vietnam, another crisis engulfed the press corps and the American leadership in Saigon and Washington. This crisis would end with the downfall of Diem and a significant shift in the relationships among the press, the United States government, and the war.

May 8, 1963 was a warm, sunny spring day in Hue, the ancient seat of emperors, the most Vietnamese of Vietnam's major cities. A festive air filled the city, as thousands of the faithful prepared to celebrate Buddha's 2,578th birthday.

But a tense anticipation of conflict soured the mood. A few days before the Buddhists' celebration, Archbishop of Hue Ngo Dinh Thuc, Diem's brother, had staged a parade, complete with Vatican flags, marking his twenty-fifth anniversary in the bishopric. Diem attended the celebration and, after seeing the church flags, reminded his brother of the law prohibiting public display of any but the saffron-and-red flag of the Republic of Vietnam. Diem then issued a statement that the Vatican flags had flown in error and that no such flags should be displayed in the future. When the Hue Buddhists were denied permission to fly their banner on their holiday, they demonstrated in the middle of the city. First the police, then troops were called in. ARVN soldiers fired into the crowd. Armored vehicles rumbled into the square. When the resulting panic subsided, nine people were dead, several children among them. Fourteen others had been wounded.[29]

"Thus began the Buddhist crisis," wrote Halberstam. "Observing the Government during these four months was like watching a government trying to commit suicide." Diem, in his stubborn isolation, didn't defuse the problem quickly by admitting the government's responsibility and offering compensation to the Buddhists. Instead, he refused to deal seriously with the Buddhists' grievances. Within a month of the incident in Hue, the Buddhist crisis had become, Halberstam reported, "a full-scale political protest."[30]

Buddhist priests, with their commitment to inner discipline, serenity, and harmony, seem at first glance an unlikely spearhead for a mass protest movement. But the Vietnamese Buddhists were of the Mahayana branch, more worldly and activist than the Hinayana Buddhism more prominent elsewhere in Asia. When the crisis began, the priests, or bonzes, showed exceptional organizational skill and a remarkable capacity for public relations. Priests who spoke French or English worked with the Western press. The movement's leadership held regular press briefings, distributed press packets, gave advance notice of events. Signs at demonstrations were written in English, as well as Vietnamese, for the benefit of American reporters and television cameras. Marguerite Higgins, a veteran New York *Herald Tribune* columnist, related an encounter with Buddhist spokesman Duc Nghiep. " 'Ah, Miss Higgins,' " he said, "you are from New York; how is the play?' Not comprehending, I said, 'Play—did you have some particular play—drama—in mind?' 'No, no, Miss Higgins,' he said, gesturing elaborately to indicate the front page of a newspaper and headlines across it. It dawned on me that he was using the newspaperman's term for whether a story is 'played' well (i.e., given prominence and space) or not 'played' well."[31]

Quang Duc's self-immolation raised the stakes in the crisis. The event had a profound effect on those who witnessed it. "Pedestrians, amazed by the awesome sight, prostrated themselves in reverence. Even a nearby policeman threw himself to the ground," said Stanley Karnow. Halberstam arrived at the scene just as the flames rose. "I was too shocked to cry, too confused to take notes or ask questions, too bewildered to even speak. . . . I had never felt such conflicting emotions: one part of me wanted to extinguish the fire, another warned that I had no right to interfere, another told me it was too late, another asked whether I was a reporter or a human being."[32]

But the impact wasn't limited to the people gathered around a Saigon street corner. The incident strengthened the extremists on both sides. The younger, more radical priests took control of the opposition. Diem had to confront his brother and sister-in-law, Ngo Dinh Nhu and Madame Nhu. Immediately after the suicide, Diem had offered to talk to moderate priests. An infuriated Madame Nhu called the president a coward and flung the tureen of chicken soup they were sharing for lunch across the table. From that point forward, the Nhus' influence rose. Madame Nhu called for more "barbecues" and offered to supply gasoline and matches. "Let them burn," she said. "And we shall clap our hands." Her husband established control over the secret police and elements of the armed forces. Nhu even made contact with the North Vietnamese and was preparing a coup against his brother.[33]

The Diem regime was clearly about to self-destruct. It had pitted itself against its own people and against the Americans—press and officials alike. The poison spread to the American community. Reporters and officials fought one another and among themselves. The question now was: Would the Diem regime take the U.S. commitment to South Vietnam with it?

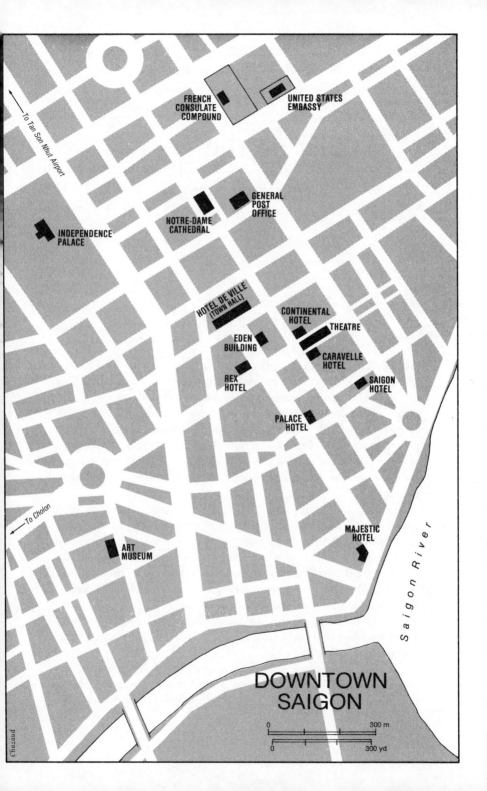

# 6

# "Get on the Team"

## The End of Diem

AUGUST 21, 1963, WAS A hellishly exhilarating day for Neil Sheehan and David Halberstam. That day, all the suspicion and irrationality of the Diem regime burst like a storm across the country. Under the cover of darkness, Special Forces troops controlled by Diem's brother Ngo Dinh Nhu attacked Buddhist pagodas in Saigon and other major cities. Priests and nuns were assaulted with automatic weapons and tear gas. Many were beaten and shot; over fourteen hundred were arrested. The pagodas themselves were ransacked and damaged.

Sheehan and Halberstam had raced around Saigon trying to gather, write, and transmit the story literally on the run. For weeks rumors ran that their names were on Nhu's death list. Friends told them that their homes would be attacked that night. So, at 4:00 A.M., physically exhausted and fearful of Nhu's next move, they appeared on John Mecklin's doorstep, seeking shelter. Mecklin was head of the Saigon USIS office and a chief adversary. He took them in that night, and they stayed with him for the next three weeks.[1] Mecklin's act of kindness that night symbolizes the story of the American press and the Vietnam War in 1963.

Like the Diem regime itself, the relationship of the American press corps in South Vietnam to senior American and South Vietnamese officials deteriorated during 1963. The optimism of top officials and the journalists they served contrasted more and more starkly with the discouragement and pessimism of the lower-level officials and the journalists they served.

But by late summer, several factors—the final days of Diem, changes in U.S. information policy, and changes in the Vietnam story itself—pushed the resident press and important elements of the American leadership in Saigon and Washington closer together. Whereas Sheehan and Halberstam moved out of Mecklin's house after three weeks, the press corps itself, once in the government's house, remained there for several years.


## "Why Didn't You Tell Us?"

Confrontations between the Buddhists and the South Vietnamese government grew more severe over the summer of 1963. Day after day, thousands of protesters took to the streets. Day after day, the government police, wielding billy clubs and rifle butts and firing tear gas, would tear into the crowds.

The pagoda raids on August 21 pushed the crisis over the edge. The raids went beyond maintaining order. Halberstam watched the raid on the Xa Loi pagoda in Saigon with Sheehan and Mert Perry. "Had Nhu wanted to arrest the Buddhist leaders it could have been accomplished efficiently in a few moments, but these troops were enacting a passion play of revenge and terror."

The raids broke the fragile society of South Vietnam wide open. When students at Saigon's universities and high schools rioted in sympathy with the Buddhists, Diem and Nhu sent the police against them, battering the children of the very elite that supported them. Soon the plotting of a coup against Diem and Nhu began in earnest.[2]

The pagoda raids also marked a final break between Diem and the American leadership. At first the crisis produced a split among American officials in Saigon and Washington. Nolting and Harkins were still committed to the regime. Others, such as Saigon Chargé d'Affaires William C. Trueheart and Assistant Secretary of State for Far Eastern Affairs Roger Hilsman, had grown more and more dubious of the Nhus and of Diem's viability.

By late summer, the entire Kennedy Administration had distanced itself from Diem. Henry Cabot Lodge's appointment to succeed Ambassador Nolting signaled that the United States was taking a tougher line against the regime. In September, President Kennedy, on the first half-hour evening news broadcast by CBS, told Walter Cronkite that the crackdown against the Buddhists had been "very serious." "I don't think that unless a greater effort is made by the Government to win popular support that the war can be won out there," Kennedy said. In October, Kennedy initiated selective cuts in aid to pressure Diem. Covert contacts with a group of generals planning a coup had been taking place for weeks.[3]

The Buddhist crisis also sparked significant changes for the American press in South Vietnam. First, the focus of the Vietnam story shifted from military to political. Earlier political tensions had been muted. They were, Halberstam said, "difficult to describe, for there were few pegs"—few specific events upon which to "hang" such a story. "The resentment was palpably there—anyone could feel it— but it did not lend itself to daily reporting." The uprising, especially the suicides and the demonstration, provided particularly dramatic material for the press.

Just as the reporters had needed steady, dependable sources concerning military action, they also needed steady, dependable sources on the details and meaning of the political crisis. Clearly the Ngo Dinh family wasn't going to be such a source. And American officials, at least at the beginning of the crisis, had little information and even less inclination to share it. As they had in the Delta, the reporters improvised.[4]

Buddhist priests were a primary source. The bonzes realized that the American press was a window to the outside world, and that publicity was a lever they could use against Diem. The similarity of the Buddhists' tactics to those being used by the civil-rights movement among black people in the American South was not lost on reporters. "As Bull Connor and his police dogs in Birmingham were to etch indelibly the civil rights movement on the minds of millions of Americans, so the Buddhists used the Government's repeated clumsiness to commit the people further to their cause and to strengthen the movement," Halberstam wrote. Thus the Buddhists gave reporters advance notice of demonstrations in order to gain the maximum emotional and political impact. The press provided maximum coverage of dramatic and portentous events. Here was mutual self-interest.[5]

By late summer, a group of reporters "had created a small but first-rate intelligence network." Its information was better than the American government's. These reporters had learned hours before the August 21 raids when and where they would occur. Immediately after the Xa Loi raid, Sheehan and Halberstam went to the embassy to check for more information. "There was nothing to learn there, for to our astonishment the embassy had been caught completely unaware by the raids. . . . One of the top officials asked, 'Why didn't you tell us?' " So deeply had the reporters burrowed into the opposition movement that they were made insiders among a group of junior officers then planning a coup, and were kept informed of the planning of the generals' coup that would pre-empt it.[6]

Coverage during the summer of 1963 portrayed a country slowly coming apart, and laid the most of the blame on Diem and his family. Halberstam described "a desperate absence of the qualities needed to win. There is around the Palace today a vast cocoon of intrigue, suspicion, distrust, separating the family from what it needs to be told and the people who are willing to tell it." *U.S. News and World Report*'s Pepper Martin wrote in September that the regime was "openly contemptuous of U.S. criticism" and that American officials were just as openly disdainful of the regime.[7]

This aggressive and critical coverage of the Buddhist crisis drove the Ngo Dinh family into another assault on the correspondents.

"The family was reluctant to expel us as a group," Sheehan said, "for fear of an outcry from Congress." Instead, the regime "decided to frighten us into staying away from the demonstrations." On July 7, plainclothes police attacked nine Western reporters, including Halberstam, Sheehan, Browne, Arnett, Faas, and Joseph Masraf, a CBS cameraman. Four policemen knocked Arnett down and began kicking him, while others tried to take Browne's and Masraf's equipment. "Halberstam charged with a bellow before they had an opportunity to hurt Arnett seriously," Sheehan remembered. "He knocked and tossed the lightly built Vietnamese aside and stood over Arnett, his grizzly-bear shoulders hunched and his great fists poised, yelling: 'Get back, get back you sons of bitches, or I'll beat the shit out of you.' " To make matters worse, the police ordered Browne and Sheehan to appear the next day to answer charges that *they* had started the fight. And when direct physical attack did not deter the reporters, the regime let word pass that their names were on assassination lists.[8]

More common and troublesome to the reporters was interference in their work. Routine surveillance, phone taps, and searches of homes and offices were stepped up. So was the monitoring and delay of dispatches. These practices reached new heights in the martial-law period immediately following the pagoda raids.

Most serious, a strict censorship was imposed, and the Post, Telephone, and Telegraph office, which operated the overseas cable, was closed. "No serious reporter wanted his name to appear over a story which had been strained through censorship," Halberstam said. The case of Joe Fried of the New York *Daily News* showed what could happen. Fried won an interview with Madame Nhu after agreeing to let her censor the dispatch personally. "He saw his dispatch waved through censorship almost unscathed, [but] with the addition of the adjectives *despicable* and *miserable* in front of all his references to monks and Buddhists."

Dispatches sent through the censorship office were completely sanitized. Reporters turned to "pigeons," sympathetic friends willing to smuggle copy out of the country for transmission from Bangkok, Hong Kong, or Tokyo. At first the reporters used servicemen, until MACV's chief public-information officer reminded soldiers that carrying such material was a court-martial offense. Reporters then moved to civilians riding on commercial airlines.[9]

Many of the reporters' sources, especially among disaffected South Vietnamese, were lying low. Martial law and its curfew made travel around the city difficult. Having to avoid censorship by sending dispatches out by plane meant that deadlines were shoved forward, leaving even less time to check with sources and compose stories.

Despite these obstacles, the correspondents, over the two and one-half days following the raids, filed thousands of words of copy that reported the events and their background accurately. For example, they knew that it was Nhu's Special Forces—not regular-army soldiers, as the regime claimed and the U.S. administration believed—that had staged the raids. On August 23, *The New York Times* ran Halberstam's story placing the blame on Nhu alongside the State Department line, reported by Tad Szulc. But because communications were so disrupted, the reporters "continued to file in a vacuum; we didn't know what was getting out, what was being printed or what play it was getting if a story was used." Meanwhile, the Kennedy Administration had acknowledged their version of the raids. When that news reached Saigon, a spontaneous party broke out in Sheehan's office. Charles Mohr of *Time* toasted Sheehan and Halberstam with beer. "You guys," said Mohr, "are the first reporters I've ever known who scooped the State Department by four days."[10]


## "The Crusaders"— Conflict Within the Press

Not all American journalists were as thrilled with the work of Sheehan, Halberstam, et al. Indeed, during 1963 the most consistent and heated criticism of Vietnam coverage came from other journalists. Once again, it was not ideology or age that created the conflict, but the demands of particular types of journalism.

Marguerite Higgins and Joe Alsop led the critics. Alsop's background is already familiar; Higgins' is quite similar. Born in China to missionary parents, she became a reporter for the *New York Herald Tribune* in 1942, serving as a combat correspondent. After the war, she was the *Herald Tribune*'s bureau chief in Berlin and Tokyo. She won a Pulitzer Prize in 1951 for combat coverage of Korea, and she remained in the Far East until 1958.

Up to this point, her career had been more like Homer Bigart's than Joe Alsop's. But in 1958 she went to Washington as the *Herald Tribune*'s chief diplomatic correspondent. With that move, her frame of reference changed, just as Alsop's had when he settled in Washington. No longer were her sources the men and women in the field, the people who knew how and how well policy was actually being carried out. Instead, her sources were policymakers—powerful people, but also those most removed from the action.

The American leadership, critical of the Saigon press corps's relative inexperience, asked news organizations to send in "mature and responsible news correspondents." In July 1963, Higgins, just such a reporter, went to the country at the Pentagon's urging, for a four-week visit. Top Washington officials briefed her. While in the country, she spoke to American and Vietnamese leaders, including Harkins, Diem, and Madame Nhu, and soldiers and others in the field.[11]

The situation she saw and reported was almost the exact opposite of that portrayed by the Saigon press corps. They had focused on the Delta, where the Vietcong threat was greatest. She concentrated on Quang Ngai Province, far to the north, described by her Washington sources as "a miraculous success story." In Diem the reporters saw an aloof and diffident man unable to deal with the problems facing him. Higgins found herself "admiring his odd impassiveness, his marked self-control in what was a time of almost intolerable tension." They saw a South Vietnamese Army whose senior commanders actually faked operations. She saw "Vietnamese officers and men so keyed up and eager for the battle they would fairly leap from the helicopter before it even touched the ground."

Higgins blamed the Saigon reporters for these contradictions. The Buddhists' public-relations savvy surprised her, and she believed that the reporters had been taken in by it. "In Saigon," she said, "the Buddhists' capacity to keep things stirred up—and catch world headlines—was seemingly boundless." She said that demonstrations were designed for "maximum impact on the American press." "It was commonplace at the Xa Loi Pagoda to hear the photographers say, 'Hey, Tic Tac Toe, when's the next barbecue going to be?' " She tried to discredit the Buddhists—and the reporters' portrayal of them—by claiming communist influence.[12]

The reporters' "accent on the negative" bothered her the most. Charles Mohr quoted her as having said, "Reporters here would like to see us lose the war to prove they're right." She denied making "so calloused and harsh a remark." She did say "the only way that the Communists could make the United States welsh on its commitment to Vietnam is if American public opinion in the 1960's was to become as demoralized as French public opinion in the 1950's. This is something the Communists are working very hard to accomplish, and there are a great many Americans unwittingly serving the Viet Cong objective of undermining the nation's will and stamina."[13]

Joe Alsop, visiting South Vietnam in September 1963, joined in. In his September 23 column, he compared the Saigon press corps to "the crusaders," journalists who had hailed Mao and Fidel Castro as saviors while criticizing Chiang Kai-shek and Fulgencio Batista. He accused them of ignoring "the majority of Americans who admire the the Vietnamese as fighters" and seeking out "the one U.S. officer in 10 who inevitably thinks all foreigners fight badly." He also blamed the "constant pressure of the reportorial crusade against the government" for transforming Diem "from a courageous, quite viable national leader, into a man afflicted with galloping persecution mania...."[14]

Though frustrated by these attacks, the reporters were even more bothered by suspicion and criticism from within their own organizations. Most celebrated was the case of *Time*, its managing editor Otto Fuerbringer, Far East correspondent Charles Mohr, and Vietnam stringer Merton Perry.

Power within the magazine was divided. The managing editor, especially a strong-willed journalist such as Fuerbringer, controlled the makeup and content of the magazine. But correspondents such as Mohr and Perry answered to the chief of correspondents, Richard Clurman. The correspondents sent in "files" every week, but what was done with the material was up to the writers and managing editor. "*Time* reporters," Halberstam observed, "have to do an undue amount of apologizing to news sources about the final product."[15]

Mohr and Perry did a lot of explaining in the late summer and early fall of 1963. Fuerbringer, reflecting his "big picture" sources like McNamara, consistently watered down his reporters' tough assessments. An August dispatch sharply critical of Madame Nhu's "destructive influence" ended up calling her "the most formidable and in some ways the bravest woman in South Viet Nam . . . a fragile, exciting beauty." Fuerbringer also killed a dispatch complimenting the Saigon press corps.

The final straw fell in September. Mohr and Perry were asked for a major assessment of the war. They put a tremendous amount of work into the assignment, filing twenty-five pages of copy in three days. Halberstam called it the toughest story yet written by a resident correspondent. It began, "The war in Vietnam is being lost." An enraged Fuerbringer rejected the dispatch. He then dictated a story for the magazine's "Press" section blasting the Saigon press corps, Mohr and Perry included. "The newsmen themselves have become a part of South Vietnam Nam's confusion; they have covered a complex situation from only one angle, as if their own conclusions offered all the necessary illumination." Like Higgins and Alsop, Fuerbringer accused the reporters of deliberately slanting their coverage. Diem was automatically "stubborn and stupid," with "justice and sympathy" just as automatically assigned to the Buddhists. Reporters

downplayed ARVN victories as contrary to "the argument that defeat is inevitable as long as Diem is in power." "When there is a
defeat," Fuerbringer claimed, "the color is rich and flowing."[16] Dick
Clurman defended his correspondents passionately. But Henry Luce
sided with Fuerbringer, the article stood, and Mohr and Perry resigned.[17]

The *Time* incident wasn't the only such case. Halberstam's superiors constantly questioned his work. *Times* managing editor, Turner
Catledge, didn't want his paper "used as a propaganda platform for
the U.S. government." But he wasn't comfortable with Halberstam's
nearly constant contradiction of American officials either. Catledge
had lived through the McCarthy period, with its sweeping accusa-
tions and creeping suspicion. No mainstream news organization
wanted to be too far out in front on a national-security story. After
Marguerite Higgins singled out Halberstam for special criticism,
*Times* editors suggested that he tone down his dispatches. "If you
mention that woman's name to me one more time I will resign repeat
resign and I mean it repeat mean it," he responded.

But *The New York Times'* top officials eventually stood by their
reporter. When the State Department was reporting one version of
the pagoda raids and Halberstam another, the *Times'* first instinct
was to run the official view on page one and place Halberstam's piece
inside the paper. James Reston, Halberstam's patron, argued that the
reporter in the field should not be disputed without very good reason.
The *Times,* in an unprecedented move, ran the two stories side by
side on the front page. At a friendly lunch with the publisher, Arthur
Ochs Sulzberger, President Kennedy suggested that Halberstam had
become too close to the story and should be transferred. Sulzberger
said no, he was quite happy with his reporter's work. The *Times* then
postponed Halberstam's long-scheduled vacation to avoid the appearance of caving in to the administration.[18]

Higgins and Alsop; Halberstam and Sheehan—their differences
reflected their geography. Top press brass and Washington-based
pundits tended to go along with "authoritative" top-level sources,
whereas reporters in the field respected their sources. Halberstam
said that Higgins' criticism "revealed the handicaps of a visiting reporter" whose "limited background might well destroy him."
"When he talked to a corps adviser, did he know that he was being
fed the opinion of General Harkins and Colonel Cao? Was he aware

of the difficulty in getting along with Cao, the resultant paralysis and loss of American freedom? Had he heard of Vann's dissents?"[19]

But soon a number of factors contributed to an easing of tension and a changing relationship between the Saigon press and the U.S. government.[20]

First, the press controversy itself got more attention in 1963. Vietnam information practices and policies played a prominent part in a new set of House Government Information Subcommittee hearings. The policies in Cable 1006 were disclosed and their intent and effect debated. The administration eventually rescinded the cable in face of public pressure.[21]

Diem's brutal treatment of the press during the Buddhist crisis also pushed the Kennedy Administration to change its own attitudes. No U.S. government could allow physical intimidation of reporters to go unchallenged. After the July 7 attack, Chargé d'Affaires Trueheart declined to file a formal protest as the reporters demanded. But he did express his "concern" and instructed Mecklin to prevent a repeat occurrence. At the same time, Assistant Secretary of State for Public Affairs Robert Manning was sent discreetly to Saigon to determine the "reasons for dissatisfaction among [the] U.S. press corps in Viet-Nam."[22]

Changes taking place within the United States government also played a part. As far back as the spring of 1962, senior officials had become concerned about the administration's policy of silence and deception. Hilsman noted his concern over the Farmgate flights, the Air Force's secret program of air support for ARVN infantry. "I'm uneasy about the tendency in Washington to attempt to keep the farm gate operations secret. I think it is an impossibility; there are just too many Americans and Vietnamese involved," he wrote. "The whole business could blow up in any number of horrendous ways."

In November 1962, John Mecklin sent a secret memorandum to Nolting excoriating the regime, particularly Nhu, for the hostile treatment of American reporters. Mecklin catalogued the press corps's complaints, agreed with most of them, and recommended a dramatic shift in information policy. "MACV should begin now to give regular daily briefings to Western newsmen on a non-attribution basis," Mecklin said. American officials should move to establish credibility by sharing limited amounts of classified information with responsible journalists. And, finally, "American advisers throughout the country should be instructed to ignore any GVN efforts to prevent them from cooperating with newsmen," even to the point of withholding American personnel or equipment from operations. "No correspondents, no choppers," Mecklin wrote.

Mecklin understood "the reality that the newsmen here will continue to find access to very much the truth of what's going on, regardless of what we may do. I think it's futile to try to 'control' them, or cut off their sources. Americans, even in the military, simply don't work that way." Mecklin, Hilsman, and others discovered that by shutting the press out the government gave up any influence over it. By cooperating with reporters, by giving them the information they needed to do their jobs, the government might have some chance to establish its point of view before the public.[23]

Mecklin had an opportunity to say this in person to Kennedy the next April, while in Washington recovering from surgery. "Kennedy appeared skeptical but willing to try," Mecklin said, and soon a series of initiatives calling for greater official contact with the resident reporters began to flow in Saigon. In May, Assistant Secretary of Defense for Public Affairs Arthur Sylvester hand-delivered a memorandum from Kennedy to Harkins and Nolting, warning them of the "unfortunate potential which rigid continuation of present press policies might aggravate" and instructing them to grant "more leeway to [the] field in making day-to-day news policy as it affects on the spot situation. This would include whenever possible taking American reporters in Saigon further into our confidence, particularly on matters which they are almost certain to learn about anyway."[24]

A second change within the government hastened acceptance of the attitude. As the Buddhist crisis escalated, so did the doubts of many American officials, in Saigon and Washington, about Diem. These doubts initially split the American brass, symbolized by the falling out between Nolting and his deputy and close friend, William Trueheart. Trueheart now doubted the viability of the Diem regime and, during Nolting's extended vacation in the summer of 1963, adopted a much tougher stance toward the South Vietnamese government. Lower-level officials within the embassy who shared Trueheart's feelings sought out reporters just as field advisers had a year before.

As the situation deteriorated into what Sheehan called "a theater of the bizarre," Trueheart's attitude began to dominate. The airport scene on the day Nolting left South Vietnam for the last time was, for Halberstam, a harbinger of the changes. Usually such events "reflected the mood of the mission": senior officials, reporters, and junior officials coalesced into separate and mutually wary groups. "But on this day there was a curious change. There was so much bitterness in the American embassy, so many civilians were fed up with our policy and its equivocations, and so tired of the family's arrogance that we correspondents were now sought out, even welcomed. For the first time the officials talked openly with us; no longer were we the enemy, no longer were they worried about being seen with us."[25]

Doubt soon became official policy after the pagoda raids and the arrival of Henry Cabot Lodge as Nolting's replacement. Soon American officials were in discreet contact with generals plotting Diem's overthrow. By October, the administration, using selective aid cuts, pressured Diem to oust his brother and to initiate reforms. An airmobility exercise code-named Running Water, actually a disguised preparation for the emergency evacuation, had been under way for several weeks.[26]

Lodge himself embodied a new attitude toward the resident press. He arrived in the wee hours of the morning of August 23, forty-eight hours after the pagoda raids, just as the full impact of martial law was felt. At the airport he "shook hands with Harkins and Trueheart and then turned toward us. 'Where are the gentlemen of the press?' " Sheehan recalled him asking. Lodge clearly valued the reporters. He agreed with them, and they offered him an alternate source of information. And Lodge, the savvy politician, knew the value of a sympathetic press. He courted them and, in turn, won their respect. One by one, Halberstam, Sheehan, and Browne lunched at the embassy. Sheehan remembers being asked blunt, candid questions and giving equally blunt, candid answers. "With the Ngo Dinhs one could only look forward to defeat," Sheehan told him. As he left, Sheehan asked, "And what's your impression, Mr. Ambassador?" Lodge, a knowing smile on his face, answered, "About the same as yours."[27]

In October, when Vietnamese police assaulted a group of American reporters, Lodge filed a formal diplomatic protest. Trueheart had declined to do so just three months before. When the regime instituted censorship and closed the PTT office following the pagoda raids, Washington instructed Lodge to give the "highest possible priority" to assisting reporters. In the first hours of martial law, reporters were allowed to use the embassy's cable to get dispatches out. Lodge also pressured Diem to lift censorship and to reopen the cable.[28]

The plottings of senior South Vietnamese generals finally bore fruit. On November 1, 1963, the rebels seized key military installations. Diem and Nhu escaped from the presidential palace, but were caught and murdered later in the day.

A new sense of hope swept South Vietnam. "Those first few weeks after the coup were a time of great frankness and soul-searching, of mutual trust in many areas," Halberstam remembered. The junta of generals now in control pursued the Vietcong with new aggressiveness. American and South Vietnamese officials, from the field to Saigon, talked candidly to one another and to the press. "For once, the job of a reporter in Vietnam was easy," Halberstam thought as he prepared to leave the country in December.[29]

But this rapprochement between the press in South Vietnam and the United States government was not based on any self-sacrifice, any real change of goals, by either party. American officials had not suddenly developed a passion for the First Amendment; the inclination to control information that had characterized the rest of Kennedy's relations with the press was still in place. Nor had the reporters given up their need and desire to cover Vietnam.

Two changes had occurred: a change in personnel, in the person of Lodge, and a change in the dynamic of the story, in the demands and opportunities it presented. For American officials the press became an instrument in their movement away from the regime, a tool to pressure Diem and to build domestic support for the policy. Reporters were vastly relieved. The American brass in Saigon, who had once shut them out and deceived them, forcing them to ferret out information elsewhere, were now themselves consistent and comprehensive sources.

Over the preceding months, American officials had realized their mistakes in handling the press. They understood that blaming the critical reporting on ideological or generational differences was not only wrong but also counterproductive. They saw that their obstructionism had cost them a significant degree of influence and control over what the reporters eventually wrote. By figuratively taking the reporters into the house, they could defuse much of the ill will and antagonism that had plagued both parties. They realized, in short, that the processes of journalism, not the politics or ages of the journalists, controlled the relationship.

The killings of Ngo Dinh Diem and John F. Kennedy in November 1963 punctuated the end of this crucial era of the war. Admiral Harry Felt earlier had snapped at Malcolm Browne, "Why don't you get on the team?" During 1963, the government and the press had gotten on the same team. But soon, further changes in the war and the story would cast Felt's question in a different light.

# 7

# "I Don't Know"

## Explaining the War, 1964–67

IN SEPTEMBER 1965, Jack Langguth, *New York Times'* veteran correspondent, had just completed a fourteen-month assignment in South Vietnam. Sorting out his thoughts on the war, he wrote, "I think often of a press briefing held last June by a very high-ranking American official." The continuing drama of South Vietnamese politics was reaching another denouement. Another "Premier of the moment" was under fire, and another government seemed about to fall. When asked pointedly by a reporter why the United States had not acted, the American diplomat replied that "I would not object to using our influence toward effecting some kind of settlement. . . . But first one would have to decide what was the best course to follow. I've been thinking about that for days now, and—maybe I shouldn't say this— but I don't know." His reporter friends were disgusted by such "an abject confession of ineptness," but Langguth remembered it "as one of the most sensible answers I had heard in Vietnam."

Langguth—no "cherry," in the GI slang of this war—had covered the war's escalation, observed and described the growing scope and destructiveness of combat. He had explored and tried to comprehend the house of mirrors that passed for politics and government in South Vietnam. As he left the country, he asked himself some fundamental questions. "If one nation begins an ugly and inhuman war, does national honor require resisting even more brutally? But, then, why shouldn't America pursue a war on its terms rather than follow rules that can only lead to failure?" And, he asked, "Will the American desperation over South Vietnam be justified 15 years from now? Will the South Vietnamese peasant be better off under today's Premier Nguyen Cao Ky, or his successors, than under Ho Chi Minh?" "Finally," he wondered, "is the United States now helping the people of South Vietnam more than it is hurting them?" Despite his experience in Vietnam, Langguth's answer was the same as that of the American official: "I don't know."[1]

Such a response typifies the state of mind of much of American society between 1964 and 1967. In those years, when United States involvement grew more intense and costly, the nature of that change should have been understood. Yet, within the government and without, confusion was the one constant.

How could this be? By the end of 1967, nearly six hundred journalists were accredited to cover the war. Over three thousand military and civilian personnel worked for the United States government in South Vietnam, their sole purpose to provide the American press and public with information about the war. With such an investment of human and financial resources, how could anyone fail to know and understand what was going on in Vietnam? Yet, when they were asked questions similar to those Jack Langguth asked himself, honesty compelled most Americans to answer, "I don't know."

Why? The answer lies in understanding how the press and the Executive Branch failed, not because of a contest between them, but, rather, because each institution tended to *complement,* not conflict with the other. Together they made Vietnam "the most covered but least understood" war in American history.

## "A New and Tougher Ball Game"

Back in November 1961, President John Kennedy had faced a major decision. Confronted by the desire to support the South Vietnamese and keep the commitment in a low profile, Kennedy chose to provide the South Vietnamese more material and advice. He resisted sending U.S. combat troops, fearing that it would only lead to more troops, just as an alcoholic's first drink leads to the next and the next.[2]

Three years had passed. Lyndon Johnson faced a similar decision. Immediately after Kennedy's death, Johnson had pledged to honor his martyred predecessor's commitment to an independent, noncommunist South Vietnam. Like Kennedy, Johnson tried to do "enough, but not too much" in South Vietnam, navigating the treacherous waters between letting the Vietcong and their North Vietnamese allies win, and increasing American involvement to the point where it threatened his "Great Society" programs. Johnson's wanted the 1964 elections to make him president in his own right, compelling him to proceed with caution.³

Johnson faced a much tougher situation in South Vietnam than Kennedy had. The fall of the Ngo Dinh family, as many of its supporters had predicted, opened the Pandora's box of conflicts latent in South Vietnamese society. Soon coup-making became the chief specialty of South Vietnamese political and military science. None of the various governments could address social needs or stem the Vietcong, who were receiving greater and more direct help from North Vietnam.⁴ By the summer of 1964, the United States government had become increasingly concerned about this threat. By June, it had developed a whole range of potential pressures against North Vietnam, including bombing of selected targets within that country.⁵

In early August, the first of these air strikes took place. For several months, American destroyers had been reconnoitering the North Vietnamese coast as part of the "DeSoto missions" that had been carried out for years in other communist waters. At the same time, South Vietnamese commandos in PT boats were conducting harassing raids in the same areas under the auspices of OPLAN 34-A, a series of covert operations against North Vietnam approved and supported by the United States. When North Vietnamese patrol boats attacked the U.S.S. *Maddox* following one such raid, the *Maddox* and another destroyer, the *C. Turner Joy,* moved closer to the North Vietnamese coast, where yet another engagement may or may not have taken place on the night of August 4. More important, American warplanes struck a North Vietnamese patrol-boat base and support facility.⁶

Despite the questionable nature of American activity and the extremely confused circumstances of the supposed second engagement between the American and North Vietnamese craft, Johnson's actions were widely endorsed. Congress, in the form of the Tonkin

Gulf Resolution, authorized the president to "take all necessary measures" to protect American forces. The press backed Johnson in editorial opinions that almost uniformly praised, as did the Louisville *Courier Journal,* the "speed, wisdom, and restraint" of the response. The public's support was no less fervent. Eighty-five per cent of those persons questioned approved of the bombing raids, and the president's general approval rating jumped from 42 to 72 percent.[7]

Lyndon Johnson's resolve had been demonstrated to the North Vietnamese leadership and the American voter. No further bombing attacks took place that year. Within weeks of the initial raids, however, the administration decided that a sustained bombing program against the North was needed to relieve the pressure on the increasingly unstable South Vietnamese government. That program began in response to a February 6, 1965, Vietcong attack on an American base camp at Pleiku, in South Vietnam's Central Highlands. Literally within hours, this retaliatory raid evolved into a long-term aerial offensive, Operation Rolling Thunder, that became a focal point of American military strategy in Vietnam. The list of eligible targets grew steadily, eventually including industrial facilities within the Hanoi-Haiphong area. The scope and intensity of the attacks grew as well. In 1965, American planes flew 25,000 sorties (a sortie was defined as one mission by one plane) and dropped 63,000 tons of bombs over North Vietnam; by 1967, those figures had grown to 108,000 sorties and 226,000 tons of bombs. At about the same time, American forces were authorized to use much broader air power in South Vietnam. Soon, aerial ordnance was being expended in South Vietnam at over three times the rate in the North. The totals fast approached and then surpassed the tonnage used in all of World War II.[8]

It quickly became clear that the bombing would not stop either the southward flow of men and material or the increase in Vietcong and North Vietnamese confidence. The question of sending in American combat troops arose again. In March, 3,500 Marines splashed ashore at Danang with a fanfare quaintly yet disturbingly out of place. President Johnson announced on July 28, 1965, that 50,000 American troops were being sent to South Vietnam immediately, with more to follow. By the end of the year, more than 125,000 American soldiers were in country. By the end of 1967, the total topped 500,000.

As these soldiers went on the offensive, the costs grew. From January 1961 through December 1964, fewer than 300 Americans had been killed in Vietnam. During 1967, the number of Americans killed in action approached 300 *per week,* and the United States was spending more than $2 billion a month on the war. Just as John Kennedy had warned, one small escalation created the logic for yet another. Whether Kennedy could have resisted this logic any better than Johnson is, of course, unknown. It's certain, however, that support for a remote anticommunist regime had, in a very short time, ballooned into a commitment that touched almost every aspect of American life. "It was," as one official said, "a new and tougher ball game."[9]

## Vietnam—"the Center of the Earth"

The American press in 1964, much like the Johnson Administration, was trying to feel its way through post-Diem South Vietnam. And, like the president, it was trying to keep a handle on the story without increasing its investment. The size of the American press corps grew only slightly during 1964, from six resident reporters and ten or so regular visitors at the end of 1963 to about ten residents and a dozen regular visitors a year later. With a low level of direct American involvement, Vietnam remained, in Peter Braestrup's words, a "journalistic backwater."[10]

The Vietnam story, however, wouldn't keep still, and neither could the American press. In a few short months, Vietnam became, in one correspondent's words, "the center of the earth." Despite these changes, the characteristics and impulses that had defined the relationship of the press and the government to the Vietnam story and each other since 1955 continued to operate, though in new ways, bringing new challenges and consequences.

The story was becoming too big for the press corps to handle. The political instability and the combat activity spreading across the country forced the already hard-pressed correspondents to sacrifice one aspect of the story for another. During 1964 and early 1965, combat coverage tended to get short shrift. Jim Lucas, correspondent for the Scripps-Howard newspaper chain, complained that, "In the six months [during 1964] I lived in the Delta, I was the only correspondent regularly assigned to working and living with combat troops."[11]

Lucas was right, but concentrating on the political crises made journalistic sense. To be sure, some American troops were certainly involved in combat, but most served advisory and support roles. South Vietnamese units bore the brunt of the fighting force; the average American reader, at least in the judgment of news executives, had little interest in the average ARVN soldier. Also, as the war spread into northern and central South Vietnam, reporters could no longer cover military action as they had when it was within a taxi ride of Saigon.

The effort to develop a stable government in South Vietnam was the defining goal of American policy. Thus, the political crises seemed to be more important to Americans than the military situation. More significantly, the political situation was concentrated in Saigon, making it a logistically easier story to cover.

The situation changed dramatically in the spring and summer of 1965. The first challenge was to adjust to the stronger American flavor of the war. The same ethnocentric impulses that had shielded the American press from the war now made Vietnam the nation's dominant news story. The AP staff in Saigon grew from four at the end of 1964 to seventeen in December 1965. UPI went from one reporter to a fourteen-person operation. *Newsweek*'s François Sully was joined by three other reporters, and *Time* and *U.S. News* established full-fledged bureaus for the first time. Television networks had previously covered the war from Tokyo. By December 1965, the networks had the largest news staffs in Saigon, more than twenty accredited employees each.[12]

The American military had for months struggled to establish a base of support for soldiers flooding into South Vietnam. So too the press corps was facing its own logistical nightmare. A basic, but by no means routine, task was finding adequate living and working space. Between 1961 and 1964, such arrangements were often crude. Neil Sheehan lived in the back half of a two-room apartment. The front half served as office space for the Saigon bureaus of UPI and *The New York Times*. Peter Grose, who succeeded Halberstam in February 1964, left the UPI office after Reuters correspondent Nick Turner "offered us more spacious facilities (i.e. one whole corner of the room rather than one side of a table)."[13]

This arrangement continued even after the *Times* bureau had grown to four employees. James Reston, visiting Saigon in August 1965, described the office at 46 Duong Tu Do from which the nation's most prestigious newspaper covered the nation's most important news story: "The office is a long rectangular room with a tile floor and a short flight of steps at back leading to a couple of radio circuits. It smells of disinfectant and the vague seeping odors disinfectant is intended to combat. It has a refrigerator with cold beer, which is good, and a toilet, which is unspeakable. I will not describe the plumbing." The office had no air conditioning, and the fans that offered the only respite from the heat and humidity were frequently inoperable, thanks to regular power outages. Charley Mohr, who had returned to South Vietnam as the *Times* bureau chief, said that he was "drenched with sweat and black with carbon" by the time he finished writing each night.[14]

Securing better facilities was easier said than done. The burgeoning American presence created a seller's market for all types of real estate, a fact not lost on Saigon landlords. In the fall of 1966, R. W. "Johnny" Apple, who followed Mohr as bureau chief, was desperately searching for new offices. He had found a dream house, very near the *Times'* current space, centrally located, equipped with an air conditioner, and including a one-room apartment on the second floor. The price was $430 a month, a figure "well within bounds of [the] local market," Apple said, pointing out to his bosses that *Newsweek* had recently rented a similar space in a "worse location than ours" for $875 a month.

Housing was no easier or less expensive to find. At the same time he was searching for offices, Apple was trying to find a house for himself and his wife, Edie. He found a "small but solid house" with "a small garden" for $640 per month; he was required to pay the full year's rent of $7,680 in advance. "A very huge amount to pay for a very small house," he admitted, but quickly added that it was "clearly the only suitable thing on the market," and that even minimal hotel accommodations ran from $600 to $750 a month—"when you can get them."[15]

The press corps confronted other logistical challenges. Communications, both within South Vietnam and between South Vietnam and the United States, topped the list. In the early part of the 1960s, the primary means of transmitting print copy was the overseas cable operated by the South Vietnamese government's Post, Telephone, and Telegraph service. Film footage was usually flown to network headquarters in New York.[16]

Frustration with the vagaries of the PTT cable ran high. The potential for copy's being blocked or manipulated by the South Vietnamese government was clear; both outgoing and incoming cable traffic was copied and examined by officials. Copy was often not transmitted for hours at a time, even though the office was supposed to be open around the clock. The process of sending a dispatch could be painfully slow. Cable charges were assessed per word, and South Vietnamese technicians counted the words meticulously. Dramatic breaking developments, when the volume of traffic and the need to send copy quickly was especially high, made the delays even worse. Many reporters marked their dispatches "urgent" as a matter of routine, for "nonurgent" copy would often wait five hours or more. Also, cable charges were high. From Saigon, the average rate per word ran around 44 cents, and as high as 71 cents a word for "urgent" copy. During 1964, when the volume of news out of Saigon was low relative to the three years that followed, the *Times'* commercial-cable costs from Saigon were projected in excess of $48,000.

The PTT's lack of security, unreliability, inconvenience, and cost moved the major news organizations to try to establish alternate means of filing. "I've been going around this town looking over Telexes like a guy looks over broads," said Jimmy Breslin, in Saigon for the *New York Herald Tribune*. The AP and UPI established their own links by leasing daily telex time to their offices in Manila or Tokyo. From these locations, copy could be cabled much more dependably and inexpensively. In late 1964, the *Times* began to buy time on the Reuters circuit for $4,200 a year. Peter Grose hoped that, even if the copy had to be routed to Singapore, Sydney, London, and finally New York, the *Times* would be "well ahead of the present erratic cable time."[17]

However, the Reuters line wasn't the godsend it had promised to be. The *Times'* London bureau held and questioned copy with even the most minor glitches, often causing stories to miss the paper entirely and infuriating the Saigon staff. Overload on the Reuters circuit was a worse problem. As the war grew, Reuters duplicated the *Times* arrangement with several other news organizations, putting the Reuters bureau chief in the position of deciding what copy would go when. "This is a clear violation of our supposed priority," Apple complained to foreign editor Seymour Topping in the fall of 1967, "and I told him [Reuters bureau chief Jim Pringle] we would not tolerate this. Further he admits Rueters [sic] now vastly overextended and in all periods of heavy copy flow they can't possible handle all their clients. . . . I personally think the time has come for us to tell him that if he can't give us better service we'll go elsewhere." Topping agreed, instructing Apple to tell Pringle that "unless kinks are taken out of system I'll insist on junking Reuters arrangement."[18]

It was just as difficult for home offices to contact their Saigon bureaus. This was not a new problem. During the August 1963 pagoda raids, Halberstam, Sheehan, and Browne waited four days to find out how their dispatches had been used, or even if they had made it out of South Vietnam. "I'm gradually getting used to the fact that I have no direct contact with the *New York Times*," wrote Grose in 1964. "I just throw my copy out into a void; maybe a couple of days later comes a message (or maybe not) and maybe (but usually not) ten days later comes a copy of the International Edition. As far as my daily work goes, the *New York Times* does not exist as the newspaper I once knew; it is only a remote spirit, abstract and inscrutable." Placing a telephone call into or out of Saigon took patience and money. International phone service between Saigon and New York was available only between 6:00 P.M. and 10:00 P.M. EST (7:00 A.M. and 11:00 A.M. the next day in Saigon). Apple told managing editor Clifton Daniel to be sure to tell the overseas operator that "you wish to place a press call to Saigon from the *New York Times*, otherwise you have to wait two weeks for a private party appointment." Even a press call took several hours to place, and calls were frequently blocked by atmospheric conditions.[19]

The inability to communicate quickly and directly was crippling. James Reston, in country in August 1964, lost a story in mid-transmission. Another was misplaced altogether, leaving the home office wondering what had happened and with a hole to fill in the paper. "We were paralyzed by a communications system that does not enable New York to flag Saigon when it falls down. . . . My concern is that this flaw could murder us some night if there is some disaster here or some big development there that New York and Saigon cannot discuss in a hurry." Though the *Times* was the only American news organization in daily phone contact with its Saigon bureau by late 1967, the difficulty and expense of the practice was prohibitive. The foreign desk told Saigon to keep looking for a "system that would give us fast two way delivery of messages."[20]

The communications problem within South Vietnam was even worse. The quaint days of 1962 and 1963, when reporters would pile into a car and drive out to the fighting, were gone. The war had spread to nearly every corner of the country. The telephone was the lifeline for any news organization trying to provide comprehensive military coverage. Reporters in the field called their dispatches back to Saigon, and reporters in Saigon called sources to verify or add to existing information. Even for coverage of noncombat stories or stories in Saigon, the telephone was indispensable.

But it's a stretch to call what existed in South Vietnam a phone "system." Three separate phone systems actually existed in South Vietnam: the civilian, government-controlled PTT; the "Tiger" network, run by the United States military; and the ARVN system, operated by the South Vietnamese military. Using any of these required luck and determination. The civilian phone system, said Reston, "is enough to justify the rebellion of the Vietnamese against the French." But, "even so," he continued, "it is better than the military phone system, which for some curious reason is nicknamed Tiger. To reach a distant province, you may have to go through as many as six or seven different operators, always with the chance you may be cut off at each relay point, and always with the awkward handicap that you can't quite hear much from the other end."[21]

## "Any Idiot Can Cover a War"

Covering even a simple story under such conditions would have been tough enough. "Doing anything in Saigon takes longer and requires more effort than in the U.S.—from getting a haircut to buying a notebook," Charley Mohr found. A story as big and complex as Vietnam required a labor worthy of Hercules, a labor that many reporters performed with Herculean dedication and skill.

Some reporters downplayed the problems of reporting military action—"any idiot can cover a war," said Keyes Beech, a longtime Far East correspondent for the *Chicago Daily News*. Even so, the war story was physically and intellectually challenging. Transportation to the field was relatively easy, by using aircraft designated for the press or by hitching rides with cooperative military pilots. Once they were in the field, though, the terrain and climate of Vietnam made reporters pay "dearly for a misspent life of martinis and cigarettes."

Thus, it was relatively rare for a correspondent from one of the mainstream news organizations to spend extended periods in the field. For those reporters responsible for providing the bulk of coverage, Vietnam simply did not lend itself to that kind of journalism. "In other wars a correspondent knew where the likely action was—at the front," the *Times'* Jack Raymond said. "He got stories by going there. He chose a unit and arranged to spend days or weeks or even months with it, knowing that it had certain military objectives." But Vietnam was a war "with a frontline that one day is miles away in the jungle and the next explodes right in one's hotel." Even the biggest news staff could not afford to place reporters in the field for days or even weeks on end, waiting for the ambush or the terrorist attack that might never come. "The Vietnam war is so complicated, so *localized*," said the *Washington Post*'s Peter Braestrup, "that conventional coverage is out of the question."[22]

To find unconventional ways to cover this unconventional war was a tremendous challenge to the American press. The mainstream American press focused on the hard news of combat, even when such combat consisted of hundreds of thousands of small engagements scattered across the country. During 1965, of the estimated twenty-eight thousand combat incidents in South Vietnam, only twenty-eight resulted in more than two hundred Vietcong or North Vietnamese deaths apiece. Bringing some sort of sense to this activity was one of the most important tasks of the American press in Vietnam, yet its ability to do so was limited.

First, the Associated Press and United Press International weren't geared for placing such news in perspective. Even though the wire services employed some of the most experienced Vietnam hands, these reporters worked furiously just to gather the basic who, what, when, where, and how many of daily war news. Because of deadline and competitive pressures, it was sometimes difficult for the wires to verify and clarify information. "AP and UPI could not wait until the fog of war cleared," said Braestrup. The wire services were also accused of occasionally yielding to the temptation to "needle up" their stories in order to catch the eyes of wire editors across the country. The tendency to sensationalize stories was fed by the lack of a ready-made context, a way to judge the significance of individual actions. "Without place names as milestones toward an enemy capital," Jack Raymond wrote, "the correspondent is almost compelled to play up the sights and sounds of battle. It takes only a few casualties in any skirmish to generate descriptions worthy of the Battle of Iwo Jima." These tendencies were most evident in the wire services, but they were seen in the coverage of virtually all American news organizations.[23]

This preoccupation with Americans in combat pushed South Vietnamese politics, except in times of extreme crisis, to a back seat.[24] Pacification—the rebuilding of the social, economic, and political structure of South Vietnam's rural areas—lacked the immediacy and drama of combat, and was also primarily a story of the Vietnamese. USIA Director Leonard Marks asked MACV commander General William Westmoreland to "stress the importance the press plays in reporting to the world the non-military aspects of our involvement . . . so that the sensational does not overshadow the significant everyday occurrences."[25]

Nor did the South Vietnamese military attract much attention. The daily ARVN briefing was held immediately after and only one block away from its American counterpart, the "Five O'Clock Follies." But the ARVN routinely attracted fewer than 20 percent of the 120 or so reporters who attended the American sessions. Chairman of the Joint Chiefs of Staff General Earle Wheeler complained to Westmoreland that the role of the South Vietnamese armed forces "is underplayed by the American press" and, as a consequence, was "vastly misunderstood by the Congress and the public." Praising ARVN operations in late 1967, Wheeler added, "I only regret that we seem unable to persuade the news media to report them."[26]

Balancing these aspects of the Vietnam story concerned nearly all responsible journalists and news organizations. The experience of *The New York Times* illustrates the problem.

In the fall of 1965, Charley Mohr complained to his editors that the *Times* was "the only outfit in town which is trying to perform the function of both a wire service and those of a 'special' correspondent—plus attempting to meet the needs of a great Sunday newspaper which has no near parallel." The *Times*, in essence, was attempting to provide the same comprehensive coverage of combat as a wire service in its own daily combat summary, the same feature and background reporting as a daily newspaper, and the same analytical coverage as a weekly newsmagazine, all with a staff of no more than four reporters and three assistants.[27]

Mohr described the virtually twenty-four-hour-a-day process required to fulfill what was, in journalistic terms, the simplest of these three functions: covering combat in the daily war summary. "I will begin at 5 p.m., which is the hour of the daily military briefing," wrote Mohr. This may break up at 5:30 or earlier but it is profitable to tarry at the USIS building for informal background. . . . The correspondent doing the daily summary will probably arrive back at the office sometime after six. He then must sit down and read a 14 page single spaced communique since only a limited amount of news is given orally at the briefing. Various items may require checking over a telephone system that is virtually beyond description and which is so overloaded that most numbers are busy a great deal of the time. . . . I write fast (too fast, I fear) but on many nights it is either difficult or impossible to get a meal.

"The Reuters wire . . . now runs until 2 a.m. and will soon begin operating until 4 a.m.," Mohr continued. "This means that when you are done you are not really done because if you learn of developments you can write new leads or whole stories and transmit them before the early [edition] has been set in type in New York. The MACV information office opens for business at about 8 a.m. and there is still time to catch the first edition. . . . The entire morning and noon hour period in Saigon corresponds to the most vital hours of a morning newspaper and it is possible to make second and third editions all morning. Since it is possible it is mandatory to keep a police reporter's eye out during this period. . . . By 4:40 or so the reporter must begin to walk over to the USIS building to begin the whole cycle over again."[28]

The "specials"—focused coverage of particular events or issues by staff reporters—put even more demands on the *Times* staff. In the late summer of 1965, the *Times* was about to add a third reporter to the Saigon bureau, a prospect Mohr viewed warily. He agreed that the paper needed more men out in the field, but he also dreaded the additional strain on the staff. Correspondents in the field could only dictate their copy back to Saigon over the Tiger phone system. "Taking dictation with the lights and fan off, in the middle of writing the daily summary, over the static-filled Tiger network is a nightmare. . . . What this is going to be like on the days when we have two reporters filing from the field to one man in Saigon staggers my imagination." Nor did it make doing the analytical pieces for the Sunday paper any easier. "Because of the pressure of getting acclimated to this," Mohr said, "I have met the problem of Sunday magazine needs by not meeting the problem at all. But we are anxious to—and must—write a number of Sunday pieces and when we begin to do our duty we are going to be even busier."[29]

Mohr feared the effect this would have on morale and quality of writing, but his main concern was how "it severely limits our ability to do the deep, thoughtful, interesting, funny, investigative, and analytical reporting which will be our real record here." His solution to the problem was "to abandon the daily summary story as a daily *Times* special. The whole term is misleading anyway," he wrote. "On a day when a great battle is being fought at Chu Lai, or five planes are lost over North Vietnam it is not a summary story at all, but the top news story of the day which we are naturally going to swarm all over. But several days a week the summary is a tedious collection of largely meaningless scraps. . . . To be blunt, *New York Times* reporters here in the past have not even read the damn things on the days when they were not personally writing them."[30]

Mohr's plea didn't persuade his editors. Mohr's boss, Seymour Topping, acknowledging the pressure on the Saigon bureau, decided to add staff rather than drop the daily summary. "We should get another correspondent into the bureau as soon as possible," Topping told Clifton Daniel. "The story possibilities are limitless, but we must provide the opportunity for staffers not working on the bang-bang fighting that has to be covered to get the time to dig thoroughly into the not-so-obvious aspects of the Viet Nam story." When Johnny Apple complained about the tendency to hold feature stories over, Topping told him that he was sorry but "We get an arbitrary space allotment and the spot news has to be covered." In late 1967, new assistant managing editor A. M. Rosenthal told a Vietnam-bound correspondent that "the Saigon bureau should give considerably more attention to the daily briefing story. As it is now, the story is usually written by our stringer," a practice Rosenthal and the other editors called "a mistake." He asked the bureau to assign the story daily to a senior member of the staff "who could bring to it his own experiences in the field. . . ."[31]

This detail from within the *Times* illustrates two important points. First, American journalists were aware of the importance of placing military action in perspective and of reporting on nonmilitary aspects of the story. But the experience of the *Times* also shows that, despite this awareness, the primary focus of the American press in South Vietnam was combat, especially combat involving Americans. When its fundamental journalistic assets—the time and effort of its reporters and space in the paper—were being allocated, the *Times* management made its priority clear. But if the *Times,* unsurpassed in its on-the-scene Vietnam coverage, its commitment to depth and breadth of coverage of foreign affairs, and the sophistication of its audience, could not buck the demands of American journalism, what American news organization could?

It somehow doesn't make sense that a press corps that at its peak numbered over six hundred persons, well over half of whom worked for American news media, couldn't cover pacification, the ARVN, or South Vietnamese internal affairs. The news-gathering and reporting capabilities of the press corps cannot, however, be judged merely by its size. First, the idea of a six-hundred-member press corps is deceptive. This figure actually refers to the number of persons accredited to news agencies by the South Vietnamese government and MACV. Security regulations required that anyone whom a news organization wished to have access to military or government facilities had to be accredited. This meant that any employee, from the bureau chief to the Vietnamese secretary who went to public-affairs offices to pick up news releases, had to be accredited. Press-corps numbers were also swelled by the fact that accreditation was routinely granted for a period of six months, even to journalists visiting for only a few days or weeks. These reporters remained on the accreditation lists even after leaving the country. Thus, the number of reporters actually in the country at any one time was usually lower than the number accredited.

Finally, accreditation was fairly easy to obtain, making the Saigon "press corps" a varied lot. To be accredited by MACV, one first had to be accredited by the South Vietnamese government. This required a valid passport and entrance visa, a letter of employment by some sort of publishing or broadcasting concern, and a record of immunization against cholera, smallpox, and the plague. Once this was done, for MACV accreditation one had only to present a letter on news-agency stationery affirming employment and stating that the employer assumed "full responsibility for his professional actions, including financial responsibility and personal conduct as these affect his professional action." A free-lancer went through a similar process, except that the news agency's letter certified an agreement to purchase copy or photographs from the person.

Thus, along with *The New York Times, Time* magazine, and CBS, the Vietnam press corps also included representatives of *Ms.* magazine, radio station WJZM in Clarksville, Tennessee, and the Bucknell College alumni magazine. In addition, quite a few correspondents, attempting to maintain some semblance of family life, obtained accreditation for their spouses. Some of these persons were actually working reporters, but the journalistic function of others was at best peripheral. When all this is taken into account, estimates of what Peter Braestrup called "fact-finding manpower," the "resident representatives of . . . those news publications, news agencies, and TV networks with national U.S. audiences," ranged anywhere from twenty to sixty persons.[32]

The reportorial force was as limited in experience as in size. The problem was not years. Although covering Vietnam remained a young persons's game—the typical Vietnam correspondent ranged in age from twenty-five to thirty-five—most of the reporters for major news organizations had sound professional backgrounds before coming to Vietnam. Rather, even the most experienced American war correspondents had little if any exposure to the mix of guerrilla and conventional combat seen in Vietnam.

The inexperience concerning Vietnam itself was a major drawback. This problem had two aspects. A very few reporters had been to Vietnam before. The degree of their preparation varied. Briefings by their employers were sometimes valuable, sometimes not. The Defense Department offered orientation lectures, and the State Department made its Vietnam Training Center available to the press. Few reporters took advantage of these opportunities. Just a handful of American reporters spoke Vietnamese before going to the country, and only a very few others picked up more than a smattering of it while there.[33]

After a while, a reporter might develop a familiarity with the country. He or she had perhaps mastered the logistics of operating there, and had developed a set of sources and a feel for the story. All just in time to be lost, for correspondents routinely rotated out of Vietnam after fairly brief tours. Out of concern for the emotional and physical well-being of the reporter, the average length of assignment in Vietnam for a print reporter was twelve to eighteen months, six months to a year for a broadcast journalist. Here was the same problem that plagued the U.S. military, which held tours of duty to one year (thirteen months for the Marines). Although there was a core of "Vietnam hands" present throughout the war, the majority of the press corps at any one time was spending a good deal of energy figuring out what the story was and how to cover it.[34]

## "Experience in Its Rawest Form"

Television resides at the extremes of our story. Popular mythology does not have it so. Rather, the effect of television coverage is seen as the most important element. Nonetheless, television was actually more subject to the problems of Vietnam coverage and to the constraints inherent in American journalism than any other news medium. Consequently, television's ability to explain the Vietnam story was even more limited, and its role in the war even more ambiguous, than was that of the rest of the American press.

Early on, the infant television networks had made limited attempts to provide film coverage of the Korean War. This effort had been thwarted by the clumsiness of the equipment and the short time available for such reports in the fifteen-minute evening news broadcasts. Nor were networks any more evident in the Vietnam of the 1950s and early 1960s. None of the three American TV networks had a bureau there, although Far East correspondents like CBS's Peter Kalischer and NBC's James Robinson visited Saigon fairly regularly, especially during the last days of Diem.

But by 1965, TV news operations had matured dramatically. CBS and NBC went to half-hour evening news broadcasts in September 1963, ABC in early 1965. The shows' audiences and advertising revenue increased. The news operations began to make money for the networks, money that in turn helped the news operations grow even bigger and more sophisticated. When the American press went to Vietnam with American combat troops in the summer and fall of 1965, television news led the way. By the end of the year, the three networks had the largest bureaus in Saigon.[35]

Television news made its first splash in Vietnam with the August 3, 1965, broadcast of the "CBS Evening News with Walter Cronkite." Read on the show that night was a description by the network's thirty-three-year-old Vietnam correspondent, Morley Safer, of a squad of United States Marines burning the hamlet of Cam Ne, near Danang. Safer said that the Marines put the mud-brick–and–straw houses to the torch after receiving only one short burst of automatic-weapon fire, and that they ignored the pleas of villagers for time to remove their belongings from the structures.[36]

Film of the report was still in transit from Vietnam. When it aired two days later, it depicted Marines moving down a line of huts whose thatched roofs were consumed in flame. A weary-looking Safer stated: "Today's operation shows the frustration of Vietnam in miniature. There is little doubt that American fire power can win a military victory here. But to a Vietnamese peasant whose house means a life of backbreaking labor, it will take more than presidential promises to convince him that we are on his side."[37]

Reactions to the Cam Ne story were immediate and visceral. Early on the morning after the film aired, CBS News President Frank Stanton was awakened by a ringing telephone. As he put the receiver to his ear, the voice on the other end bellowed, "Frank, are you trying to fuck me?" "Who is this?" asked the groggy Stanton. "Frank," the voice drawled, "this is your President, and yesterday your boys shat on the American flag." Johnson, sure that Safer was a communist, ordered a background check of the reporter. When nothing incriminating turned up, Johnson had the Marine officer in command at Cam Ne that day investigated, equally convinced that Safer had bribed him to set the huts on fire. Pentagon spokesman Arthur Sylvester echoed that charge, and called upon CBS to remove Safer from Vietnam. The Defense Department also began monitoring network evening news shows. The public reacted just as strongly. CBS was flooded with calls and letters critical of Safer's report and the negative light it cast upon American servicemen. From that point on, television became a lightning rod for discussion of the role of the press in the war.[38]

If television coverage sparked more extreme reactions than that of other news media, it also faced more extreme obstacles. Consider the logistical problems. Operating in Vietnam was tough enough for a print journalist, whose equipment consisted of notebook and pencil, and perhaps a camera or a typewriter. A television correspondent, however, was linked by cable to a cameraman and a soundman whose equipment together could weigh upward of a hundred pounds. A print reporter might lurk on the edge of the action, later combining what he'd seen with other reports to make a story. Not so the television correspondent, who had to be right in the action if possible. As one reporter put it, "New York has an insatiable appetite for film."[39]

Naturally, it was even more difficult—and expensive too—for a television correspondent to file his or her reports. Each day, TV reporters sent cables advising their bosses in New York what sort of film they had or planned to have; how each piece of film was handled depended on its immediate newsworthiness and the need to match the competition. If the film was of a breaking story or of some particularly dramatic development, it would be flown to Tokyo, where it would be developed, edited, and transmitted by satellite to New York. Such treatment was rare, though—to send a three-minute piece of film this way cost $4,000 or more. Much more often, stories were transported by plane all the way from Saigon to New York.[40]

Cost considerations had influenced coverage of Vietnam since the 1950s. Their effect on television coverage was especially pronounced. The equipment was expensive and required relatively large staffs to operate. Television reporters were generally better paid than their print colleagues. The logistical costs were also higher. By 1967, the three networks together spent more than $5 million a year on coverage of the war. The networks tried to hold down costs where possible, and one prime opportunity was in the use of film stories. Though the producers of the evening news shows may have had an "insatiable appetite" for film, such stories actually made up a fairly small portion of the total network coverage of the war. Most TV coverage was composed of wire-service dispatches read by anchormen. In order to hold costs down as much as possible on the film stories that were used, correspondents were encouraged "to produce film reports analogous to newspaper feature stories, which would 'hold up,' if necessary, for several days," allowing the film to be shipped by air rather than transmitted more expensively over satellite or cable.

Because of its nature, television focused centrally on combat reporting. "Television is the transmission of experience in its rawest form," said NBC News commentator John Chancellor. Television news lived and died on its emotional immediacy, and this was especially true in a story as emotion-laden as Vietnam. An unidentified CBS cameraman said that he felt "so inadequate being able to record only a minute part of the misery, a minute part of the fighting. . . . When I am halfway through the story, and I feel it is good, I become greedy. Greedy to capture more on film, more drama, more excitement. This is when you are fully committed, and emotionally involved." As in other media, this emphasis on action pushed out other stories. "A good fire fight is going to get on over a good pacification story," said an ABC News executive. And, like other news organizations, the networks were most concerned with action involving Americans. A survey by Lawrence Lichty and Thomas Hoffer quoted in Peter Braestrup's *Big Story* found that, of 187 film reports from Vietnam appearing on the evening news shows from September 1967 through January 1968, 159 dealt exclusively or primarily with American troops.

All of these pressures and characteristics combined to make television coverage of the war less explanatory, less "newsy." TV coverage was more impressionistic, more interested in the viewers' hearts and guts than in their heads. Viewers may not have known how important what they saw was, but they knew how it felt. "Combat in living color is often wanting in perspective," said *Time*, "but rarely in impact."[41]

Just what that impact is, remains up for grabs. Some observers agreed with ABC News Vice-President James Hagerty, who argued "that the coverage of the sight and sound of the war in Vietnam by American television was exposing the false glory of war. . . . By doing so, such coverage was contributing . . : to a growing public consciousness that war should no longer be tolerated."

Others believed that repeated coverage of Vietnam actually dulled Americans' sensitivity, making them more tolerant of war. "What we are getting is a hawk's eye view of life and death," said psychiatrist Frederick Wertham. "War is becoming routine." Still others felt that TV coverage only reinforced existing feelings and preconceptions. More recently, in an echo of Hagerty's view, the assumption has been that, rightly or wrongly, television, along with the other news media, turned Americans against the war.[42]

To assess these views, it helps to have some sense of just what TV film coverage did and did not show. One assumption has taken on the certainty of fact—that television showed all the agony and gore of combat, and that such coverage lay at the root of whatever impact television supposedly had. Because of TV, *Newsweek* breathlessly said, Americans "will know how it is for Americans to die in battle and how they kill."[43]

But this assumption isn't very accurate. Network news executives were extremely sensitive to the limits of the public's taste for reality. The networks routinely deleted particularly graphic footage, and also refrained from showing in close-up the faces of wounded Americans, at least until the families had been notified. The bodies of dead Americans were usually shown only after they'd been covered or placed in body bags. Even the depiction of Vietcong and North Vietnamese dead, about whom American producers and viewers were less concerned, could go too far. CBS learned this lesson when its film of forty-eight dead Vietcong being loaded into a cargo net inspired dozens of complaining calls.

Instead of blood and guts, most coverage of "combat" consisted of American troops walking through the bush; American troops exchanging fire with an unseen enemy; Americans waiting for something to happen. Some evidence indicates that such coverage could have, at least indirectly, increased support for the war. A Louis Harris poll commissioned by *Newsweek* in the summer of 1967 was one of the first relatively scientific studies of media impact on public opinion concerning the war. The survey found that only 31 percent of those questioned said that TV moved them to oppose the war. The same group was then asked if television made them more inclined to "back up the boys in Vietnam" or more inclined to oppose the war. By more than two to one, respondents said television coverage of the war caused them to want to support the troops rather than to oppose the war they were fighting.[44]

This poll, and the other studies, finally reveal a complex message. TV coverage of the war, as befits its nature, could inspire a whole range of emotional reactions—anxiety, confusion, or stubborn resistance to new ideas. But a better understanding of the war was rarely a product of television news.

A television critic wrote in *Life* that "difficult war aims and delicate policies are simply not rendered any clearer by the genuine bravery of a correspondent putting on tape his own entrapment by Vietcong snipers." Instead, he continued, television left its viewers "an appalling record of surprise and death, its only cohesion being the Kilroyesque figure of the groggy GI slogging through the unfriendly terrain of any war, calmly convinced that he is getting a job done, the sooner the better."[45]

The Vietnam story had changed. From 1964 to 1967, the story was a bigger, more American war. The press had changed too. Lured by the drama of a wider war, the press corps's growth paralleled that of the U.S. troop contingent. During this period, the American press's own characteristics, along with conditions in Vietnam, shaped the story significantly. Another important factor—the press's sources and its relation to them—changed as well.

# 8

# "Fighting in the Open"

## Sources and the Story, 1964–67

A MAJOR ELEMENT of the press story in Vietnam had always been the relationship between reporters and their sources. The Kennedy Administration denied information to reporters, driving them to other, more critical sources. From 1964 to 1967, the way reporters dealt with sources, even the sources themselves, changed. But did this mean that the American press—and American people—were getting any better understanding of the war?

## "Behind the Lines"

A significant new development in the press's attempt to cover the war was access to the other side. Like the advent of television, this access would add both a new dimension and a new burden to the press.

Unplanned contacts between reporters for American news organizations and opposing troops had taken place during the course of the war, as journalists were occasionally captured and held for short periods. Such encounters occurred with some regularity, especially after the ground war escalated throughout South Vietnam and, in 1970, spilled over into Cambodia. For example, the *St. Louis Post-Dispatch*'s Richard Dudman and UPI's Kate Webb spent several days as prisoners of the Khmer Rouge. To be sure, these brief interludes made exciting reading and provided interesting glimpses into the lives of guerrilla fighters in Indochina. Conversely, they obviously offered highly personal and pressure-filled perspectives on the "other side."

American news organizations also made occasional use of reports about the Vietcong by journalists either sympathetic to the Vietcong–North Vietnamese cause or from neutral countries. The best-known such reporter was Wilfred Burchett, an Australian newsman who made a career out of reporting from the communist side of various issues and conflicts. During 1964, Burchett spent four months in the Mekong Delta with the Vietcong. However, reports by Burchett and others identified with communist causes were generally dismissed as slanted and propagandistic, even if factually accurate.[1]

Much more important than these contacts was a glimpse into North Vietnam via the bombing of the country by the United States. From the beginning of Rolling Thunder, President Johnson had been extremely concerned about a possible backlash against the image of the world's most powerful nation trying to pound a Third World country into submission. Because of this concern, particularly over the civilian casualties, the administration tried to control both the extent of the bombing and its portrayal in the American press. Such control grew even more important in the summer of 1966, as the bombing expanded to include the major industrial and population centers of Hanoi and Haiphong.

In early June, Earle Wheeler alerted Westmoreland and the commander of U.S. forces in the Pacific, Admiral Ulysses G. Sharp, that authorization to strike at petroleum storage and transmission facilities near the North Vietnamese capital was on its way. "You should know," Wheeler added, "that this first intrusion into the Hanoi/Haiphong sanctuary will raise some specters of large numbers of civilian casualties in the target areas. In order to satisfy sensibilities here [Washington] I have placed in the draft execute message certain admonitions as to briefings, weather, crew experience and weaponry which I would normally oppose presenting to a field commander." The public-affairs guidance that accompanied the authorization two weeks later put strict controls on what briefing officers could and could not say. The guidance also made clear Washington's intent to monitor public statements about the raid very closely. Arthur Sylvester instructed Westmoreland to tape the briefing and to transmit it to the Pentagon immediately.[2]

From the beginning of the air offensive, in the late winter of 1965, through most of 1966, this sort of control worked pretty well. *The New York Times* account of the large raids on March 2, 1965—the first raids not justified solely as retaliatory actions—was taken straight from the Saigon briefing by a Colonel Hal Price. Colonel Price described the location and nature of the targets, the type and amount of ordnance used, losses to American forces, and the success of the raid. Such stories became standard coverage as the air war in the North expanded and intensified. They suited the needs of both government and press. The government was able to control the characterization of the bombing, emphasizing its precision and effectiveness, because the press had no alternate source. And reporters were, as a State Department official said, "glad to have the detailed reports of the air strikes, since it satisfies their primary need for the hard news on U.S. participation in the war."[3]

Observers in North Vietnam provided occasional glimpses of the effects of the bombing from observers in North Vietnam itself. A journalist for the Polish government press agency reported that towns in southern North Vietnam had dug whole networks of trenches and anti-aircraft bunkers. Commercial activity, he went on, was conducted at night. Claiming that one town he was in during a raid had no military significance, the journalist called the bombing an act of terrorism. He also said that the attacks "have had just the reverse effect than that expected in Saigon and Washington," as the local people declared their "unflagging will" to resist the Americans.

A London *Daily Mail* article by a British woman working at Hanoi's Teacher Training College told how just the threat of attacks had disrupted the life of the city. She described a city where teachers and bureaucrats spent days digging bomb shelters, where children had been evacuated to the countryside, and where playgrounds were now the sites of civil-defense and military drills. A series from Hanoi by British journalist James Cameron similarly depicted a city and a country under siege, but also one in which the bombing had not touched the people's "totally unshakable determination to win the war, on their terms." After the attacks reached Hanoi and Haiphong, Agence France Presse reporter Jean Raffaelli, the lone Western correspondent stationed in Hanoi, disputed the claims of the American government and reports in the American press. Instead of surgically precise bombing inflicting crippling damage on North Vietnam, Raffaelli said that the summer-1966 attacks on oil facilities had been "off target and costly in civilian lives." The raids would not force Hanoi to "capitulate," he continued.[4]

These reports received limited circulation in the American news media, and were usually written off as either propaganda or the products of poor journalism by non-Americans. It would be much more difficult for the American press, government, and people to ignore reports from North Vietnam by a respected representative of an important American news organization.

Beginning the day after Christmas 1966, such reports began to appear in *The New York Times,* written by Harrison E. Salisbury, the paper's veteran foreign correspondent and assistant managing editor. Salisbury had been trying off and on for several months to get into North Vietnam. The North Vietnamese approved his visa in December 1966, and, after hurried preparations, he arrived in Hanoi late that month. Before leaving the country in early January, Salisbury had filed a total of fourteen articles based on his own observations and on information furnished to him during tours conducted by North Vietnamese officials in Hanoi and surrounding towns.[5]

The series largely echoed earlier reports by non-Americans. Salisbury was taken to the small city of Nam Dinh just south of Hanoi, a town described by its mayor as "a textile producing center of limited military significance." Salisbury reported seeing "block after block of utter destruction." He also quoted, without initially citing their source, North Vietnamese statistics on damage to nonmilitary structures and civilian casualties. In this and other stories, Salisbury directly and indirectly disputed official American characterizations of the bombing.[6]

Salisbury's reports, unlike those by earlier, non-American visitors, weren't ignored. Rather, they ignited a brief but telling controversy that ran through both the American government and press. Members of Congress lined up on both sides of the issue. Senators Richard Russell and George Smathers "urged President Johnson to forget world opinion and bomb Hanoi flat," whereas Senator Bourke Hickenlooper acidly said, "It's strange to me that they [North Vietnamese officials] will let a *New York Times* reporter in but not objective reporters." Others, including House Government Information Subcommittee members John Moss and Ogden Reid, used Salisbury's dispatches as a platform from which to question official descriptions of the bombing and the air offensive itself.[7]

The administration had a mixed response. The White House and Pentagon had no advance knowledge of what each article would bring. They were initially put on the defensive and forced to react to individual aspects of Salisbury's stories. Reconnaissance photographs confirmed some of Salisbury's reports, and the government conceded that, though "all possible care is taken to avoid civilian casualties," bombs aimed at military targets had on occasion missed their mark and hit nearby civilian areas.

Despite private acknowledgment that they had oversold the bombing's accuracy, Defense and other officials did their best to chip holes in the series. Intelligence personnel dissected the articles "line by line," according to Deputy Assistant Secretary of Defense for Public Affairs Phil Goulding, and their analysis was used to refute some of Salisbury's assertions publicly. Senior American commanders in South Vietnam were to convince the press corps there that the bombing, civilian casualties aside, was affecting Hanoi's war-making ability.

The anger in the Pentagon over the series ran "deep and strong," Goulding said. "No newspaper writing or television commentary in my four Pentagon years so disturbed me, and none so disturbed more of my associates in government." Goulding's boss, Arthur Sylvester, referred publicly to Salisbury as "Harrison Appallsbury" and to his employer as "The New Hanoi Times." An unidentified member of the administration told *Time* that the series was "a stinking job of reporting . . . the kind of report one would expect from a Communist source, without balance or reflection or skepticism or doubt."[8]

That was the problem. For over a year and a half, the American press in Saigon and Washington had accepted without "skepticism or doubt" the official characterization of the bombing's accuracy and effectiveness. Reports to the contrary by the foreign press could be dismissed. But when the country's most respected news organization presented such reports, they were blasted with a precision that would have been a bomber pilot's dream.

Salisbury's articles made even some of his press colleagues nervous. *Washington Post* Pentagon correspondent Chalmers Roberts— "the very embodiment of an establishment reporter," according to

Halberstam—said the articles were part of a new Ho Chi Minh tactic, "one as cleverly conceived as the poison-tipped bamboo spikes his men implanted underfoot for the unwary enemy." ABC's Howard K. Smith accused Salisbury of practicing sloppy journalism and of allowing himself to be taken in by the North Vietnamese. "The *Times'* carelessness about the simple basic practices of fair and accurate reporting has become suspicious," Smith said. "If one were given to phrase mongering one might say that it has dug its own credibility gap."⁹

To be sure, the series had flaws. Most notable was the failure to identify North Vietnamese sources more frequently and clearly. One must ask, though, what "independent" statistics Salisbury was expected to find while being guided through Hanoi by North Vietnamese officials. The series most disturbed the American press, however, by making abundantly clear its dependence on the United States government for information about the war. The press reaction to the series also revealed how wary even the most powerful news organizations were of going too far out on a limb.

Most telling is the response of the *Times* itself. The paper accepted praise from some quarters for its courage in running the reports. The *Times* also not-so-discreetly backed away from the series. The day after the first installment, Hanson Baldwin wrote a four-page memo to Clifton Daniel, outlining in detail the journalistic, factual, and interpretive errors he found in the story. What bothered Baldwin was how sharply Salisbury's assertions differed from the government's. "The whole tone of this story gives the impression that the United States is deliberately undertaking saturation and population bombing and it swallows the Communist line almost hook, line and sinker," he told Daniel. The stories "seem to put Mr. Salisbury and the *Times* squarely on the side of North Vietnam." "My chief concern," Baldwin concluded, "is the effect that these stories will have upon the country and upon the *Times*."

Daniel shared that concern. He ran a front-page news analysis by Baldwin, based on Pentagon sources, that essentially refuted Salisbury's conclusions. Baldwin even used one quotation that directly attacked the reports as "grossly exaggerated." The *Times* further distanced itself from the articles in an editorial three days later. "The targeting restrictions in the North have been so precise and definite that the military feels some American pilots have given their lives because of this," the editorial said. Nor did the paper's caution end here. Daniel privately called on his editors to "do everything we can in the coming weeks to balance the Salisbury reports."[10]

Despite the controversy, Salisbury's articles from Hanoi were, as *Newsweek* called them, "easily the biggest news beat of 1966." They opened the door to North Vietnam for American civilians. The day Salisbury left Hanoi, American journalists Harry Ashmore and William Baggs arrived, acting as official representatives of the Center for the Study of Democratic Institutions and as unofficial agents of the State Department. A year later, CBS sent correspondent Charles Collingwood to Hanoi. For the rest of the war, a fairly steady stream of Americans, journalists and others, went to Hanoi.

Through them the American public had an unprecedented view of a wartime enemy. Americans in the twentieth century had become accustomed to regarding enemies as less than human, rabid beasts to be exterminated. Two factors were behind this phenomenon. First, World Wars I and II were total wars, requiring significant sacrifice from the home front. Thus, the government turned its propaganda efforts toward keeping commitment to the war effort at a fever pitch. Second, these efforts were not countered by an American press reporting from Berlin or Tokyo. During Vietnam, however, the government was trying desperately to avoid the implications of "total war," and thus could go only so far in stirring sentiment against the enemy. Also, beginning with Salisbury, the American people could see their enemy not as animals but as another people trying to make a life for themselves and their children amid hardship and sacrifice.[11]

## "Like Sand between Your Fingers"

Logistics, a tendency to focus on military action involving Americans, the cost of news coverage, the advent of TV, and access to North Vietnam all complicated the task of reporting the war. But, as the Salisbury affair demonstrated, another factor loomed even larger—the ambiguous relationship between the American press and the United States government concerning information on the war. In the end, this factor would combine with the others to leave the press, the government, and the people alike feeling that a true understanding of the Vietnam War was, in the words of one official in Saigon, "like sand between your fingers. You can't put your hand on anything."[12]

Two philosophies of press relations operated in the Johnson Administration and the military. James L. Greenfield, assistant secretary of state for public affairs, represented one approach; his Pentagon counterpart, Arthur Sylvester, the other. Their differences were on display at a meeting in Presidential Press Secretary Bill Moyers' White House office late in the afternoon of August 10, 1965.

Arrayed around the room were senior information officials of the Executive Branch: Moyers himself, John Chancellor and Barry Zorthian from the USIA, Greenfield from State, and Sylvester from Defense. Still fresh on all their minds was Morley Safer's report on the burning of Cam Ne. Sylvester blamed such reporting on "unfriendly correspondents in Viet-Nam." He blasted Safer, impugning his professionalism and his motivations. Safer, a Canadian, was for Sylvester an example of foreigners who, while working for American news organizations, "are known to be less than fully sympathetic with our efforts and [who] appear to miss no chance to embarrass us." He even hinted that Safer had concocted the whole incident.

Greenfield shot back immediately. "We couldn't pull a curtain on the problem. . . . It isn't just a problem of a few bad apples. We have to get used to fighting in the open," he said. "This is a new kind of war, a war in which the basic goal is people, not territory. You can't win the people in Viet-Nam by burning their villages. This may have worked at Iwo Jima, but it won't work in Viet-Nam. We have to take steps to prevent these things from happening, not just to make sure reporters don't see them."[13]

These two approaches appeared to clash, but they shared the same old and ultimate goal: control and manipulation of information. No less than the Truman, Eisenhower, and Kennedy administrations, Lyndon Johnson's Executive Branch found it easier to conduct national-security policy in a context of its own choosing and design. Though the philosophies represented by Greenfield and Sylvester differed in tactics, each aimed to give Johnson control of the public's knowledge and perception of the Vietnam War.

Greenfield's viewpoint represented a line of thinking that went at least back to the fall of 1962, when John Mecklin had called for a more open, cooperative press policy. Mecklin had pointed out that American reporters were finding information and filing dispatches from other, usually unfriendly sources. The government had a much better chance of getting its view of the war's events, aims, and progress across if it provided the information the press required to fulfill its own professional obligations. This idea came into practice during 1963, as the Diem regime began to lose the support of important American officials in Saigon and Washington. They came to agree with reporters in Saigon and began to use the press as a tool by which to exert further pressure on the South Vietnamese president and his brother.

Greenfield wholeheartedly agreed with this approach. He told his colleagues that "the press will write whether or not we brief. You can't prevent stories by not providing information. . . . Whenever we have taken pains to keep the press abreast of what is happening it has worked to our advantage."[14]

Greenfield was not alone in this belief; during 1964, the idea of cooperation with the press became official policy, and it remained so for the remainder of the American involvement in the war.

The policy first appeared in the form of Operation Maximum Candor, a concentrated effort in the summer of 1964 to redress the chief irritants between the press corps and American officials in Saigon. Barry Zorthian, a career USIA official, was named overall coordinator of information for the entire U.S. mission, answerable only to the ambassador. Also, Colonel Rodger Bankson, one of the army's most senior public-affairs officers, replaced Colonel Basil Lee Baker, chief military-information officer during the discredited Harkins-Nolting era. The staffs of the civilian and military information operations were enlarged. MACV expanded its regular briefings, and provided greater amounts of more accurate information on a more timely basis. Access to top officials was made easier. Reporters were given more help in getting to the field. Facilities for the press, both in Saigon and the field, were improved.

The patterns laid down by Maximum Candor continued to develop over the next three years. By 1967, the civilian and military information operations in South Vietnam had grown into a small army, from Zorthian all the way to the provincial and battalion levels. In short order, this operation became extremely effective at furnishing the American press what it needed most—the information and logistical support required to report the hard news of American activity, primarily military, in Vietnam.[15]

In addition to such assistance, the press in Vietnam worked under extremely light official restrictions. Formal military censorship was considered briefly at the behest of President Johnson on two occasions in the spring of 1965, but was rejected both times. Any effective censorship would, as a legal and practical matter, have had to involve the South Vietnamese government. The memory of Diem's attacks on American reporters was fresh, and his successors' willingness to restrain the domestic press clear. U.S. officials believed that putting the American press at the mercy of the South Vietnamese again would be a grave mistake. Imposition of censorship would have negative political repercussions in the United States. Finally, they acknowledged that the stories sparking Johnson's concern did not affect military security.[16]

Instead, reporters in Vietnam agreed to abide by a set of ground rules detailing types of information that could and could not be released. Though they changed slightly from time to time, restricted information fell generally into the following categories:

(1) Future plans, operations, or strikes.

(2) Information on or confirmation of Rules of Engagement.

(3) Amounts of ordnance and fuel moved by support units or on hand in combat units.

(4) Exact number and types or identification of casualties suffered by friendly units.

(5) During an operation, unit designations and troop movements, tactical deployments, name of operation and size of friendly force involved, until officially released by MACV.

(6) Intelligence unit activities, methods of operation, or specific location.

(7) The number of sorties and the amount of ordnance expended on strikes outside the RVN [Republic of Vietnam].

(8) Information on aircraft taking off for strikes, enroute to, or returning from target area. Information on strikes while they are in progress.

(9) Identity of units and location of air bases from which aircraft are launched on combat operations.

(10) Number of aircraft damaged or any other indication of effectiveness or ineffectiveness of ground anti-aircraft defenses.

(11)  Tactical specifics, such as altitudes, course, speeds, or angle of attack. (General terms such as "low and fast" may be used.)

(12)  Information on or confirmation of planned strikes which do not take place for any reason, including bad weather.

(13)  Specific identification of enemy weapon systems utilized to down friendly aircraft.

(14)  Details concerning downed aircraft while SAR [search and rescue] operations are in progress.

The potential penalty for breaking these restrictions was severe. "Deliberate violation of these conditions or ground rules," reporters were warned, "will be regarded as a basis for suspension or cancellation of accreditation." Loss of accreditation meant loss of access to American and South Vietnamese facilities, loss of access to information, perhaps even loss of the right to remain in South Vietnam. Certainly at risk was the ability to perform one's job. However, so carefully did the press comply voluntarily with these guidelines that, from 1965 through 1967, only two reporters had their accreditation suspended for violating them. Only one of these, Jack Foisie of the *Los Angeles Times,* worked for an American news organization.[17]

This didn't mean, however, that the millennium had arrived in terms of press relations with military and government in Vietnam. Greenfield represented a more sophisticated approach to press relations, one in which the government took advantage of the dynamics of the American press. Arthur Sylvester represented the other side— the belief that the best way to deal with the press was not to deal with it at all, to deny it information or, when necessary, to lie. The attitude embodied in Maximum Candor was official policy from 1964 through the rest of the war. Even so, some of the old philosophy, its roots reaching deep back into the Cold War, remained.

*"The Maximum Candor policy pays off in Viet-Nam,"* one State Department official said. "Nearly all problems with the press result from departures from the policy." Such departures occurred frequently, and took a variety of forms. At times the government simply attempted to deny information to the press. One such instance involved a supposed encounter in the Gulf of Tonkin between United States Navy destroyers and North Vietnamese PT boats on September 18, 1964. Unlike the high drama and publicity surrounding the first engagements, a few weeks earlier, a lid slammed shut on the

details of this incident—an apparent attempt to keep the Vietnam situation in the background until after the November elections. Instead, the attempted secrecy drew even greater notice to the incident, fostering, as a *New York Times* editorial said, "suspicion at home and abroad." The whole event took on a comical tone when, after administration efforts to keep the names of the ship involved secret, the details of the encounter were revealed by a proud mother who shared a letter from her son serving on one of the destroyers.[18]

On other occasions, the government tried to deter reporters by blocking physical access to important areas or denying adequate facilities. During the spring and summer of 1965, Danang became one of the chief staging areas for the bombing campaign against the North. Officials barred reporters from the air base there, claiming that dispatches about the raids filed over open phone lines assisted the enemy and put American pilots in "unnecessary jeopardy." Even granting a genuine concern for security, the effectiveness of such restrictions was questionable. If the Vietcong and the North Vietnamese wanted advance notice of air raids, they could have easily acquired it through their own observers, without eavesdropping on the conversations of American reporters.

However, the restrictions went beyond simple concern for security. Reporters were also denied access to military clubs and restaurants, either on the base or in the city of Danang. Fliers operating outside South Vietnam were under orders not to speak with the press. The military enforced these restrictions firmly. Several newsmen trying to view the airfield were taken into custody for brief periods by American and South Vietnamese military police. And, in a move reminiscent of the Diem era, American officials tried to disavow responsibility for the restrictions by claiming that they had been imposed by the South Vietnamese "without notice to United States authorities."[19]

The restrictions eased somewhat when they inspired the anger of the press corps and the interest of the Moss subcommittee. Failure to provide adequate facilities and support for the press still limited access to the air base and its personnel. For example, reporters were eventually allowed onto certain areas of the base if they were under military escort at all times. However, only two men were available to escort the thirty or so reporters working at Danang. Also, access to the base required special passes that could be obtained only in Saigon and only after negotiating with the South Vietnamese bureaucracy. In addition, the press center in Danang was woefully inadequate. "This is the only press center in the world without a telephone," one reporter said. Most reporters understood that officials would need time to provide proper facilities, but they also found "the military unprepared or in some cases . . . unwilling to meet their needs and their demands in keeping the world informed."[20]

Casualty figures provide a final example of departures from Maximum Candor. Under Westmoreland, the United States developed a military strategy based on destroying the enemy's forces faster than they could be replaced. Eventually, it was hoped, a weakened Vietcong would be forced to negotiate. A significant measure of progress in this strategy was, obviously enough, the enemy casualty rate. The military told correspondents that, although no figure on enemy killed in action could be exact, it was felt that "duplication and other errors on the high side" were offset by uncounted casualties. These numbers included enemy dead and wounded carried away from the battlefield, those who died later of wounds incurred during the battle, or those killed by artillery fire or air strikes not followed by a ground patrol. However, even though MACV believed its figures were "conservative in the long run," both the accuracy of the figures and their validity as a measure of progress were widely questioned. Charles Mohr wrote in late 1965 that "one characteristic of a guerrilla war is the extreme difficulty of telling how it is going," and that "statistical measures had very little meaning." He discounted estimates of enemy killed. "So great is the pressure for body-count figures," Mohr said, that troops began "to joke . . . about Saigon's request for the 'WEG,' or 'wild-eyed guess.' " Throughout the period, and especially in mid-1967, the size of the VC–North Vietnamese force was sharply debated within the government. The military was claiming greater effectiveness in reducing those forces than that found by civilian estimates. But when, in March 1967, MACV's own assessments revealed greater enemy capability than expected, Wheeler implored Westmoreland to "do whatever is necessary to insure that these figures are not repeat not released to news media or otherwise exposed to public knowledge." "If these figures should reach the public domain," Wheeler warned, "they would, literally, blow the lid off of Washington."[21]

American casualty figures were also controversial. Claiming security considerations, the American military in July 1965 stopped reporting specific figures for individual actions. Instead, they characterized American battle losses as "light, moderate, or heavy." These descriptions created problems from the beginning. The meaning of the terms varied from person to person. In fact, MACV spokesmen agreed to tell reporters specific casualty figures off the record so that they could select their own adjectives if they disagreed with those assigned officially. Also, the press suspected the military of manipulating the reporting process to downplay American casualties. For example, the losses of a company nearly wiped out in an ambush could be diluted when they were reported as part of the casualties for all the units involved in a total operation. By early 1967, the military went back to reporting specific casualty figures for individual actions, complaining that the previous system resulted in inflated estimates of American losses in the press. This was a tacit but nonetheless clear admission by the military that political and public-relations considerations, at least as much as security, governed its decisions on casualty information.[22]

All of this points to the central factor—and the central problem—of the relationship between the American press and the American government and military over Vietnam information. The Maximum Candor approach largely achieved its goals. It made the press dependent upon the government for information concerning the war and, consequently, usually made what the government wanted told the first and most prominent aspect of any particular story. One of Greenfield's aides told him, "The preoccupation of the press with each day's story can be made to our advantage to minimize the impact and duration of unfavorable events, but only if we tell the story whole, all at once. It's never a good idea to conceal from reporters what they may find out for themselves—because in Viet-Nam they will. And when they do they'll write it *their* way, not in a context of our choosing."[23]

The extent of the press's dependence on official sources is clear. During the war, news organizations themselves were concerned that "coverage of Vietnam . . . suffers from undue reliance on centralized sources."[24] Despite some misgivings, the press was by and large comfortable with this dependence, for it was getting what it needed to cover the war in the way that the characteristics of American jouranlism dictated. Maximum Candor accommodated itself to those characteristics and turned them to the government's advantage.

The press was imprisoned by a paradox. The press became dependent on the government for the information it needed. Yet, in order to protect its function, the press was also forced to suspect and sometimes question that very information and the government that was its source. What the news consumer saw, then, was a press that eagerly reported what the government told it, but also occasionally said that the government and its information were less than trustworthy. Left in the middle was the poor public, not quite knowing whom to believe.

The American press faced unprecedented challenges in covering the Vietnam War. Reporters in Vietnam had to contend with a difficult physical setting in which to work. The tendency of American journalism to cover its wars like a police beat oversimplified an extremely complicated situation. The process was also complicated by the new challenges presented by television and by access to the enemy capital. Finally, reporting of the war was caught up in the ambiguities of the press's relationship to official information and the government that supplied it.

Small wonder, then, that, despite their ingenuity, skill, and commitment, reporters were frustrated. "It's the only story I've been on in my life where I get a hopeless feeling when I try to get on top of things," said Dan Rather of CBS. "We're drowning in facts here, but we're starved for information," said the *Los Angeles Times*' William Tuohy. If the reporters who were living and breathing the story every day could not make sense of things, what chance did the public have?[25]

# 9

# "Buddha Will Understand"

## The Crisis of Confidence, 1967–68

FIGHTING WAS STILL GOING on at several places in and around Saigon that Thursday morning, but near the An Quang pagoda in central Saigon it was momentarily quiet. The Vietcong occupying the building had been forced out by South Vietnamese Marines. One of the captives was a man in a plaid shirt and baggy black shorts, a small man, his arms tied tightly behind his back. He had been beaten, but as he was moved down the street away from the pagoda he appeared calm, not frightened by the armed and angry men around him.

Just then, another man arrived at the scene. Brigadier General Nguyen Ngoc Loan, chief of the National Police, walked toward the prisoner. Larger than the prisoner, more imposing in his green military fatigues and flak jacket, Loan stopped three or four feet from the man in the plaid shirt, drew a pistol, and pointed it toward the prisoner. No word passed between the two. Loan simply fired a single round, and the man in the plaid shirt collapsed, his life and soul rushing onto the dirty Saigon street through the hole in the side of his head. Loan turned to the reporters standing a few feet behind him. "They killed many Americans and many of my men," he said quietly in English. "Buddha will understand. Do you?"[1]

On February 1, 1968, one man killed another in South Vietnam. So what? Men had been killing one another with an almost mechanical regularity for the better part of thirty years in Vietnam. What made this death worth remembering and thinking about for even a moment, much less for decades afterward? Two factors.

First, it occurred during the North Vietnamese–Vietcong "general offensive" of early 1968, commonly known as the Tet Offensive, commencing as it did on the first day of the Vietnamese holiday that marks the lunar new year. The offensive was one of the boldest and most dramatic military campaigns by either side during the war, reaching across the country and into the heart of South Vietnam's most important cities. It was to have political and diplomatic consequences even beyond its military significance.

But this wasn't enough to make a single death so remarkable. Nearly 9,000 American and South Vietnamese soldiers died during the Tet Offensive. Over 14,300 South Vietnamese civilians perished. More than 58,000 North Vietnamese and Vietcong troops were killed.

Eddie Adams, an AP photographer on his third tour in Vietnam, came upon the South Vietnamese Marines at the An Quang pagoda that morning. NBC correspondent Howard Tuckner and his cameraman, Vo Suu, were there too. "The shooting occurred so quickly that I got the picture through reaction," Adams said. "As Loan's hand holding the pistol came up, so did my camera—but I didn't expect what happened. I just shot by instinct." Similarly, Suu followed the prisoner, followed Loan's arm as he raised it to shoulder level and fired, and followed the prisoner as he fell backward.

Everyone who saw them knew immediately that both pieces of film were special. Adams caught the instant the bullet entered the prisoner's skull. "When the AP developed the film there was jubilation. . . . Everyone knew it was a prizewinner," Tet historian Don Oberdorfer said. Tuckner told his bosses in New York that if Suu "had it all it's startling stuff." NBC News executive producer Robert Northshield and correspondent John Chancellor sat in shock as they screened the film just moments before that night's "Huntley-Brinkley Report." Within hours of the event, the photograph and film had been seen by millions of people around the globe; millions of people had witnessed the last moment of life for the man in the plaid shirt.

This death, then, is not memorable because of the prominence of either the killer or the killed. It didn't change the tide of battle. Rather, the photograph and film speak of the presence and characteristics of American journalism. Adams, Tuckner, and Suu were skilled reporters with an instinct for the dramatic incident. The pictures they shot that day were valued examples of that sort of reporting. Adams won almost every possible award that year, and Northshield hailed the film as "an important and powerful statement of the reality of war."[2]

What was that reality? Descriptions of Tet '68 emphasized the suddenness of the event. "A surprise offensive of extraordinary intensity and astonishing scope," said Stanley Karnow. "The biggest single convulsion the war has yet produced," *Newsweek* said. These descriptions, in one sense, aren't far off. Despite intelligence warnings that something was to happen around the time of the Tet holiday, the offensive was, in the words of MACV combat-operations coordinator General John Chaisson, "surprisingly well coordinated, surprisingly intensive and launched with a surprising amount of audacity."

The effect on American political and public opinion was described in similar terms. "The Tet Offensive shocked a citizenry which had been led to believe that success in Vietnam was just around the corner," wrote Oberdorfer. Shana Alexander, writing in *Life* at the time of the attacks, said that "The entire tree of American opinion about the war, its branches drooping with doves, hawks, eagles, owls, now shudders in the lash of the new fire storm."[3]

A mythology has grown up around the Tet Offensive and its coverage that encapsulates the controversy over the press's role in the Vietnam War. This myth says that Tet was a watershed in public support of the war. It portrays public opinion before the event as supportive of or at least apathetic toward the effort, and claims that afterward public opinion swung against the war.

Those who view Tet this way point to press coverage as one of the prime catalysts. In recent years, the press has been blamed for distorting the character of the offensive, exaggerating both Vietcong–North Vietnamese success and American and South Vietnamese desperation. The press supposedly turned a military triumph for the United States and the South Vietnamese into a "psychological victory" for the enemy. In his memoirs, Westmoreland bitterly attacked the press for misrepresenting the actual course of events. Robert Elegant, who had written critically of the Diem regime while working for *Newsweek* in the early 1960s, blasted the press in 1981 for sapping the American public's will to pursue the war, and cited Tet as a particularly grievous example of the press's failure.[4]

But this view fails to understand the characteristics of the American press in Vietnam, what motivated it, what drove it. Second, it fails to understand the full range and complexity of the relationship that had grown up between the press and the government concerning the war. And, finally, it fails to understand the development of public attitudes toward the war in the year preceding the offensive. All of the elements came together by late 1967 to create a crisis of confidence in the government, in the press, and in the public, of which Tet was more climax than cause. Buddha may have understood the meaning of the Vietcong's death, but such understanding was harder for the less divine to achieve.

## "They Began Throwing Stones"

Walter Cronkite, the soul of journalistic objectivity and authority, standing in the CBS newsroom reading wire-service dispatches during the offensive, yelled, "What the hell is going on? I thought we were winning this war!" "MORE OF THE SAME WON'T DO," declared the title of a March 18, 1968, *Newsweek* article that went on to say, "Only the deluded can console themselves with the comforting feeling that suddenly the war will turn a corner and the enemy will wither away." "A satisfactory conclusion for the U.S. is nowhere in sight," said *U.S. News and World Report* a month earlier. "How did the U.S. reach this critical point? What went wrong"[5]

As discussed earlier, the American press and the United States government had developed a vital yet paradoxical relationship in the years leading up to the Tet Offensive. Two different philosophies of press relations within the Johnson Administration defined that relationship. On the one hand was the Maximum Candor approach, aimed, in the words of one official, "to cooperate with (i.e., exploit), the press" by making it dependent on government support. On the other hand, an older approach, reaching back to the earlier days of the Cold War, aimed to deny reporters information outright. As time passed, the interaction of these two philosophies upon the characteristics of American journalism produced a steadily increasing suspicion and tension between the press and the government.

Much the same set of forces was at work in the United States, as the Johnson Administration attempted to manipulate the type and amount of information available to the public through the domestic press. Lyndon Johnson was first elected to the Senate in 1948, the year when the Iron Curtain fell across the face of Europe, and he adopted the same apocalyptic world view as most of his countrymen. He bought the Cold War equation of secrecy with security. This viewpoint, commonly held by most American leaders and citizens, combined with Johnson's own more personal inclination to control information. Born during his student days at San Marcos College, nurtured during his years in the Congress, Johnson's "powerful inner inclination toward secrecy," as Doris Kearns described it, was a well-known factor in his leadership by the time he became president.[6]

Vietnam was just one of the issues that colored Johnson's relationship with the press in the years before the Tet Offensive. In December 1963, Johnson led journalists to believe that the fiscal-1965 budget would be, much to his distress, in excess of $100 billion. For three weeks, the press wrote reports based on this authoritative information. When the budget was revealed, however, it was $97.9 billion, $1 billion *less* than Kennedy's last budget, making Johnson look like a "financial wizard." But members of the press felt used. Johnson, pleased with himself, called this technique "showing a little garter." This and other early episodes quickly led to open criticism of Johnson's public-relations and press practices. "There may be those who claim that the White House has not attempted to 'manage the news,' " *The Saturday Evening Post* said. "They have a point. 'Mismanage' is a better word."[7]

The tension continued to escalate over the weeks and months that followed. During the spring of 1964, stories surfaced on the investigation of longtime Johnson aide Bobby Baker, on Johnson's financial dealings while in the Senate, even stories detailing his careening around the LBJ Ranch with a steering wheel in one hand and a beer in the other. Nor did Johnson's evident discomfort with the formal press conference help. His preference for spur-of-the-moment, casual gatherings with the press at settings outside the White House disrupted reporters' logistical and journalistic routines. He continued to manipulate the White House press corps on appointments and policy decisions. In May 1965, the term "credibility gap" was used publicly for the first time.[8]

Johnson's uncertainty in foreign affairs made him even more sensitive. He feared triggering World War III if he moved too aggressively in Vietnam. Yet he also feared the diplomatic and political consequences of doing too little. He apparently believed Joe Alsop's warning that "losing" Vietnam would be to him what "losing" China had been to Harry Truman. He believed that doing too much or too little would also invigorate the right wing of American politics and start calls for total war.

Finally, he feared for the Great Society. "I knew from the start," he told Doris Kearns, "that I was bound to be crucified either way I moved. If I left the woman I really loved—the Great Society—to get involved with that bitch of a war on the other side of the world, then I would lose everything at home. . . . But if I left that war and let the Communists take over South Vietnam, then I would be seen as a coward and my nation would be seen as an appeaser." A dream he claimed to have had repeatedly in early 1965 reveals the depth of Johnson's fear. "Every night when I fell asleep I would see myself tied to the ground in the middle of a long, open space. In the distance, I could hear the voices of thousands of people. They were all shouting at me and running toward me: 'Coward! Traitor! Weakling! They kept coming closer. They began throwing stones.'"[9]

Consequently, the Johnson Administration produced a domestic Vietnam-information policy based on manipulation and deception. Various formal and informal groups comprising officials from the White House, State, Defense, and other agencies met to assess current information issues and to devise new tactics. These groups continually monitored congressional, press, and public opinion on the war. The administration also sought to influence domestic press coverage and opinion. In the summer of 1964, Operation Maximum Candor transported groups of Washington-based reporters to South Vietnam at government expense. The State Department, in addition to its regular daily briefings, also held major national conferences on American foreign policy. In the first half of 1965, State held two such gatherings in Washington and one each in Pittsburgh, Dallas, and Portland, featuring such administration heavyweights as Vice-President Hubert Humphrey, Secretary of State Dean Rusk, and Undersecretary of State George W. Ball.[10]

Johnson used other direct and indirect means to shape the information given the public on the war. He enlisted private individuals and groups as conduits of the official viewpoint. Community opinion leaders such as educators and ministers took government-sponsored trips to South Vietnam to assess firsthand—amply aided by civilian and military officials—the situation there. During the "teach-in" movement in 1965, the administration also sent "truth teams" of Executive Branch officials to give lectures and participate in debates on college campuses.

Other actions required a more discreet government presence. Bill Moyers approved an idea offered by the Young Democrats' executive director, Fred Ricci, to develop a "cadre . . . of articulate and respected students" on college campuses to encourage support for administration policy in Vietnam. These groups would be guided by the administration and funded by the Democratic National Committee but, Ricci said, "we suggest that there be no traceable identification with either the Youth Division or the Democratic National Committee, but separate stationary [sic], post office box, and supporting information such as favorable editorial reports, costs of mailings, etc. should be provided on a separate account basis."[11]

The White House also quietly supported the American Friends of Vietnam. At the first meeting of the *ad hoc* group on Vietnam information, in August 1965, White House aide Chester Cooper pointed out that "we have an instrument for public information on Vietnam in the shape of the 'American Friends of Vietnam.' While we have been careful to keep our hand fairly hidden, we have, in fact, spent a lot of time on it and have been able to find them some money." Cooper later praised the AFV for its work in "counteracting the teach-in movement." He added that "the organization can undertake more extensive programming with the likelihood of considerably more success provided additional funds required can be obtained." "We can't get too involved," Cooper cautioned, for if the AFV "became too closely identified with the U.S. Government, its credibility will be badly affected." The administration also played a significant behind-the-scenes role in establishing and supporting the Citizens Committee for Peace with Freedom in Vietnam, the so-called Douglas Committee, headed by former Illinois Senator Paul Douglas. The committee was a "who's who" of foreign-policy, military, and political figures from both parties, and served as a "private" validator of Johnson policy.[12]

These activities represent just the barest portion of the time, energy, imagination, and money put into controlling the information environment in the United States concerning the war. But, this effort notwithstanding, Johnson ultimately abdicated any real leverage over domestic press and public perception of the war by deliberately choosing *not* to provide them a simple and satisfactory context. Johnson tried to conduct Vietnam policy remote from press and public scrutiny, just as his predecessor had done. What Johnson did not remember, or chose to ignore, was that Kennedy's attempt at control failed, in both Vietnam and the United States, as the press filled the vacuum created by this policy with its own sources and their perceptions. And this was at a time when only thirteen thousand or so American troops were in Vietnam and American casualties were light. How much more difficult would it be for Johnson, and how much greater the ultimate failure, when nearly half a million American soldiers were in Vietnam, dying at the rate of two hundred or more each week?

From the beginning of his presidency, Johnson attempted to ratchet American involvement up without alarming either the press or the public. He successfully sidestepped Vietnam during the 1964 presidential election. GOP nominee Barry Goldwater called on the president to make a "full, frank revelation of what our Vietnam policy actually is," adding that such a report "is long overdue." But Johnson refused to take Goldwater's bait, following Moyers' advice to "keep the public debate on Vietnam at as low a level as possible" and not to "take risks the dangers of which outweigh the advantages." The one bold move Johnson made during the election regarding Vietnam, his response to the Tonkin Gulf incident, was politically masterful. As Congress, the press, and the public rallied to support him, praising his forcefulness and his restraint, Johnson was able to keep Vietnam out of the campaign.[13]

After his decisive victory made him president in his own right, Johnson continued to follow a strategy of diversion and deception on Vietnam. Over the months that followed, each major escalation was downplayed either as a specific response to North Vietnamese–Vietcong pressure or as a logical extension of previous actions that didn't change the U.S.'s fundamental role. "Johnson thus took the nation into war by indirection and dissimulation," George Herring wrote. "The bombing was publicly justified as a response to the Pleiku attack and the broader pattern of North Vietnam's 'aggression,' rather than as a desperate attempt to halt the military and political deterioration in South Vietnam. The administration never publicly acknowledged its shift from reprisals to 'sustained pressure.'"[14]

These measures proved insufficient, and Johnson decided in July 1965 to send combat troops to South Vietnam. True to form, he attempted to disguise the significance of the move. He rejected the advice of McNamara and the Joint Chiefs, who recommended that he mobilize public support by declaring a state of emergency, calling up the reserves, and increasing taxes. He told both hawks and doves what they wanted to hear—that he would safeguard South Vietnam and that he was committed to pursuing a diplomatic end to the war. To everyone he maintained that, despite the decision, the nature of American involvement had not changed. Johnson's desire to soft-pedal the decision even shaped the arrangements for the decision's announcement. The commitment of American combat troops to a land war in Asia was announced as part of the opening statement of a noon press conference, along with Abe Fortas' nomination to the Supreme Court and John Chancellor's appointment as head of the Voice of America.[15]

"By pretending there was no major conflict," Doris Kearns wrote, "Johnson believed he could keep the lever of control in his hands." But from the first weeks of his administration, his attempts at manipulation and deception produced suspicion and resentment. In February 1964, *Newsweek* "placed the U.S. Government yet again in the harsh light of apparent ignorance or ineptitude or duplicity in its reports to the American people on how the war is faring in Vietnam."[16]

As the situation in South Vietnam continued to deteriorate during 1965 and 1966, the press criticized Johnson for failing to explain things to the American people. The *Atlanta Journal* said in March 1965 that "It is good strategy to keep your enemy confused," but, the paper continued, "the trouble with Mr. Johnson is that he doesn't stop there. He confuses everyone."

Russell Baker lampooned the whole question. He conducted his own poll in "Washington's best informed drawing rooms" and found that 4 percent of those questioned approved of Johnson's Vietnam policy, 3 percent disapproved, 18 percent were undecided, and 52 percent were confused. Baker also found that "the big confused bloc felt, on the whole, that while there probably was a United States policy on Vietnam, it would be hopeless for them to try to understand it in the limited lifetime available to them. As one confused respondent put it, 'Look, I'm only human. For the last three years I've been laboring to get a firm understanding of our policy in the Congo, and I think I'm getting close. But Vietnam? A man doesn't have that many years.' "[17]

Such criticism continued through the rest of 1965 and on into 1966 and 1967. *The New York Times* charged that "maximum secrecy" had replaced Maximum Candor. The *Des Moines Register,* trying to understand the president's policy, asked, "What is he up to? He goes around making speeches for peace—and sends more thousands of fighting men to South Vietnam and more thousands of bomb loads to North Vietnam." Commenting on Johnson's 1966 State of the Union address, *Newsweek* said that "the speech did little to lift the cloud of misunderstanding that has cloaked much of the public discussion of U.S. aims in Vietnam."[18]

In August 1966, concern had grown so great that the Senate Foreign Relations Committee called Arthur Sylvester in to discuss Vietnam information policy. Sylvester denied telling a group of reporters in Saigon that they should be "handmaidens of the government," and added that "the only place where news is managed, the only place where it can be managed, the only place where it should be managed and is managed, is in every news office."[19]

By the spring of 1967, an informal poll of newspaper editors revealed that, even among the majority who still supported the president's policy in Vietnam, many felt that he had failed to communicate the logic and aims of that policy to the public. "It's more than just a credibility gap," said one. "It's an understanding gap."[20] Some months earlier, *The Nation* had asked simply, "Can this Administration ever be believed again?"[21]

This question would become the definitive expression of the paradoxical relationship between the press and the government concerning the Vietnam War. The press depended on, needed to believe, government information. But Johnson's information policy fostered in the press a self-protective suspicion that increasingly strained the relationship. By the end of 1967, the question "Can this Administration ever be believed again?" would take on a poignant, even desperate tone.

As early as January 1965, *Newsweek* warned that "the hope of fighting the Communists to a standstill is unlikely to have much success with a people who, traditionally, have shown scant patience for wars that do not offer the clear possibility of unequivocal military victory." This point became a critical concern for the Johnson Administration. Its military-political strategy—like that of its adversary—was based on exerting ever greater pressure, until the enemy's willingness and ability to pursue the war were drained.[22]

Showing a steady improvement in the situation, and countering any statements to the contrary, was one of the government's prime concerns. In June 1966, Johnson's decline in the polls sounded alarms at the White House. A Louis Harris survey found that "the people are in a 'foul mood' regarding Vietnam. . . . [T]hey don't see how a country of our size and power can seemingly make so little progress in the situation. In one word the mood is *frustration,*" and the middle ground that Johnson was attempting to hold was an "isolated little island." Moyers and other aides agreed with the pollsters' conclusion that "what the President needs to do is offer 'some ray of hope' " and that "the grim 'bite the bullet' attitude is no good." But Harris warned that such optimism had to be credible. "Were the President to speak hopefully now of either a military success or progress toward negotiations and six months from now nothing had materialized, we would be in a more disastrous position that we are now."[23]

Demonstrable progress was not that easy to find. Studies by two different intelligence agencies in the second half of 1966 concluded that "the North Vietnamese transport and logistic system is now functioning more effectively after almost 18 months of bombing than it did when the Rolling Thunder program started." By the end of the year, the military had feared the growing perception that the war was becoming a stalemate. Admiral Sharp told Wheeler and Westmoreland, after his own informal test of public and congressional opinion, that "we had better do what we can to bring this war to a successful conclusion as rapidly as possible. The American people can become aroused either for or against this war. At the moment, with no end in sight, they are more apt to become aroused against it. It's up to us to convince our people and Hanoi that there is an end in sight and that it is clearly defeat for Hanoi." "Let's roll up our sleeves and get on with this war," Sharp said. "We have the power. I would like authority to use it. . . . When Hanoi screams in anguish, we should hit them again."[24]

In the spring of 1967, sentiment grew in the military and in the administration to demonstrate progress. Johnson authorized an increase in military pressure against North Vietnam. He called Westmoreland back to the United States for "consultations" and, more important, to offer public reassurances that American efforts in Vietnam were paying off. In speeches to the Associated Press Managing Editors Association and to a joint session of Congress, Westmoreland struck a cautious but optimistic tone. "I foresee, in the months ahead, some of the bitterest fighting of the war," he said, but he was also confident that "we will prevail in Vietnam over the Communist aggressors."[25]

But these efforts changed neither the perception that the war was settling into a bloody draw nor the deepening skepticism inspired by government claims of advancement. The American Society of Newspaper Editors criticized Johnson for "consistently trying to make the news sound or seem better than it is." "Is 'tremendous progress' being made, with the enemy being steadily ground under, as top U.S. officials keep publicly insisting . . . or are the facts something else again?" *U.S. News and World Report* asked. Answering its own question, the magazine said that the facts in Saigon "tell a story far less optimistic that the one Americans hear from officials in Government." In a special July 10, 1967, issue devoted entirely to the war, *Newsweek* declared that, "cleft by doubts and tormented by frustrations, the nation this Independence Day is haunted by its most corrosively ambiguous foreign adventure."[26]

CBS and *Time* show what was going on in the press in the summer and fall of 1967. CBS News was headed by Dr. Frank Stanton, LBJ's close friend of thirty years. CBS also had Cronkite, that rock of objectivity. Early in the war, CBS and Cronkite reported the official perception of the war. But victory didn't materialize, or even appear appreciably closer as time went on. Television magnified the seemingly interminable nature of the struggle. In Halberstam's words, "the war played in American homes, and it played too long." By the autumn of 1967, Cronkite and others in the home office of CBS News, continually exposed to the doubts of correspondents in the field, doubts that were reinforced by the misgivings of members of Congress, academe, and the business community, moved away from such unquestioning attitudes. The course of the war bothered Cronkite, "the disproportion of it, the fraud of it, [the] increasing doubts about the credibility of the men running it." But he gave no hint of his concern, at least not on the air.[27]

The change in attitude at Time-Life, Inc., occurred more openly.

*Time* and *Life,* under the direction of Henry Luce, had long been champions of America's anticommunist crusade in Asia. But Luce had stepped aside as editor-in-chief, turning the position over to Hedley Donovan. Donovan, like Luce before him, supported the war. The Saigon bureau of *Time* continued to run into a brick wall named Otto Fuerbringer. Fuerbringer continued to have access to the upper levels of the Executive Branch, and through him Johnson was able to dilute or kill the less optimistic reports coming from *Time*'s people in Vietnam.

But Donovan read these reports, and he confirmed them for himself during an April 1967 trip to South Vietnam. His concerns showed first in his report on the trip, published in the June issue of *Life*. He admitted that "Some over-optimistic Americans (this writer included) had expected to see by now the beginnings of a real momentum in Vietnam. . . . It certainly hasn't happened yet." The shift became even more evident during late summer, when Donovan personally edited *Time* while Fuerbringer was on vacation. By fall, the transition was nearly complete. In October, *Time* said that "Conscience and practical politics alike dictate that the Administration devise and pursue every conceivable alternative to warfare within its power."[28]

In the last half of 1967, LBJ was getting pressure from both sides of the Vietnam issue within Congress. Senate Preparedness Subcommittee hearings concluded that the war was not being fought hard enough. The House Foreign Operations Subcommittee claimed that pacification was not being pushed hard enough. Johnson had for years resisted increasing taxes to pay for the war. But in September 1967 he confronted fiscal reality and asked for an income-tax surcharge. Finally, at the same time that the war called for a greater portion of the American treasury, it also demanded a greater toll in American flesh and blood. The series of battles staged by the North Vietnamese as a prelude to the Tet Offensive inflicted tremendous casualties on American forces.[29]

As Louis Harris had warned, Johnson's middle ground was now an island quickly sinking in a sea of frustration. To stem the tide, the administration implemented a formal effort to demonstrate progress in all phases of the war. Beginning in September 1967 and continuing up to the Tet Offensive itself, a flurry of cables and memoranda swirled within and between Washington and Saigon, detailing a variety of measures to reassure the press and public. Harold Kaplan, a former aide to Barry Zorthian in Vietnam, came back to Washington to coordinate this "progress campaign." A Kaplan memo to Walt Rostow reveals how serious this campaign was. "I would suggest that a little exhortation is in order. American public opinion has become the 'X factor' in the entire Vietnamese equation," Kaplan said. "It is absolutely essential that this weekly meeting of key Washington officers involved in Vietnam information problems not, repeat, not, peter out and disperse as past efforts of this kind have done. We understand that participants all have other things to do. But nothing is more important than this."[30]

Plans were developed and executed across the public-relations front. Their goal, in Kaplan's words, was "to demonstrate to the press and public that we are making solid progress and are not in a stalemate." Reporters received captured enemy documents describing the difficulties inflicted upon North Vietnamese and Vietcong forces by the American presence. Examples of special achievements, whether by a particular combat unit or a particular village or district in the pacification program, were identified, and strenuous efforts made to steer reporters to them. The South Vietnamese armed forces were portrayed more prominently and positively, as was the South Vietnamese government. Efforts to use private individuals and groups to validate claims of progress were stepped up. Statistical measurements of progress, such as infiltration rates, enemy troop strength, enemy casualties, and the figures making up the so-called hamlet evaluation system were all re-examined for use in the campaign.[31]

Westmoreland had earlier been reluctant to participate in such public-relations efforts, for fear that he would be drawn into the politics of the war. The state of public opinion and Johnson's concern, however, moved him and other commanders to join the progress campaign.

"It has become apparent," Westmoreland told Wheeler and Sharp, "that a vocal segment of the news profession is equating a lack of major combat operations with a stalemate at best, or a loss of initiative on our part at worst. Nothing could be further from the truth, of course." Westmoreland found Johnny Apple's piece in the August 7 *New York Times* a particular pain.

"Vietnam: The Signs of Stalemate" listed several indications that the effort in Vietnam was not proceeding as well as the United States government claimed. Apple quoted an unnamed American general in South Vietnam who said, "Every time Westy makes a speech about how good the South Vietnam Army is, I want to ask him why he keeps calling for more Americans. His need for reinforcements is a measure of our failure. . . ." Westmoreland criticized Apple's reporting, telling Wheeler and Sharp that "I have watched Apple become more critical and argumentative during recent months. Barring some dramatic and irrefutable turn for the better here we can expect him to continue to play the role of doubter and critic. He is probably bucking for a Pulitzer Prize."

Stories like this moved Westmoreland, as he told his superiors, "to initiate several actions designed to clarify the mind of the public. Of course, we want to make haste carefully in order to avoid charges that the military establishment is conducting an organized propaganda campaign."[32]

The progress campaign reached its height in November 1967. Johnson himself declared during a November 17 news conference that "we are making progress." Vice-President Humphrey did the same during an appearance later in the month on NBC's "Meet the Press." The top leaders of the effort in South Vietnam—Ambassador Ellsworth Bunker, pacification chief Robert Komer, and Westmoreland—came back to Washington for a blitz of speeches and public appearances. In an address before the National Press Club, Westmoreland stated that he was "absolutely certain that whereas in 1965 the enemy was winning, today he is certainly losing." Though Westmoreland warned that significant fighting remained, he was equally assured that "the end has begun to come into view."

Because of the prominence of the speakers, the press in the United States reported these statements prominently. Many commentators accepted them at face value. For example, *U.S. News and World Report* ran two articles, one from Washington and the other from Saigon, in its November 27 issue, and the degree to which these reflected official optimism is seen in their titles. "Vietnam: War Tide Turning to U.S.," said the Washington article; the dispatch from South Vietnam declared that "The Coin Has Flipped Over to Our Side."[33]

However, the press also reacted against what it saw as obvious attempts at manipulation and control. At the same time as it conveyed to the public the positive statements of American officials, the press strongly questioned their credibility. Hedrick Smith of *The New York Times* reported that members of Congress and even some important administration officials were skeptical of the claims of progress. James Reston criticized the effort for having stifled dissent in Washington. David Halberstam, on a return trip to South Vietnam for *Harper's,* had hoped to find "American optimism . . . at least tempered," but he quickly discovered that "the illusions still exist. When you pay $30 billion a year you buy at least a fair share of illusions." *Newsweek* contrasted the optimistic views of Bunker, Westmoreland, Komer, and others with the more pessimistic assessments of veteran Vietnam correspondents Johnny Apple, Peter Arnett, Mert Perry, and Bob Shaplen. Hubert Humphrey, in South Vietnam in the fall of 1967, asked a group of journalists to "give the benefit of the doubt to our side." "Benefit of the doubt?" replied one reporter. "Hell, what do they think we've been doing the last six years?"[34]

## "Should Something Unexpected Happen"

Confusion and tension reigned between the press and the government in the fall of 1967. A similar confusion and tension were enveloping other important relationships: between civilian and military officials, between the Congress and the White House, and, most important, between the American people and their federal government. Nearly three years earlier, the editors of *Newsweek* had pointed out the essential danger of such a situation. "The riddles posed by the deadly and delicate struggle in Vietnam are endless," they wrote in January 1965. "But as this frustrating war continues, it is crucial that the American public understand the stakes and the alternatives, so that there will be no bitter disillusions should something unexpected happen."[35]

As they had done for a number of years, the Vietcong announced and the United States and South Vietnam agreed to a cease-fire to mark the opening days of the lunar new year, or Tet, celebrations. The Tet holiday was described to Americans in Vietnam as "a combination of All Souls' Day, a family celebration, a spring festival, a national holiday and an overall manifestation of a way of life," an event with no parallel in the West. The North Vietnamese and Viet-cong had planned their general offensive/general uprising for this time in hopes of catching their adversaries at less-than-peak fighting readiness.

While many—but not all—South Vietnamese units joined the rev-elry, the United States forces were on alert. The coming Tet Offensive was one of the worst-kept secrets of the war. For many weeks prior to the offensive, American intelligence had picked up strong indica-tions of a major enemy military effort sometime around the Tet cease-fire. In mid-November, a copy of the order for the offensive had fallen into American hands, and its contents were released to the press. But the government did little to push the story, so as not to dull the sheen of the progress campaign. Also, the American commanders concluded that whatever action the North Vietnamese and Vietcong took was merely a diversion. Westmoreland believed the main enemy objective to be Khe Sanh, the Marine outpost near the Demilitarized Zone (DMZ).[36]

What was unexpected was the breadth, the strength, and the sheer gall of the attacks. Within a four-hour period beginning just after midnight on the morning of January 30, the North Vietnamese and Vietcong struck many of the major cities of central and northern South Vietnam, including Danang, Nha Trang, Kontum, Pleiku, and Ban Me Thuot. Twenty-four hours later, they launched similar as-saults across the rest of the country. The North Vietnamese and Vietcong hit 39 of the 44 provincial capitals, 71 of 242 district capi-tals, and dozens of other civilian and military targets. Around Saigon alone, the Vietcong attacked the Bien Hoa and Tan Son Nhut air bases, the United States Embassy, the presidential palace, the Ameri-can III Corps command post, the headquarters of the South Viet-namese Joint General Staff, and many other facilities. By the morning of February 1, it seemed that the whole country was engulfed in combat.

But by mid-month American and South Vietnamese counterat-tacks had pushed the Vietcong back into the countryside. The major military action was concentrated at Hue, where American and South Vietnamese soldiers engaged in house-to-house fighting with the North Vietnamese, and at Khe Sanh, which was enduring heavy bombardment and occasional ground probes against the razor-wire perimeter. On February 24, after twenty-five days of fierce fighting,

Hue was retaken. The siege of Khe Sanh, which had begun January 21, continued until early April, although the North Vietnamese began to reduce their pressure against the base a month earlier.[37]

The Tet Offensive's exact effect on the course of the war is still controversial. Some observers maintain that it was a watershed, that Tet shocked and shattered both the confidence of the public and that of the Johnson Administration, even though the United States defeated the North Vietnamese and Vietcong in strict military terms. As Bernard Brodie wrote, Tet was "probably unique in that the side that lost completely in a tactical sense came away with an overwhelming psychological and hence political victory."[38]

Almost without doubt, the American public was as startled by the scale and audacity of the attacks, as was the American brass in Saigon. But the changes of opinion often associated with Tet had been in the works for a long time. In October 1967, for the first time, more Americans answered "yes" than "no" to the question "Do you believe United States involvement in the Vietnam War to have been a mistake?" Concern in Congress had been growing practically from the day the Tonkin Gulf Resolution was passed. Major news organizations, even those that previously had been supporters of administration policy, had become openly skeptical by late 1967. The doubts of some senior administration officials grew. McNamara, for example, had become so concerned that in 1967 he authorized the secret compilation of a history of American policy in Vietnam, a study that he perhaps hoped would help him understand just what had happened and why. Even Lyndon Johnson, whose March 31 announcement that he would not seek re-election cast him as the final casualty of Tet, had actually been contemplating retirement for some months.[39]

Thus, it's incorrect to blame—or credit—either Tet or the press coverage of it with creating a great turn in public or press opinion. The Tet Offensive was the war in microcosm—superior American firepower against superior North Vietnamese political will. Similarly, press coverage of the offensive, and the relationship between the press and the government in those weeks, reflected the way the press approached the story and the way it related to the government throughout the war. Tet was less the occasion of a sudden shift in such opinion than it was a confirmation of characteristics and trends that had been around a long time.

*Big Story* is former *New York Times* and *Washington Post* Vietnam correspondent Peter Braestrup's thoroughly detailed study of how major national American news organizations covered Tet. His research demonstrates that the same characteristics of American journalism that had shaped its approach to the Vietnam story for years operated to shape its coverage of Tet.[40]

Economic considerations were at work at Tet. Despite the fact that Vietnam was American journalism's hottest story, the investment of American news organizations in South Vietnam still had its limits. Reporters for the major news outlets were, in the best of circumstances, hard-pressed to keep up just with military developments, much less with other facets of the story. Tet, most assuredly, was not the best of circumstances. When the offensive broke, the Saigon bureaus could not be everywhere, even within the city itself. As Peter Arnett told Braestrup, not even the wire services had "enough bodies" to cover everything that was happening. The pressure on other news organizations was still greater, as reporters operated under extreme physical, psychological, and professional strain.[41]

The offensive pushed the press's fragile logistical base to the limit. Communications within the country and between South Vietnam and the United States had frustrated reporters and editors for years. During Tet, when fast, reliable communications were needed most, the system broke down. The civilian and military phone systems overloaded, making it difficult for reporters to dictate dispatches from the field or to verify information with sources outside Saigon. It was almost as difficult to get information out of the country. The AP, UPI, and *Time* had their own direct communications links with New York. *The New York Times,* the *Washington Post,* and all other print organizations, however, still depended on the unsatisfactory arrangement with Reuters wire. The TV networks found it tough to get film out of the country when commercial air traffic was suspended in the first hours of the attack. MACV helped out by carrying film— including NBC's film of the VC prisoner's execution—to Tokyo, Manila, and other points outside the country aboard military aircraft.[42]

These conditions, combined with competitive pressures, pushed reporters to produce and file stories as quickly as possible. For Braestrup, coverage of the Vietcong commando raid on the United States Embassy complex highlighted the problems this created.

At about 2:45 A.M. on January 31, a squad of nineteen highly trained Vietcong troops drove up to the gates of the embassy and fired at the two American military policemen standing guard. A few moments later, the Vietcong blew a hole in the wall of the embassy grounds and then attempted to blast open the chancery building's doors with rocket fire. Though they tried in vain to enter this building, the Vietcong did get into a villa on the grounds occupied by retired Colonel George Jacobson, an administrative assistant to the ambassador. For the next few hours, American MPs and Marines hunted down the Vietcong one by one. The battle for the embassy compound ended when Colonel Jacobson, holed up in a second-story room in his house, killed the last commando with a pistol tossed up to him by an MP.[43]

As soon as he found out that the embassy was under attack, Barry Zorthian called the bureaus of the major news organizations. Based on Zorthian's call, the two wire services issued bulletins and continued to file new material as their correspondents reached the scene. Reporters could get no closer than a hundred yards or so to the compound until just before Jacobson shot the last commando. In the darkness, the reporters could see little, and they depended on the MPs, who could see no more than they, for information. As the fight went on, the reporters filed what the MPs told them, which was that the Vietcong were in the embassy building. "My God, yes," Arnett remembered an MP captain telling him, "we are taking fire from up there. . . . [K]eep your head down." So, for the first hours of the offensive, the press repeated, and even embellished, the mistaken information that the Vietcong had occupied the embassy building itself.[44]

The coverage of the embassy attack also illustrated two other press characteristics.

The first of these traits is the fixation on American activities. Dozens of South Vietnamese targets, including the presidential palace, were hit that night, but the focus of attention was on what one American officer called a "piddling platoon action" at the embassy. Of course, the attack resonated with symbolism. The embassy, legally and diplomatically recognized as United States soil, was a tangible representation of the American presence in South Vietnam, and an attack on it represented an attack on the United States itself.

This focus carried through the rest of the offensive. Of the hundreds of sites hit across the country, most were South Vietnamese, not American. The fact that inviting American targets were passed by for South Vietnamese installations even gave rise to the incredible rumor that the United States, the North Vietnamese, and the Vietcong had together engineered the offensive. This was supposed to provide cover for a trade in which the United States would allow the North Vietnamese and the Vietcong to dominate a coalition government in exchange for permanent military bases in the South. Only one major center of media attention, the battle for Hue, involved a strictly Vietnamese setting. Even then, the press followed the American Marines, not the South Vietnamese soldiers who did the bulk of the fighting and dying for the Citadel, the core of the city. At Khe Sanh, an ARVN Ranger battalion that absorbed the only ground attacks on the main base camp went almost completely unnoticed by reporters. The South Vietnamese armed forces were, in Braestrup's words, "almost as 'faceless' as the North Vietnamese and the Vietcong."[45]

Embassy-attack coverage demonstrated a second characteristic. The embassy story dominated the early coverage of the attack on Saigon because, as Braestrup said, "(1) it was American, (2) it was close at hand, and (3) it was dramatic." In a similar way, military action, especially major military action involving Americans, dominated the Vietnam story for several weeks. After the fighting eased in Saigon, attention shifted to Hue. After Hue was retaken at the end of February, the press's focus shifted to Khe Sanh, where it would remain for most of March. According to Braestrup, during February and March "roughly nine out of ten firsthand newspaper stories, wire-service dispatches, and TV reports from the battlefield were from Saigon, Khe Sanh, and Hue."[46]

This had a twofold effect. First, the major fighting across the country had pretty well abated after mid-February. But the concentration on Hue and Khe Sanh made it seem, as Braestrup said, "that, well into March, the outcome on the Vietnam battlefield was very much in doubt." Second, the focus on Saigon, Hue, and Khe Sanh drained the limited resources of the American press away from the smaller, less dramatic, less accessible action that, nonetheless, involved the bulk of American troops and casualties. These events were left to the daily war summaries that provided little by way of a larger understanding of the war.[47]

The same relationship that had existed between the press and the government since the earliest days of the Johnson Administration was still present during Tet. The press depended heavily upon the information provided by military briefers, who themselves depended on the confused and incomplete reports coming in from the field. Only in relatively rare instances did reporters have the opportunity to confirm the information independently.

One haunting example makes the point. On March 16, units of the Americal Division brought together as Task Force Barker were conducting an operation in the northern coastal section of South Vietnam. The summary of that day's activity prepared by Americal public-information officer Major Patrick Dionne reported that Task Force Barker had killed 128 Vietcong near a village six miles from the city of Quang Ngai. The MACV Office of Information made the report part of its daily handout, which was reworked into the war summaries of the wire services and *The New York Times*. Not for another year and a half would Americans find out that something else had happened that day at the village near Quang Ngai. The name of the village was My Lai.[48]

The government's aggressive public-relations efforts reinforced the press's dependence on official information. Johnson ordered Westmoreland to speak briefly to the press at least once a day during the offensive, in order to "convey your confidence in our capability to blunt these enemy moves, and to reassure the public here that you have the situation under control." The information operation continued to churn out forests of briefing papers and communiqués. The military continued to provide transportation throughout the country. Officers and men in the field continued to talk with reporters. Even Colonel David Lownds, commander at Khe Sanh, held a daily briefing in his bunker for the reporters who shuttled in and out of the besieged base camp.[49]

But, at the same time, the government began to plan restrictions on information, particularly in connection with Khe Sanh. Sharp told Westmoreland on February 24 that "I am concerned that much sensitive information is being released to the press." Sharp was particularly disturbed that news reports were discussing the number and effectiveness of the North Vietnamese artillery rounds falling daily on the base. Sharp instructed Westmoreland to withhold such information from the press and to encourage reporters not to publish "bombardment/casualty data they may observe." "We cannot," Sharp concluded, "continue to serve as spotters for enemy artillery." Two days later, Westmoreland issued a new directive to the press, restricting the information that so worried Sharp. The flood of reporters to the northern section of the country strained press facilities in the Danang area. It also, as Westmoreland told new Secretary of Defense Clark Clifford, "sharpened competition [that] is producing information that can assist the enemy." In response, MACV limited the number of reporters allowed at the string of bases below the DMZ. The cap at Khe Sanh was fifteen, with each of the TV networks allocated two spots, AP and UPI two each, one for Reuters, and a four-person pool for the remaining American news organizations. "If the above procedure does not prove effective," Westmoreland said, "censorship in some form should be invoked."[50]

The press accepted these restrictions with only minor grumbling. Officials took care to cast them as necessary to safeguard American troops. Indeed, the only major violation of the ground rules took place in June, months after the offensive ended, when John Carroll of the *Baltimore Sun* broke an embargo on the news that Khe Sanh was being evacuated.[51]

The stark contrast between the Tet attacks and the progress campaign, set against a background of years of tension and suspicion between the press and the government over Vietnam, nonetheless produced dismayed and skeptical reactions in the press. *The New York Times* declared on February 2 that the Tet attacks "throw doubt on recent official American claims of progress. . . ." *Time* called the offensive "a humiliating surprise." *Newsweek* said that "the American people have not been given a realistic assessment of the situation in Vietnam." *The New Republic* said that the government's "prophecies are as discredited as the policies they serve." Events had so disturbed Walter Cronkite of CBS and Frank McGee of NBC that they overcame television's traditional fear of expressing an opinion on the air. Both called upon the United States to look vigorously for a diplomatic settlement.[52]

The Tet Offensive of 1968 broke like an earthquake through the physical landscape of South Vietnam and the political landscape of the United States. It's clear that its antecedents ran far back into the history of Vietnam and the American involvement there. Similarly, the coverage of the offensive by the American press is cited by some as the product of political and ideological biases and as the catalyst for a dramatic abandonment of the administration by the American people.

But the coverage of Tet, with all the limitations and flaws described by Peter Braestrup, was instead the product of characteristics of American journalism and government information policies that had been developing for years. To fulfill its fundamental purpose— filling space on a page or time in a broadcast, preferably with news of American activity—the press had come to depend mightily on the information and support provided by the government. Most of the coverage of the war reflected that information virtually unchanged and unchallenged. However, attempts to confront the press or to deny information threatened the press's ability to do its job and inspired its anger and suspicion.

Thus, the American people were confronted with the picture of news organizations reporting government information as fact at the same time that they were questioning that information and the credibility of the officials who released it. Despite reporters' bravery and initiative, the same confusion, misunderstanding, and frustration that the press-government relationship had long produced was again evident during the Tet Offensive.

But the American people had over the years been coming to the conclusion that the policy of slow escalation had to end. Whether calling for a diplomatic settlement or all-out war, Americans came to realize that the cost in lives and treasure was simply too great to sustain without some successful end in sight. The Tet Offensive, despite its drama and intensity, was but one important milestone on the road to that realization.

In March 1968, after two soldiers from the small Alabama town of Brewton were killed during the Tet fighting, the local weekly paper shifted from its previous support of President Johnson's policy to a call for American disengagement. Two Americans sacrificed for a confusing, inconclusive war that neither the government nor the press could explain were two Americans too many when they were *your* sons, *your* husbands, *your* brothers. "Like hundreds of communities across the country," the paper's editor said, "the war came too close when it got to Brewton." Buddha would understand.[53]

# 10

# No More Bodies

*Turning Away from Vietnam,*
*1969–75*

IT WAS ONE of those summer days in Saigon that, back in 1962, when
he was a twenty-six-year-old AP correspondent fresh in Vietnam,
could almost have made Peter Arnett forget there was a war going
on.

The war seemed far away. The city's population of six hundred
thousand had yet to feel the influence of the growing but still-small
American presence. Sitting on a park bench, Arnett could watch the
Vietnamese girls, demure yet alluring in their close-fitting *ao dai*s, go
by. He could smell the jasmine blossoms in nearby trees as their scent
competed with the joss sticks burning at family altars and the char-
coal fires of dozens of outside food stalls.

But it wasn't 1962. It was the summer of 1970, and even in Saigon
it was harder and harder for Arnett to forget about the war. Saigon
had become a refugee camp, its population swollen to nearly two
million by peasants who had fled the fighting. Vietnamese bar girls in
halter tops and miniskirts had replaced the Vietnamese schoolgirls in
traditional dress. The odor of exhaust fumes and garbage over-
whelmed the fragrance of the trees. And, after eight and one-half
years in Vietnam, Arnett had decided that, at thirty-five, he was too
old to cover the war any more.

As they sat in a Saigon park, his old colleague Morley Safer asked
Arnett if he had become hardened to the killing. After all, Arnett had

probably seen more than any American soldier. Surely he had become inured to the death by now. "No," Arnett told his friend, "I probably was a reverse case. I took a hardboiled approach to the Vietnam War from the very beginning. . . . I've seen as many as 120 Americans on a battlefield at the Nha Trang Valley, and I've seen 200 at a time North Vietnamese just chopped to pieces by artillery, and I've always tried to look past that." But by the time of the spring-1970 invasion of Cambodia, he had had his fill. He told Safer about what he found in the rubber-plantation town of Snoul. "The North Vietnamese had dug in," he said, "and there was a battle for the town. We went in on the tanks next morning and the enemy had fled. Left in the marketplace were five bodies, a woman, looked like three kids, and a man, [who] had sort of been all fused together by napalm." It was at that moment, Arnett said, that he decided "I just don't want to see any more bodies."[1]

Arnett's exposure to the war's suffering was obviously more immediate and intense than that of the average American. But in a way the reporter and the reader had made the same sort of mental and emotional journey. Years of seemingly inconclusive death and destruction steadily taxed resources of patience and endurance. Finally, Arnett's wish in that little Cambodian marketplace became the defining thought of the period, limiting and directing both the policies of the United States government and the functioning of the American press in Vietnam. For the government it meant a gradual end to direct American involvement in the war. For the press it meant that the same internal characteristics and external forces that had shaped its coverage of the war from the 1950s would continue to operate. For both institutions it meant fulfilling Arnett's and the American people's desire not to see any more bodies.

## "The Color of the Bodies"

Continued increases in the number of American combat troops in South Vietnam were no longer an option after the Tet Offensive. Impatience and frustration with the Johnson strategy had grown steadily in both the press and the public. Tet gave shape and direction to this dissatisfaction, a fact not lost on the candidates of both parties in the 1968 presidential contest. Richard Nixon, who bested Vice-

President Hubert Humphrey in the general election, had benefited from the notion that he had a "secret plan" to end the war.[2]

Nixon had no such plan. Two assumptions were in his mind as he took office in January 1969. First, public opinion and his own ambitions demanded that he get the United States out of the war. "I'm not going to end up like LBJ," he said, "holed up in the White House afraid to show my face on the street. I'm going to stop that war. Fast." The second assumption was that, no matter how strong the public's desire to end the war, a withdrawal that appeared too fast or left South Vietnam immediately vulnerable could be disastrous for his political and diplomatic goals. "We would destroy ourselves," he told *New York Times* columnist Cy Sulzberger, "if we pulled out in a way that wasn't really honorable."[3]

Nixon at first tried to end the war quickly through a combination of violence and diplomacy that he called "the Madman Theory." He tried to make the North Vietnamese believe he would do anything, even resort to the use of nuclear weapons, to end the war. The North Vietnamese, however, were no more cowed by this than they had been by Johnson's gradual escalation. By the fall of 1969, Nixon fell back on a remnant of Johnsonian policy that came to be known as "Vietnamization." This approach aimed to build up the South Vietnamese military so that it would take over combat operations and allow the United States to withdraw from all but a few support roles.[4]

Nixon made this policy his own in a televised speech to the nation on November 3, 1969. He tried to give a little something to everyone. To those who still wanted victory, or at least didn't want the sacrifice to have been in vain, he promised continued support to South Vietnam. To those who wanted the United States out of the war—and by no means were these two groups mutually exclusive—he held out a plan for the withdrawal of American combat troops. At the conclusion of the speech he cast himself in the role of Great Conciliator when he appealed to the "great silent majority of Americans" for support. "Let us be united for peace. Let us be united against defeat," he said, because "let us understand: North Vietnam cannot defeat or humiliate the United States. Only Americans can do that."[5]

The speech certainly didn't end concern and conflict over the war. As the withdrawal commenced and continued, increasing numbers of Americans grew impatient with its deliberate pace. As early as March

1970, significantly more respondents to a Gallup poll favored either an immediate withdrawal or one that would be complete at the end of eighteen months. The joint South Vietnamese–American invasion of Cambodia in May and June 1970 sparked massive protests on college campuses across the country, as well as inspiring a movement in Congress to limit the president's war-making ability. Both developments led to what Nixon's legal counsel Charles Colson called a "siege mentality" taking over the White House.[6]

Despite all this, the "silent majority" speech and the Vietnamization policy were successful political maneuvers. Nixon was shrewd enough to understand that the level of American interest in the war was tied directly to American ground-combat involvement. If that involvement could be reduced, and especially if the number of American casualties could be lowered significantly, the American people would lose interest in the war. This would give Nixon a freer hand in Indochina, just as his old nemesis John Kennedy had had in 1961 and 1962.

Sure enough, as the withdrawal gained momentum and as fewer and fewer Americans came home in aluminum caskets, the war diminished in American thinking. As early as the end of 1969, for example, the environment was beginning to supplant the war as a primary concern among college students. The withdrawal of American troops from Cambodia in June 1970 pulled the plug on that episode. *Newsweek* reported in October that, "by working steadily toward an end to U.S. fighting in Viet Nam, the President has dampened discord and virtually removed the war from active political debate in the 1970 election campaign." In early 1971, *New York Times* columnist Anthony Lewis wrote, "Vietnam does not dominate our consciousness as it did." The reasons, he said, "are lower American casualties and gradual American withdrawal."[7]

The "silent majority" speech, more than the Tet Offensive, marked a real watershed in U.S. involvement in Vietnam. In it Nixon permanently altered the nature of the issue. No longer was the question *whether* the United States was going to get out, but, rather, *how* and *how fast*. Under Vietnamization, Nixon did not so much introduce new factors into the Vietnam equation as he recognized, re-emphasized, and exploited old ones. By reducing American casualties, Nixon, in essence, turned the clock back to a time when the American public knew little and cared less about what was going on

in Vietnam. What Nixon promised the American people was not an end to the killing in Vietnam but, rather, an end to the killing *of Americans*. "Vietnamization," said one critic of the policy, "means only that the color of the bodies is now different." But for the American public—and for the American press—that made all the difference in the world.[8]


# "As If the Past Ten Years
# Had Never Happened"

It was September 1971 and Ellsworth Bunker was tired. He was in his last assignment, United States ambassador to South Vietnam, at the end of a long and distinguished diplomatic career. He had come to South Vietnam in late 1967, and presided over the whole of the Vietnamization process, with all its hopes of South Vietnamese security and American withdrawal.

But this assignment was turning sour. The South Vietnamese military hadn't recovered from the licking it had received during the invasion of Laos earlier that year. Doubts about ARVN's ability to survive without American air power grew steadily. And just that month, South Vietnamese President Nguyen Van Thieu forced his chief opponents out of the presidential race, seizing the presidency for himself and dashing the illusion of incipient democracy. As he sat down to meet with a group of reporters, Bunker was clearly disappointed at this turn of events. "Bunker's replies were largely uninformative," *Time*'s Stanley Cloud remembered, "and he was reduced to mouthing the slogans of the Cold War." As he sat there watching, Cloud thought that "It was almost as it were 1959, as if Bunker were discussing whether the U.S. should become involved in Viet Nam. It was as if the past ten years had never happened."[9]

From the beginning of the Vietnamization process to the signing of the truce accords in early 1973, time did seem to run backward. No longer did the people or the press focus on American fighting, largely because American troops were doing less of it. The viability of South Vietnam, of its military and government, and its effect on American disengagement, became the prime story for the American press. As Vietnamization proceeded, the press's approach to the Vietnam story in the Nixon years came to bear a striking resemblance to its approach during the Kennedy years.

As the American combat role diminished, the public's and the press's attention moved away from the story *in Vietnam*. As always, the press was most concerned with the American angle of the story, and that angle was increasingly to be found somewhere besides Vietnam. The peace talks in Paris, despite their fitful pace, became an important facet of the story. The domestic aspects of the story also drew attention. Just what are the president's policies and goals for the war? Will the public buy them? Will Congress? What is the antiwar movement, where is it going, and how effective is it? Can the president neutralize his critics? How will all this affect his initiatives at home? How will it affect the political scene? What is the war doing to American society? These questions couldn't be answered from Vietnam. The effect of Nixon's Vietnam policies on his larger diplomatic ambitions, especially regarding the Soviet Union and China, also emerged as significant topics. These stories were covered out of Washington, New York, Geneva, Moscow—not Saigon.

This ethnocentricity made Vietnam more and more a domestic story, but it also had a profound effect on the coverage from Vietnam. For American news organizations in Saigon, Vietnamization became the major story. American reporters in Saigon during this period spent most of their time trying to answer one central question: Will South Vietnam become strong enough quickly enough to allow the United States to get out of the war?

In the immediate aftermath of the "silent majority" speech, Vietnam correspondents answered this question with charitable skepticism. Reporters acknowledged signs of progress. *Time* bureau chief Marsh Clark contended that, "by most of the familiar statistical indicators, there is evidence of improvement for the U.S." Clark concluded that "the chance of success for the often repeated U.S. object in Viet Nam—to guarantee the South Vietnamese the right of self-determination, free from outside aggression—has vastly improved during the past year, because gradually an environment has been created in which the South Vietnamese can fend for themselves."[10]

After the Cambodian incursion, however, the press in Vietnam became less charitable and more skeptical about Vietnamization. An active "front" in Cambodia demanded even more of South Vietnamese forces. At the end of his fifteen-month tour in Vietnam for

*The New York Times,* Terence Smith reported "widespread doubt among the most experienced American observers [about] the efficacy of the Vietnamization program. . . ." "The United States still faces vast problems extricating itself" from the war, Smith concluded. In a similar end-of-assignment overview, *Newsweek* Saigon bureau chief Maynard Parker said that Vietnamization was not "a withdrawal strategy" but a formula "for a long war and a continued American involvement."[11]

In the January 26, 1971, *New York Times,* Saigon correspondent Iver Peterson reported the often noted caveat that, whatever progress had been made, "no one knows what would happen if new enemy pressure should catch them with their lines overextended." Since the beginning of Vietnamization, American reporters and officials had wondered how the South Vietnamese would respond to a significant North Vietnamese action. "Saigon's Armed Forces Improving, but Big Test Is Still Ahead," ran the headline over Peterson's story. As it turned out, that big test was just days ahead.[12]

For years the American military had contended that a strike at the Ho Chi Minh Trail in the panhandle of southern Laos would slow or stop the flow of supplies from North Vietnam. The domestic and diplomatic ramifications of an American entry into Laos stayed Johnson's hand. But after the Vietcong lost their supply routes through the southern ports of Cambodia in March 1970, the Trail became even more important in both North Vietnamese and American eyes. In early 1971, Nixon approved the plans for "Lam Son 719." South Vietnamese infantry and armor would enter Laos, supported by American air power, but not American ground troops or advisers.[13]

For the first several days, the South Vietnamese met little resistance as they moved west on Highway 9 toward the Laotian town of Tchepone, where several branches of the Trail met. But the North Vietnamese finally countered savagely, sending the South Vietnamese reeling back across the border and inflicting casualties estimated as high as 50 percent on the twenty-six-thousand-man invasion force. The slaughter would have been even worse but for the thousands of support and evacuation sorties flown by American helicopters, fighters, and bombers.[14]

The invasion had been touted by the administration as the long-awaited major test of Vietnamization. According to the American press, the ARVN failed, and that boded ill for the whole policy. News dispatches told of the massive losses endured by the South Vietnamese as they pushed back along Highway 9. *Time* described an ARVN Ranger battalion that held a base for three days against a much larger North Vietnamese force. "By the time the survivors hacked their way through to another base two miles away, no fewer than 323 of 500 Rangers were dead, wounded, or missing." Dozens of other accounts like this painted a picture of a beaten and humiliated South Vietnamese Army. Still photographs and film of ARVN soldiers clinging to the skids of American helicopters in desperate attempts to escape destruction became the lasting image of the operation.[15]

Despite an administration publicity campaign to portray the invasion as a success, American reporters concluded otherwise. *Newsweek* called Lam Son 719 "a costly miscalculation." *Time* described an operation plagued from the beginning by poor intelligence, poor planning, and poor leadership. Literally within days of the operation's end, news organizations were reporting that truck traffic on the Trail was, if anything, heavier than before the invasion. Stepped up North Vietnamese activity in the South "deflated" claims of success for Lam Son 719.[16]

The bottom line, for press and public, was, in *Time*'s words, "What It Means for Vietnamization." *Newsweek* correspondents furnished an answer when they quoted an American official in Saigon. "As usual, we've been guilty of self-delusion," the official lamented. "Vietnamization was to be the theme upon which we were going to slide out of this mess. And nobody wants to recognize the fact that Vietnamization does not reflect the reality on the ground." Nixon had claimed that Lam Son 719 showed that the South Vietnamese could "hack it" on their own; even so, *The New York Times'* Alvin Shuster discounted the invasion's significance to Vietnamization. "The operation was certainly no test of Vietnamization," Shuster said. "If anything, it showed how dependent the South Vietnamese remain on the United States for air power." Shuster quoted an ARVN officer who participated in the invasion. "They brought us in, they brought us out," he said, "and they can let us die."[17]

This scenario played again a year later, during the so-called Easter Offensive. In early April 1972, the North Vietnamese launched "a classic World War II–style assault," pouring thousands of troops, supported by long-range artillery and armor, across the DMZ in the north and out of Cambodia toward Saigon. Once again the American press in Vietnam described the staggering South Vietnamese setbacks. Once again the big question for the American press, government, and public was "What does it mean for us?" *Newsweek* said that the offensive "threatened to make a mockery of President Nixon's carefully constructed policy of disengaging from an unwanted war in an orderly and honorable fashion." When Nixon responded to the Easter Offensive by mining Haiphong Harbor and unleashing Linebacker I, *Newsweek* went on to say that "it only underscored the frailty of the Vietnamization program and demonstrated just how deeply the U.S. was still ensnared in Vietnam." *Time* concluded that the president reacted as he did "out of an almost obsessive fear of national and personal humiliation in Viet Nam."[18]

Even though South Vietnamese troops and an armada of American aircraft eventually halted the North Vietnamese, American reporters at the end of the year were still describing a South Vietnamese Army on the defensive. In November 1972, with a cease-fire imminent, the North Vietnamese and Vietcong started a series of small but intense actions, hoping to intimidate peasants and spread the ARVN forces thin. *Time*'s Barry Hillenbrand reported that Saigon was virtually surrounded. "Watching the action on Highway 13 to the north of Saigon is like watching mortar rounds being walked in on a position. Each day, when one drives up the highway through the flat open rice fields, progress is stopped closer to Saigon."[19]

The press also questioned Thieu's viability. Not long after the declaration of Vietnamization, *Newsweek* said that even though Thieu's "political position seems unassailable . . . he is still far from popular with his people." In 1971, Thieu ran for a second term. American officials hoped the election would signify, as *Time* put it, "a long step toward open and competitive democracy, vindicating Nixon's policy of Vietnamization and justifying a stepped-up U.S. withdrawal." But when Thieu ordered the name of Nguyen Cao Ky, his vice-president and chief rival, stricken from the ballot, *Time* continued, "he turned the election into an all but meaningless referendum on his own performance in office."[20]

Thieu became even more autocratic and withdrawn during 1972. He ordered Vietnamese newspapers to print only official reports of the war and closed down papers that dared to criticize him. He also lashed back at his increasingly vocal and broadly based political opposition, including the Buddhists. After the 1971 election fiasco, tension between Thieu and American officials in South Vietnam increased, climaxing in bitter confrontations over the proposed truce agreement. He was, as one American official told Robert Shaplen, "his own Nhu."[21]

It did indeed seem that the last ten years had never happened. Watching events in South Vietnam from 1969 to 1973 was like watching a film running backward. American troops were leaving, until there were only a handful of advisers left. The enemy was once again on the advance, spreading its influence closer and closer to the major cities. The South Vietnamese Army was again on the defensive, and the leadership of the nation was isolated and increasingly paranoid. Watching, one almost expected to see Ngo Dinh Diem spring from the grave and resume his place in the presidential palace. In a very real sense, he had.

The American press's approach to the Vietnam story was also going backward. For over four years, reporters had concentrated on the United States' combat presence, covering the day-to-day details of Americans at war. Now that story disappeared. The center of United States policy and press interest became—under Nixon, as it had been under Kennedy—the ability of the South Vietnamese government and military to resist the communists and, most important, the effect that this would have on the United States' involvement in the country.

From 1971 through 1973, as from 1961 through 1963, the American press was pessimistic concerning these issues. Indeed, in reading the coverage of the later years of American involvement, one is struck again and again by its similarity to dispatches written ten years before. The same corrupt, politicized, passive military. The same autocratic government. The same divisions within South Vietnam, within the American community there, and between the two. The same disciplined, aggressive enemy. Just change the names.

There is one important difference. Bigart, Sheehan, Halberstam, Arnett, and Browne had tried to figure out whether the United States would intervene more directly to give South Vietnam the time to grow. Their successors were trying to figure out whether the United States could ever withdraw completely, and whether this withdrawal would at least give South Vietnam time to die with dignity.

Tragically, the last ten years *had* happened.

## "Nothing to Report"

For years a Saigon correspondent routinely paid a visit to the Joint
U.S. Public Affairs Office when it opened each morning at eight o'-
clock, there to gather up the reams of summaries and news releases
on the previous day's action. These documents, chock-full of details
on ground engagements, bombing, activity by naval forces, and on
and on, had long been the foundation of the coverage of the war.

But on the morning of January 9, 1971, reporters did not find the
usual stack of papers arranged neatly on a long table near the
briefer's podium. Instead, an official spokesman appeared to tell
them that MACV would issue no morning release. "Normally we
report B-52 strikes in Vietnam," the spokesman said. "There were no
indirect fire attacks. Normally we report ground action involving
U.S. troops. There were no ground actions. . . . There just wasn't
anything to report."[22]

This scene captured in one moment a significant element of the
story of the American press and the war during this period. Vietnamization had turned the clock back in terms of the press's approach to
the story. It did the same regarding the American press's relationship
in Vietnam to the U.S. and South Vietnamese governments and militaries. Under Johnson, the government and the military over-
whelmed the press with combat information, and encouraged the
South Vietnamese to do the same.

Nixon, however, didn't face Johnson's task of building support for
the American presence. Rather, he was trying, just as John Kennedy
had done, to limit Vietnam as a political liability. He took a couple of
lessons from his old adversary. To avoid charges of "losing" Vietnam, he provided the Thieu regime with massive material support.
Next, to give himself more freedom of action in Indochina, he reduced the American public's interest in and knowledge of Vietnam.
He cut back the American combat role and limited sharply the American press's access to information in Vietnam. Nixon's goal, like
Kennedy's, was for the press to have nothing to report.

Under Nixon, the crude balance between "maximum candor" and
what one wag had earlier called "maximum mum" tilted toward the
latter. This shift had two aspects. First, MACV and the United States
Embassy in Saigon became more close-mouthed, claiming that as

American activity declined there was simply less to report. Maintaining that the South Vietnamese now carried the burden of combat, American officials shifted the burden of dealing with the press to the South Vietnamese.

This shift became evident early in Vietnamization. In June 1969, the South Vietnamese government banned an issue of *Newsweek* that reported that several government and military officials had made secret escape plans in the event of a communist takeover. The Information Ministry summoned the magazine's bureau chief, Maynard Parker. Officials told him that other recent articles had been found "unsuitable," and that such reports could result in the magazine's staff's being permanently banned from the country. Though the United States Embassy protested, it also told *Newsweek* and other news organizations that the South Vietnamese government had a right to "protect its morale." The long-held South Vietnamese wariness of the foreign press became even more evident during the rest of 1969 and into early 1970, as ARVN commanders either refused to speak with reporters or banned them from their areas of operation altogether.[23]

Things also got hotter between the American press and United States information officials. Reporters, who had long derided the daily briefing in Saigon as the "Five o'Clock Follies," became even more critical, as evidenced by an essay in *Time*. The briefings, the essay said, had become "a ritual recitation of memorized details, a reduction of experiences to a set of quantifiable data." As time went on, MACV held details of American activity closer. As the air war took center stage, American officials cut back on what they would say about it. They discussed air operations in Laos and Cambodia, if at all, only in the vaguest language. American air bases in Thailand remained, as they had been throughout the war, off limits to American reporters. As one American officer said, "We may not be down to a low profile in Indochina yet, but we sure have got down to low visibility, and we intend to keep things that way."[24]

Other sources of tension arose. Two Americans and two Vietnamese, accredited as newspersons to an organization called the American University Press, turned out to be employees of the U.S. Army's Criminal Investigation Division. Their cover blown, MACV quickly revoked the men's accreditation and claimed to have reprimanded and reassigned the person responsible. MACV also maintained that the men weren't spying on reporters but investigating black-marketeering among American GIs. Speculation ran strong, though, that what *The New York Times* called "growing dissatisfaction in the military in Saigon and Washington over the reporting by United States newsmen of 'unfavorable' reports" was behind the episode.[25]

The invasion of Cambodia meant more restrictions. MACV insisted that the South Vietnamese were responsible for the operation and any press arrangements, and refused to allow American reporters to accompany American units into Cambodia. Nor did the South Vietnamese make accommodations for reporters.[26]

Thus, for the first time in several years, American reporters had to get to the story on their own. Time-Life had a jeep for its bureau, and photographers Sean Flynn and Dana Stone rode into battle on Honda motorcycles. Rented cars became the vehicle of the day for most reporters.

The struggle to reach the story was oftentimes less difficult than the struggle to get the story once correspondents reached the fighting. The South Vietnamese were merely uncooperative, but Cambodian-government troops and communist guerrillas were dangerous. CBS correspondent George Syvertsen was killed when his jeep was hit by a Vietcong grenade. Photographers Flynn and Stone, along with NBC's Welles Hangen, disappeared. All told, twenty-four journalists were killed or captured during the two months of the operation. Nor were all the dangers from the guerrilla side. Members of a CBS camera crew had warning shots fired close over their heads as they approached a Cambodian-government position. When several reporters discovered government troops threatening ethnic Vietnamese in the town of Takeo, they shielded the civilians for several hours against the tense and hostile troops.[27]

These dangers underlined just how dependent the American press had become on the logistical support of the United States government and military. "Instead of traveling lonely roads in rented cars, as they do in Cambodia, war correspondents [in Vietnam] are taken to the scene of action by planes and helicopters and put down only where there are friendly troops," said *The New York Times'* Henry Kamm. "Compared to Cambodia, covering the war in Vietnam is like touring with American Express."[28]

During the rest of 1970 and into 1971, official American sources shut their doors to reporters. Early in his tour as MACV commander, Creighton Abrams met with the bureau chiefs of the major news organizations fairly frequently, but dropped the practice in early 1971. Well before that, MACV ended the background-intelligence briefings that had been held as often as twice a week earlier in the war. Even in the field, American sources were clamming up. UPI correspondents, for example, reported several cases in which United States officers refused to allow their troops to speak with reporters or even to provide them with accommodations. These actions sprang partly from a growing animus between correspondents and officers. "You guys have been shafting us for years so now we're shafting you right back," a colonel told UPI's Kenneth Braddick and Stewart Kellerman. It also came from the clear desire of higher authorities to keep the war, and especially the American role in it, out of sight and out of mind. "The word has gone down the line," wrote UPI's Arthur Higbee. "The war is over, we in the military are doing nothing but going home, it's an all-Vietnamese war now, so don't write about us Americans."[29]

The watershed in this process was Lam Son 719. A number of developments during this operation made it clear that the days of maximum candor were over.

First, MACV imposed a six-day embargo, or blackout, on the news of the impending invasion. Such embargoes has been imposed several times during the war. But Lam Son 719 was one of the few cases in which the embargo itself was embargoed, meaning that reporters could not even tell readers that there was something they could not tell them. Embargoes could and did have legitimate security functions.[30]

Reporters in Vietnam protested the embargo on Lam Son 719 strongly, however, for that security function was quickly shot in this case. For weeks prior to the invasion, American bombers had been hitting the target area extremely hard. Also, movement of American troops into the old Marine fire bases along the DMZ clearly signaled that something was up. So heavy was the flow of men and materiel to the area that, in late January, newspersons were denied seats on aircraft heading to the northern province of Quang Tri, the invasion's base. And, finally, rumors of the invasion had been running rampant for days. Surely, reporters rightly pointed out, the North Vietnamese could smell out the impending move. The only people confused by the embargo, they said, were the people of South Vietnam and the United States.[31]

MACV complicated matters for reporters even further. Just before Lam Son 719 began, the United States officially halted its daily briefings on South Vietnamese activities. American officials couldn't comment on South Vietnamese operations inside Laos, nor were the South Vietnamese themselves much more cooperative. American officials barred correspondents from American helicopters flying into Laos. Reporters had to rely on South Vietnamese–piloted craft that were both rare and more risky than those flown by experienced American pilots. Only after four photographers were killed in an ARVN chopper did Defense Secretary Melvin Laird relent and make a limited number of American helicopters available. However, the invasion's South Vietnamese commander controlled access to them.

Because of these restrictions, reporters in South Vietnam had to turn to unofficial sources to find out what was going on in Laos. For many journalists, the only readily available sources were the American helicopter pilots and the South Vietnamese soldiers they shuttled in and out of combat.[32]

Such sources gave the same kind of information that they had eight years earlier, in that other much-ballyhooed test of the South Vietnamese military, the Battle of Ap Bac. They painted for reporters a picture of the South Vietnamese Army, which had entered Laos with such bravado, now being hammered and humiliated. For example, Gloria Emerson of *The New York Times* spent many days at Khe Sanh, the rear base for the invasion, interviewing the men who had seen the fighting firsthand. Stories of clouds of anti-aircraft fire, of casualty rates of 50 to 80 percent in some South Vietnamese units, of North Vietnamese armor and infantry attacks sending the South Vietnamese back across the border in near-panic, jarred against the comments of the American spokesman who blithely said, "I have nothing to report today. Everything was quiet," and claims by the Nixon Administration that the operation was a great success.[33]

Such practices again inspired charges of official deception and misinformation. Correspondents questioned—but still reported—both enemy and friendly casualty figures supplied by the United States and South Vietnam. American officials, in an attempt to minimize the beating that American helicopters were taking, reported only those aircraft that were completely destroyed, not the hundreds more that were shot down but later recovered. The U.S. administration tried to prove Lam Son 719's success in cutting the flow of supplies by displaying a section of gasoline pipeline supposedly destroyed during the invasion. But its credibility slipped even further as reporters discovered that the pipe had actually been seized months before in a commando raid. Frustrated by the savage North Vietnamese counterattack, Nixon lashed out at the press for emphasizing the negative aspects of the operation. But, as *Time* pointed out, very little information had been furnished concerning the invasion, and almost no reporters could get into Laos to cover the action firsthand. Thus, *Time* concluded, "the President was in effect criticizing the press for not entirely accepting the official version of the story."[34]

*New York Times* bureau chief Craig R. Whitney wrote at the end of Lam Son 719 that the continued Vietnamization of the information process boded ill for reporters. "As sparing of information as the Americans have been in this war, the Vietnamese are even less forthcoming. . . . If the operation in Laos is any indication, then reporting on this war may become even more dangerous in the future than it has in the past."[35]

All this sparked little reaction from the American public. Whereas the Cambodian invasion a year earlier had triggered a tidal wave of protest, Laos hardly caused a ripple. The main differences were, first, another year's worth of troop withdrawals and, second and most important, the fact that no American ground troops entered Laos. Senator Edward M. Kennedy expressed "disappointment and dismay" at the nation's placid acceptance of the invasion. So uninterested was the public that, when Nixon did a prime-time television interview with ABC's Howard K. Smith to explain and defend the operation, the show drew only 14 percent of the audience, the rest preferring an NBC movie or Doris Day and Carol Burnett on CBS.[36]

As 1971 gave way to 1972, official South Vietnamese briefings, never very informative, became exercises in hostility and frustration for spokespersons and reporters alike. For example, most of the ground action in Indochina during these months took place in Cambodia, but the South Vietnamese government refused to give even the sketchiest details on the operation there. A Reuters correspondent described South Vietnamese information practices as consisting of "a succession of official and semiofficial reports and firm official denials." With authorized information so sparse, reporters turned to sources within the amorphous structure of South Vietnamese military officers, government officials, and official and semiofficial radio and television stations and news agencies. The correspondent gave the January 29, 1972, briefing as a typical example. First the ARVN spokesperson, Colonel Le Trung Hien denied an armed-forces radio report that fighting was taking place just a few miles outside Saigon. He next denied a report that the commander of the South Vietnamese Rangers had asked permission to raid the North Vietnamese port of Vinh; Hien himself had issued that very report to Vietnamese journalists. Finally, he quashed a rumor that the Saigon area was on full military alert against an impending attack. Hien concluded the briefing with a terse warning to correspondents about reporting such rumors. "Don't do it," he said.[37]

At the same time that it limited official information, the South Vietnamese government tried to silence unofficial sources. In July and December 1971, the government toughened its information guidelines, putting a tighter lid on the release of data and more stringent punishment of its use. Colonel Hien pulled no punches as he announced the second of these steps, telling reporters that "when you get these new rules you will be restricted very much in reporting on military operations."[38]

Reporters felt the full weight of these practices during the 1972 Easter Offensive. As the North Vietnamese streamed across the DMZ and out of Cambodia, the South Vietnamese government tried to shut reporters off completely from information. News organizations trying to beef up their reduced staffs during the offensive found their reporters' visas being delayed or denied outright. Briefings were even less helpful than usual. Reporters were again forced to find their own transportation. But finding a car and driver did not guarantee access to the fighting, for reporters were banned from the battle areas. Civilian traffic was allowed to pass checkpoints established on major roads, but anyone holding a press card was turned back.[39]

Reporters who managed to avoid the checkpoints faced a cool reception at the other end. South Vietnamese commanders, traditionally wary of foreign reporters, became downright hostile during the Easter Offensive. An ARVN captain told Malcolm Browne, back in Vietnam for *The New York Times*, that "the press is the agent of the Vietcong, so don't be surprised by what happens to you newsmen here." Browne told of an ARVN artillery officer who tried to send him into the hands of the North Vietnamese by giving deliberately misleading directions to a South Vietnamese position. NBC's Bob Jones, anxious to film the South Vietnamese raising the flag over the recaptured citadel in the city of Quang Tri, asked an ARVN officer the quickest way to the event. "Just walk across that field, and someone will show you the way," the officer said. Jones could see that the field was under heavy fire. The officer smiled at Jones and said, "You go. I'll stay here."[40]

Even as the offensive waned in the summer of 1972, the crisis between the foreign press and the South Vietnamese government intensified. The government harangued reporters about what the government considered distorted and pessimistic reporting. Journalists were warned repeatedly that such reports would result in expulsion from the country. In a particularly ominous move, President Thieu instituted a martial-law decree that made circulating news or pictures "detrimental to the national security" a criminal offense.[41]

South Vietnamese hostility, the malevolent inaction of U.S. officials, the increasing physical danger, and, not least, the indifference of the American public—all this took its toll on the Saigon press corps. Reporters asked themselves if the story was worth the trouble any more. Can the South Vietnamese hold on, will the North Vietnamese make another big push, will a cease-fire be signed, will it hold, what will happen, what will the United States do, who cares? Arnett, back in Vietnam after a two-year hiatus, said that in earlier days reporters had felt their work meant something. But now, standing amid the rubble of a generation's shattered dreams, he lamented that "reporting the war is no longer the noble act it once was."[42]

## "The Story Belongs to the People"

The war hadn't completely lost its ability to grab headlines. The invasions of Cambodia and Laos and the 1972 Easter Offensive all brought the war blasting back onto front pages, magazine covers, and evening news broadcasts.

In fact, some of the most dramatic stories, those that helped to generate the image of a superpress, able to leap the walls of official secrecy in a single bound, broke during this period. Three such stories—the My Lai massacre, the secret bombing of Cambodia and

North Vietnam, and the Pentagon Papers—have important things to say.

The My Lai massacre occurred March 16, 1968, in the wake of the Tet Offensive, at a small village in the northern coastal region of South Vietnam. Troops from the Americal Division entered the hamlet of My Lai, known to GIs as "Pinkville" because of the longtime Vietcong presence there. According to charges filed against Lieutenant William Calley, in command of the particular unit involved, American troops murdered several hundred innocent civilians, mostly old men, women, and children.[43]

No reporters were there that day, no TV cameras. The only photographer was Sergeant Ronald L. Haeberle, who worked for army public information. Company commander Captain Ernest Medina told his troops not to talk about the incident. This "conspiracy of silence" went all the way up to division commander Major General Samuel W. Koster.

These instructions worked; the massacre remained a secret many months. The division's news release that day reported that units of the Americal had swept an area near My Lai, killing 128 Vietcong. For a year afterward, the incident remained locked in the memories of those who had seen or heard about it. In March 1969, an ex-GI named Ronald Ridenhour, who had not been at My Lai but had heard about it from participants, broke the silence. He was skeptical about the first reports. "But in the following months I was to hear stories from such a wide variety of people that it became impossible for me to disbelieve that something dark and bloody did occur. . . ." Ridenhour wrote a five-page letter to President Nixon, twenty-three members of Congress, the secretaries of state and defense, and the chairman of the Joint Chiefs of Staff. His letter prompted an investigation by the army inspector general that eventually led to charge's being filed against Calley and others.[44]

But even then the My Lai story didn't become news. No major news organizations had it. That left the field to Seymour Hersh, a young former AP correspondent. Hersh had been tipped off by an informant in mid-October that charges were about to be filed against Calley at Fort Benning, Georgia. After interviewing Calley for five hours, Hersh traveled thousands of miles, talking to other participants and witnesses, piecing together an account. Still, none of the major news organizations would take the story. "*Look* turned me down," Hersh said, "and an editor at *Life* said it was out of the question." Only the tiny Dispatch News Service would touch Hersh's report, and only after DNS began to market the story did it break.[45]

With the United States pulling its ground troops out of Vietnam, the Nixon Administration depended increasingly on air power. As the air war went on, the administration became less and less cooperative in informing reporters in South Vietnam about the campaign. Two major bombing campaigns were contrived and carried out in secret.

The first campaign, known as Operation Menu, involved the bombing of Cambodia from March 1969 through May 1970. Early in his first term, Nixon was alarmed at the buildup of North Vietnamese and Vietcong forces in Cambodia, but he held back from openly attacking a supposedly neutral Cambodia. For weeks, Nixon, in Kissinger's words, "marched up the hill and down again" over whether or not to strike secretly at the base areas. A complex dual reporting system was finally devised. This system kept the raids secret for fifteen months, even from the secretary and chief of staff of the Air Force. Nixon authorized the campaign in an Oval Office meeting on March 16, 1969—the first anniversary of My Lai.

Almost immediately, though, the story began to leak. Several publications noted the rumors, but dropped the matter when the White House denied them. Only William Beecher, *The New York Times'* Pentagon correspondent, kept working. On May 9, he published a detailed description of the Menu campaign. But when the story caused no public reaction, Beecher dropped it as well. Not until four years later, when it came out as part of the Watergate investigations, did the story cause even a brief stir.[46]

The second secret bombing campaign didn't appear to have such high-level authorization. In August 1971, General John D. Lavelle took over as commander of the Seventh Air Force. His frustration with the limits placed on his air power grew as he watched the North Vietnamese prepare for the Easter Offensive. In November 1971, Lavelle decided to ignore these restrictions. Over the next five months, he launched at least 147 unauthorized sorties into North Vietnam, covering them up as "protective reaction strikes," pre-authorized retaliatory strikes on anti-aircraft emplacements.

As with My Lai, the story came out only when someone far down the chain of command blew the whistle. Sergeant Lonnie Franks, a former intelligence specialist at Udorn Air Force Base in Thailand, described the activity in a letter eventually read by Air Force chief of staff General John Ryan. After a quick investigation confirmed the charges, Lavelle was reduced in rank and given quick retirement, supposedly for "health reasons." Only after Representative Otis Pike kept questioning the unusual nature of Lavelle's separation from the service did the whole story come to light.[47]

The final case involved *The New York Times*' June 1971 publication of the Pentagon Papers, the top-secret documentary history of American involvement authorized by Robert McNamara.

Daniel Ellsberg had enjoyed a meteoric career as an academic and a defense analyst. In fact, his Harvard doctoral thesis, titled "Risk, Ambiguity and Decision," outlined some of the ideas that eventually became Nixon's "Madman Theory." Ellsberg went to work for the Rand Corporation, a favorite Pentagon think tank, and eventually became a special assistant to Assistant Secretary of Defense John McNaughton. Later he went to Vietnam, first working for Edward Lansdale and later as a pacification analyst.

Before going to Vietnam, *Time* said, Ellsberg was a "superhawk," but his exposure to the war turned him into a "superdove." After returning to the United States, Ellsberg turned to antiwar activities. He was convinced that, if the Pentagon Papers, which he had helped write, were made public, a popular outcry would bring the war to a quick end. Ellsberg photocopied the documents, and immediately began to look for an effective conduit. Political figures, such as Senator George McGovern and Representative Paul McCloskey, to whom he offered the papers, kept a wary distance of them and him.[48]

Ellsberg finally found a partner in Neil Sheehan, who was now working for *The New York Times*. Sheehan was equally obsessed with the war. In March 1971, he wrote for the *Times*' *Book Review* section a survey of thirty-three books on Vietnam. The review was in actuality a searing examination of whether or not the United States had committed war crimes in Indochina. After mutual assurances that the papers would be published, Ellsberg turned the material over to Sheehan. The *Times* devoted a team of top reporters, led by Sheehan, and over $100,000 to preparing a series based on the documents, a process the paper called "Project X." Extended and sometimes heated discussions took place among the *Times*' management and its attorneys concerning the publication of the series. Finally, publisher

Arthur Ochs Sulzberger decided that the series would commence with the June 13 edition.

The Nixon Administration first thought that, since the material dealt with Democratic administrations' taking the country deeper into war, it might actually be helpful to the GOP. However, Nixon's deep sense of secrecy and his concern for Executive freedom of action won out. On Tuesday the 15th, the Justice Department was granted an unprecedented injunction barring the *Times* from further publication of the series until the matter could be decided in court. For the first time in peacetime, the government had been granted the power of prior restraint, the ability to stop a publication from publishing a story. The case, which soon involved the *Washington Post* as well, quickly made its way to the United States Supreme Court. The Court, in a six-to-three decision issued on June 30, overturned the injunction.[49]

These stories illustrate some simple but important ideas concerning the press, the Vietnam War, and the United States government.

First, neither the My Lai incident nor the secret-bombing stories were broken by Vietnam correspondents. Reporters there, committed to covering the day-to-day action of the war and, increasingly, the issues surrounding American withdrawal, didn't have the time to take on long-term investigative projects.

Second, insiders broke all three stories. This is, of course, not to make light of the courage and hard work that such reporters as Sy Hersh, Neil Sheehan, or William Beecher brought to these stories. But the fact remains that, had it not been for Ron Ridenhour, the murder of the people of My Lai might yet be unknown to all but a few Americans; that without Daniel Ellsberg the Pentagon Papers would still be "top secret," gathering dust deep in the bowels of the Defense Department or the National Archives.

Last, consider the reaction of the Nixon Administration to the Cambodian bombing story and the Pentagon Papers. Few people noticed Beecher's May 1969 article. But the leak upon which it was based inspired Nixon and Kissinger to begin a program of domestic surveillance that bent the law beyond its breaking point. Kissinger asked FBI Director J. Edgar Hoover to find Beecher's source. The same day, the FBI tapped the phone of Kissinger aide Morton Halperin and other suspects. Kissinger, thanking Hoover for his quick response, supposedly assured the FBI director that the administration would "destroy whoever did this if we can find him, no matter who he is."

As the Beecher investigation went on, Nixon approved the Huston Plan, which advocated the use of illegal wiretaps, interception of the mails, and burglary to accomplish its goal of identifying and eliminating sources of dissent. Although Nixon dropped the plan when it proved to be too much even for Hoover, it did show the depths to which the Nixon White House was willing to descend. This didn't mark the end of such activity, however. The Senate Select Committee on Intelligence (the so-called Church committee) found in 1975 that intelligence agencies employed many of these methods without presidential authorization.[50]

Nor did the White House give up the game. Nixon, thwarted in his effort to use the legal system to stop publication, quickly adopted "extra-legal" means. On the day after the Supreme Court's Pentagon Papers ruling, Nixon met with several close aides. There began the discussions that eventually led to the formation of the Plumbers, a group of secret White House operatives. Its mission was to destroy what Nixon saw as a conspiracy to undermine his presidency through leaked information.[51]

Nixon's attempt to use the law to stop the *Times* was not a complete failure. The Supreme Court's decision was hailed by many at the time as a clear-cut victory for the First Amendment. However, as Harrison Salisbury points out, the Court's decision was not a sweeping, definitive statement on freedom of the press. The decision can be seen as a step *backward* for freedom of the press. The Court did *not* say that the government had no right to prior restraint in peacetime, as had been understood since the early days of the Republic. Rather, the Court said merely that the government "carries a heavy burden of showing justification for imposition of such a restraint." All the Supreme Court did was to decide that, in the case of the Pentagon Papers, the "Government had not met that burden." A door, seemingly closed tight, had been left ominously cracked open.[52]

Certainly Nixon brought his own obsessive ideas regarding Executive authority, secrecy, and the press to the White House, and his assault on the news media has been thoroughly discussed elsewhere. But Nixon's attitudes and practices were not aberrations. They were examples of tendencies that had been developing since the beginning of the Cold War. Nixon's efforts to control the press were cruder, more personal, and more vicious than those of Eisenhower, Kennedy, or Johnson. They were nonetheless based on the same belief that the Executive Branch, and particularly the White House, had not only the right but the obligation to restrict and manipulate information. The stories of My Lai and secret bombing campaigns and the Pentagon Papers made clear the government's ability to do just that. "The story belongs to the people," Neil Sheehan had said. But it was a hard story to get.[53]

## "Hoa Binh"

During 1972, the United States and the North Vietnamese moved fitfully toward a cease-fire. After last-minute complications, recriminations, and violence on all sides, an agreement was reached, and the formal truce accord signed in Paris on January 27, 1973. But the hopeful exclamations of *"hoa binh"*—"peace"—were to prove hollow for both the Vietnamese people and the American press in Vietnam.

By the end of March, the last American troops had left South Vietnam, and with them went most of the remaining American press corps. The number of accredited news personnel was over six hundred during the 1968 Tet Offensive; of them, four hundred or so worked for American news organizations. By the end of 1971, accredited employees of the American press in South Vietnam had declined to fewer than two hundred. September 1973 saw only fifty-nine persons accredited to American news media.[54]

Soon the Thieu regime unleashed the full force of its repressive tendencies on the foreign press. Within days of the signing of the accords, the South Vietnamese government barred reporters from speaking with the Vietcong and North Vietnamese truce representatives, who were virtual prisoners in their compound at Tan Son Nhut airport. Reporters trying to contact them were forcibly restrained, and their press cards, notes, and film were seized. ARVN military police let it be known that they were authorized to shoot intruders at the base.[55]

The government kicked a number of correspondents out of South Vietnam during 1973 and 1974 for "distorted" coverage and "un-Vietnamese activities," and many others were threatened with expulsion. The South Vietnamese paid special attention to reporters who had contact with the communists. Correspondents such as *The New York Times'* James Markham, *Newsweek*'s Ron Moreau, and ABC's Steve Bell, who visited Vietcong-held areas of South Vietnam, were routinely detained and had their notes and film taken from them. South Vietnamese officials seized the passport of Le Lieu Browne, Mal Browne's wife, after she accompanied her husband to Hanoi.[56]

Physical assaults not seen since Diem's days broke out again. A plainclothes policeman severely beat a CBS correspondent covering an antigovernment demonstration. Paul Leandri, a correspondent for Agence France-Presse, was summoned to Saigon police headquarters for questioning concerning the sources for a recent article. When Leandri protested the questioning and attempted to drive away, he was shot and killed by a Saigon police officer.[57]

Reporters and American officials in Saigon went after one another with renewed venom. Graham Martin, who replaced Ellsworth Bunker as ambassador in August 1973, was more secretive and more suspicious of the press than any of his predecessors. Immediately upon his arrival, Martin dramatically restricted press access to the embassy. He made no effort to hide his hostility. He said on one occasion that "The editorial page of the *New York Times* . . . has long been generally regarded as having a deep emotional involvement in the success of North Viet Nam's attempt to take over South Viet Nam by force of arms." When *Times* correspondent David K. Shipler wrote a story portraying continued heavy American support for the Thieu regime—certainly no secret—Martin wrote a "splenetic reply." Martin suggested that Shipler's article "be made available to the Columbia Graduate School of Journalism as a case study of propaganda under the guise of 'investigative reporting.' "[58]

In early 1975, the North Vietnamese launched another major offensive. By mid-March, the end was clearly at hand for South Vietnam. As the North Vietnamese surged forward, Thieu abandoned the northern provinces and the Central Highlands, withdrawing into a defensive enclave comprising the Mekong Delta, the southern coastal cities, and Saigon.

Like everyone else in South Vietnam, reporters were caught up in the maelstrom of confusion and panic that swept over the country. Bureaus had been cut to the bone after the American withdrawal, and now news organizations tried to rush in reinforcements. Trying to get to the fighting—especially up north, near Hue and Danang—was very difficult. Military aircraft had long since ceased to be an option and, as the situation worsened, many commercial flights were suspended. This left reporters, said an NBC News executive, "in the hands of the various crooks who run charter services." Reporters faced very tough restrictions on what they could and could not report.[59]

However, the fighting quickly came to the press. One after another, the major cities fell, leaving Saigon virtually surrounded. The evacuation of American personnel and dependents, along with selected South Vietnamese, had gone fairly smoothly for several days. But Ambassador Martin delayed the evacuation's final stage, and by the time it was initiated, panic had seized the city. Reporters were given instructions on when and where to meet for transportation to the airport. After North Vietnamese shelling closed it, reporters were sent to the United States Embassy, where helicopters shuttled nonstop to aircraft carriers out in the South China Sea. "It's complete, it's total, it's bye-bye, everybody," was the embassy's not-so-subtle evacuation signal to the press corps.[60]

Emotions ran high for the reporters there at the end. Some reporters thought about staying behind after the fall of the city, and quite a few did. But most, like NBC's David Butler, "stopped thinking of possibilities, and thought only, and this with great clarity, about what I had to do . . . in order to be a part of the evacuation." Many reporters worked around the clock, trying to cover the story and to get as many South Vietnamese out of the country as they could. They were on an adrenaline high, almost giddy with excitement, nervousness, and not a little fear.

But the futility of it, the fatigue and sheer sadness, soon took hold. For many reporters, such as Robert Shaplen, a part of their lives was coming to a close. Shaplen had come back to South Vietnam for the last days, come to witness the disintegration of something to which he had been personally and professionally committed for more than twenty years. When the final evacuation was ordered, he boarded a bus with several other reporters. As they looked out the windows at the crowd, Shaplen sat quiet and sad, tears rolling silently down his face.[61]

The scene at the United States Embassy became one of chaos and desperation in the evacuation's last hours. Americans and Vietnamese fought through the crowd, trying to make their way past the guards and through the gate or over the wall, to the line leading to the roof, to helicopters, to safety.

In the midst of this madness one small scene embodied the tangled web of the American press, the American government, and the war. A young Vietnamese shouldered and sighted an M-1 rifle, preparing to fire on the group of Marines guarding the embassy gate. An American television camera crew, looking to get the last bit of combat footage from South Vietnam, filmed the man as he took aim, then turned to film his victims. At that same moment, the Marines saw the Vietnamese and the cameraman. After knocking the Vietnamese down and taking his weapon, one of the Marines seized the camera and smashed it to the ground.[62]

# Conclusion

LONG BEFORE THE last American fell in combat in Vietnam, long before the last helicopter whirled from the roof of the U.S. Embassy in 1975, a search began for the cause of American failure in that tortured and torturing country.

Too often this search has turned to scapegoating. A succession of different people, groups, and institutions has been tagged with varying amounts of blame—or credit—for the outcome. At the center of this hunt has been the American press. Whether thought of as savior or villain, the press has enjoyed a virtually unanimous reputation as a powerful actor whose adversarial relationship to the United States government and military played a large part in ending American involvement in the war.

Creators of such images have made a simplistic morality play out of what is a complicated, important story.

A belief that the press, for good or ill, was politically and ideologically opposed to the war has been a central assumption since the war's end. However, an examination of how the press actually covered the war in Vietnam makes it clear that not politics, but the demands of journalism, motivated reporters in Vietnam and their superiors back in the United States.

These demands shaped coverage of the war in several ways. The relative lack of investment in foreign reporting kept Vietnam in a journalistic backwater long after the United States' investment in the

Diem regime had become significant. The press's traditional ethnocentrism contributed to this lack of attention. American news organizations cared little about Vietnam while it was primarily a fight between Vietnamese. But when American soldiers began to fight and die with regularity, journalistic interest and investment increased. An intense focus on spot reporting of day-to-day combat activity, to the detriment of coverage of less dramatic, less easily packaged, but equally important social and political stories, also typified American journalism in Vietnam. During the height of American military involvement, even the most interested, diligent news consumer could conclude that the war in Vietnam was primarily an American effort in which nonmilitary issues were either nonexistent or unimportant.

The way the press and the United States government and military related to each other also shaped coverage. These institutions were far from the simple adversaries they have been painted. Rather, the relationship between the press and the government/military was based on a fluctuating mix of confrontation and cooperation. In the early and late years of the war, when the Kennedy and Nixon administrations wished to downplay American involvement, the government and the military restricted the press's access to official information concerning the war. In both periods, these attempts turned the press toward other sources, sources that usually had their own points of view, contrary to those of American and south Vietnamese officials. Most of the stories that have fed the popular mythology of an adversarial press broke during these periods. Not coincidentally, it was also during these periods that the American press's coverage of the war was at its most courageous and imaginative.

But during the peak of the United States' combat involvement, the press and the government/military largely cooperated. Even in the Kennedy years, officials realized that the negative coverage of the effort flowed from their refusal to provide information to reporters. Under Lyndon Johnson, the "maximum candor" approach flooded the press with the information it needed to report the daily story of Americans in combat. By packaging and distributing that information in ways of its own choosing, the Johnson Administration influenced significantly the picture of the war. For the most direct and intense period of United States involvement in Vietnam, then, the interests of the press and the government complemented each other much more than they conflicted.

None of this intends to diminish the efforts of the American press corps in Vietnam. Most reporters covered the war with bravery, intelligence, and dedication. But the constraints they worked under can't be dismissed. Given these limits, the work of most American journalists in Vietnam was admirable. But given these conclusions, it is difficult to maintain that the press was the profound, even decisive, influence over public opinion and the course of the war that it has been portrayed to be. The press was more a paper soldier than an antiwar, antigovernment crusader.

The forces that shaped American attitudes toward Vietnam are not my subject, but some basic conclusions seem plausible. Rather than the press, it was the military policies of the United States and North Vietnamese governments that determined public support, or the lack thereof, for the war. The United States attempted to fight a limited war against an enemy prepared to fight a total war. The level of violence and the level of sacrifice increased gradually, with little tangible progress. In the end, the American people simply tired of pouring more of their blood and money into Vietnam. Their impatience grew virtually from the beginning of direct United States involvement, and eventually moved Lyndon Johnson to turn seriously toward negotiations. And public doubt and discouragement became the basis of Richard Nixon's Vietnamization policies.

A clear picture of the press's role must be part of a larger understanding of the war. It's clear that the whole fabric of American society—not just the press—determined how the war was fought, and that a variety of influences played a part in its outcome.

One fascinating aspect of American diplomatic history is the way in which social, cultural, and domestic political influences, in addition to the traditional questions of international relations, shape the foreign policies of the United States. All these factors have to be taken into account to understand how American foreign policy evolves. By studying the press and the government as institutions, by understanding the demands that shaped their behaviors and how these behaviors related to one another, Vietnam can be a useful frame of reference for further study of American foreign and national-security policy.

Finally, the story of the press and the Vietnam War has a deep significance for our political culture. When our Founders gathered in Philadelphia in 1787 to devise a new federal union, a prime concern centered on Executive power. Many delegates had fought during the

Revolution against what they saw as a distant Executive, beyond the accountability of the people. They were determined that no such creature be part of their new scheme of government. These wise men, were they to visit us today, would be shocked by the power that has flowed into the Executive Branch.

The catalyst for this shift has been the Cold War. With weapons so terrible, and a threat so profound, the Executive was entrusted with power far beyond that envisioned by the Founders.

A chief tool of this Executive power has been control of information. Many cases, when lives or important agreements might be jeopardized by premature or inappropriate disclosure, justify some limited controls. However, a cult of secrecy that goes far beyond legitimate security considerations has evolved in American government. This obsession with secrecy, from the Bay of Pigs to the Persian Gulf, has bent and occasionally broken the machinery of American system of government. As the Vietnam War showed, the ability and inclination of the Executive Branch to restrict and manipulate information is largely beyond the press's ability to resist.

This secrecy goes to the heart of the Constitution. Near the end of the war, public-opinion polls began to indicate that the relationship between the press and the government had resulted in the public's growing lack of confidence in the credibility of both institutions. The people seemed to be saying that they did not know whom or what to believe. Such an attitude can only lead to cynicism and, worse, apathy.

The Cold War that created this cult of secrecy is over. The effect that will have on our domestic and international political culture is still unclear. But at a time when much of the world is yearning for democracy, we surely cannot allow it to wither here. If we as a people are to prevent our system of government from becoming the last casualty of the Vietnam War, we as a people must demand more honesty and openness from our leaders, more aggressiveness and skepticism from our press, and more involvement and vigilance from ourselves.

# Acknowledgments

FIRST I WISH to thank the staffs of the many libraries and other archives at which I have done research. Librarians and archivists are the unsung heroes of the history profession, for it is their work that forms the foundation of any research project, and I have encountered individuals of exceptional skill and helpfulness. The members of the staff of the Margaret I. King Library at the University of Kentucky have been particular examples of such traits. Special thanks go to the members of the staff of the Grace Doherty Library at Centre College, all of whom are friends and who have extended to me no end of patience and support.

This book is a reworked version of my doctoral dissertation. There are many friends who have taken a kind interest in this project. No group of people has been more helpful or supportive than my friends at the Alumni House at Centre College. Donna Campbell and Marlene Hart have been friends above and beyond the call. Donna turned a mass of my bad typing into a presentable dissertation. Marlene rescued the dissertation from computer oblivion and turned it into a book. Ann Garner has lent a sympathetic ear on many occasions. All three have helped this project, and me, more than I can say. Shawn Lyons and Bill Breeze, and Rick Nahm before them, gave me the opportunity to earn a living while also giving me the freedom to work on the dissertation. I am also grateful to Centre President Dr.

Michael F. Adams, who, upon his arrival at Centre invested his time and confidence in me.

I would be remiss if I failed to mention the individuals who instilled in me a love of history. At Centre College, Drs. David Newhall, Max Cavnes, and, especially, Charles Lee made history exciting. The history faculty at the University of Kentucky provided me with a graduate experience second to none, and I am particularly thankful to the members of my doctoral committee, Drs. Lance Banning, Robert Ireland, and Raymond Betts. I am also grateful to Dottie Leathers for her guidance, advice, and friendship.

No one could have enjoyed a more supportive family. My in-laws have encouraged me all through this process. My late father and mother instilled in me an early and deep appreciation for learning; there is no way that I could repay the sacrifices they made so that I might have opportunities that they missed. The affection and encouragement of my brother and sister have always meant much. I am especially grateful to my son, Andrew.

Of all the persons to whom I owe thanks, however, there are two to whom the debt is greatest. If George Herring had only been my dissertation director, my obligation to him would still be significant. He has been a model for which any graduate student would be grateful: an excellent teacher, demanding but caring; an internationally renowned scholar, whose discipline of mind and ease of expression are exceptional. How much greater, then, is my obligation to the George Herring who has become over the years a close friend, one who has shared his time, his encouragement, and his confidence.

The other person to whom I owe a special debt is my wife, Mona. She has been unfailingly patient, unfailingly wise, and unfailingly supportive. She has given me her confidence, her faith, and her love.

It is to these two, George Herring and Mona Gordon Wyatt, that I dedicate this work.

# Notes

CHAPTER 1: A Different Kind of World

1. "The Snag in Atom Control," *New York Times,* August 2, 1946, p. 18. See also "Bomb Legislation," *New York Times,* June 2, 1946; "Atom Control Bill Signed by Truman," *New York Times,* August 2, 1946, p. 7; Harry S. Truman, *Memoirs,* vol. 2: *Years of Trial and Hope* (Garden City, N.Y.: Doubleday, 1956), pp. 2–8, 11, 15.

2. Stanley Karnow, *Vietnam: A History* (New York: Viking, 1983), pp. 152–57; Allan V. Cameron, ed., *Viet-Nam Crisis: A Documentary History,* vol. I: *1940–1956* (Ithaca, N.Y.: Cornell University Press, 1971), pp. 80–84.

3. "We've Made a First Move to End Needless Government Secrecy," *Saturday Evening Post,* December 27, 1958, p. 10.

4. Peter Braestrup, background paper in *Battle Line: Report of the Twentieth Century Fund Task Force on the Military and the Media* (New York: Priority Press, 1985), pp. 27–43; "Who Keeps the Secrets?," *Newsweek,* July 15, 1957, p. 57; reports by Byron Price and Elmer Davis to Government Information Subcommittee of House Government Operations Committee, hearings, 88th Cong., 1st ses., *Government Information Plans and Policies,* pt. 2: *Office of Emergency Planning,* June 5, 1963 (Washington, D.C.: Government Printing Office), pp. 206–56; Phillip Knightley takes a somewhat different point of view, feeling that reporters were more co-opted and controlled than cooperative. See *The First Casualty* (New York: Harcourt Brace Jovanovich, 1975), pp. 330–32.

5. Francis E. Rourke, "Administrative Secrecy: A Congressional Dilemma," *American Political Science Review,* September 1960, pp. 687–88.

6. "Censorship with a Sting," *Business Week,* September 29, 1951, pp.

140–41; David Lawrence, "Our Own 'Iron Curtain,' " *U.S. News and World Report,* October 5, 1951, p. 76.

7. V. M. Newton, Jr., "The Iron Curtain in America," *Look,* February 18, 1958, pp. 115.

8. "Barring the Door," *Time,* October 8, 1951, p. 50; Lawrence, "Our Own 'Iron Curtain,' " p. 76.

9. "Security and Information," *Time,* November 9, 1953, p. 88; "Who Keeps the Secrets?" p. 59; Newton, "Iron Curtain in America," p. 115.

10. "House Group Warns on Barring of Data," *New York Times,* November 4, 1955, p. 11; "Pentagon Accused of 'News Control,' " *New York Times,* January 23, 1959, p. 7: "Secrecy Scored by House Panel," *New York Times,* September 4, 1959, p. 5; "Editors Urge Curb on Federal Secrecy," *New York Times,* November 16, 1958, p. 52; "Transcript of the President's News Conference on Foreign and Domestic Matters," *New York Times,* February 19, 1959, p. 14; "Transcript of the President's News Conference on Foreign and Domestic Matters," *New York Times,* November 5, 1959, p. 16; "We've Made a First Move to End Needless Government Secrecy," *Saturday Evening Post,* December 27, 1958, p. 10; "The Pentagon's Closed Door," *Time,* March 2, 1958, p. 46; "Journalism Group Scores U.S. Secrecy," *New York Times,* November 12, 1959, p. 12.

11. Michael R. Beschloss, *Mayday: Eisenhower, Khrushchev, and the U-2 Affair* (New York: Harper and Row, 1986), pp. 20–23, 140–42; "Flight to Sverdlovsk," *Time,* May 16, 1960, pp. 15–18; "Tracked Toward Trouble," *Time,* May 23, 1960, pp. 12–13; "The Flight of the U-2," *Newsweek,* May 16, 1960, pp. 27–32; "Excerpts from the Questioning of Powers at His Espionage Trial in Moscow," *New York Times,* August 18, 1960, p. 10.

12. Dwight D. Eisenhower, *Waging Peace, 1956–1961* (Garden City, N.Y.: Doubleday, 1965), p. 548; Beschloss, *Mayday,* p. 37; "Excerpts from Censored Transcript of Senate Panel's Hearing on U-2 and Summit," *New York Times,* May 21, 1960, p. 2.

13. "Khrushchev's Remarks on U.S. Plane," *New York Times,* May 6, 1960, p. 2; Osgood Caruthers, "Premier Is Bitter," *New York Times,* May 6, 1960, p. 1; Beschloss, *Mayday,* p. 39.

14. U-2 pilots had been instructed, in what had been considered the unlikely event of capture, to acknowledge as much of the nature of their mission as any evidence made obvious. They were also to identify themselves as civilian pilots for the CIA in order to avoid any interpretation of the flight as an armed attack. ("Tracked Toward Trouble," p. 13; Beschloss, *Mayday,* p. 28.)

15. Eisenhower, *Waging Peace,* p. 549; Beschloss, *Mayday,* p. 47; "Excerpts from Censored Transcript of Senate Panel's Hearing on U-2 and Summit," *New York Times,* May 28, 1960, p. 2.

16. Beschloss, *Mayday,* p. 50.

17. Osgood Caruthers, " 'Confession' Cited," *New York Times,* May 8, 1960, p. 1; Eisenhower, *Waging Peace,* pp. 549–50; Beschloss, *Mayday,* pp. 58–61.

18. "Mr. K Thunders on the Left," *New York Times,* May 7, 1960, p. 22.

19. Beschloss, *Mayday,* pp. 243–44, 246–49; Eisenhower, *Waging Peace,* p. 550; "Excerpts from Censored Transcript," May 28, 1960, p. 2; "Text of the U.S. Statement on Plane," *New York Times,* May 8, 1960, p. 29; James Reston, "Action Explained," *New York Times,* May 8, 1960, p. 1.

20. Beschloss, *Mayday,* pp. 140, 249, 251–53; James Reston, "Flights Stopped," *New York Times,* May 9, 1960, p. 1; Dana Adams Schmidt, "Angry Congressmen Urge Inquiry on Spying Activity," *New York Times,* May 9, 1960, p. 1; Stephen E. Ambrose, *Eisenhower,* vol. II: *The President* (New York: Simon and Schuster, 1984), pp. 574–75; "Many Here Decry Timing of Flight," *New York Times,* May 9, 1960, p. 1; "Crisis in the Cold War," *New York Times,* May 9, 1960, p. 28.

21. Dana Adams Schmidt, "Senate Explodes In Policy Clash," *New York Times,* May 24, 1960, p. 1; Dana Adams Schmidt, "2 Senators Decry U-2 Coordination," *New York Times,* June 6, 1960, p. 5; Russell Baker, "Senators' Report Scores Handling of U-2 Incident," *New York Times,* June 26, 1960, p. 1; "Excerpts from Senate Report on U-2 Incident and 2 Senators' Dissent," *New York Times,* June 26, 1960, p. 31; Russell Baker, "Senate Unit Asks Silence on Spying," *New York Times,* June 17, 1960, p. 1; "Aftermath of the U-2—the Argument Goes On," *U.S. News and World Report,* July 11, 1960, pp. 88–90; Dana Adams Schmidt, "Fulbright Voices Doubt on U-2 Step," *New York Times,* May 30, 1960, p. 1.

22. "Editorial Comment on U.S. Flight Over Soviet Union," *New York Times,* May 10, 1960, p. 15.

23. Ibid.; James Reston, "What Kind of President Do You Want?—III," *New York Times,* May 11, 1960, p. 38; Arthur Krock, "The Enigma in the Pilot Powers Case," *New York Times,* May 10, 1960, p. 36; "Lessons of the U-2," *New York Times,* June 5, 1960, p. 10E.

24. Beschloss, *Mayday,* pp. 234–35; Jack Raymond, "Capital Explains," *New York Times,* May 6, 1960, p. 1; William J. Jorden, "U.S. Asks Details of Plane Incident," *New York Times,* May 6, 1960, p. 1; "U-2 Is Civilian-Piloted, Unarmed Research Jet Plane," *New York Times,* May 6, 1960, p. 7; "List of Clashes on Plane Given," *New York Times,* May 6, 1960, p. 7; "Text of the U.S. Statement on Plane," *New York Times,* May 6, 1960, p. 7. See also other *New York Times* coverage, May 6–11, 1960,

25. "A Peculiar Moral Climate," *Nation,* May 21, 1960, pp. 433–34; Beschloss, *Mayday,* p. 249; "The Press & the U-2," *Time,* May 23, 1960, pp. 34, 36; Norman Cousins, "What Do We Do When We Are Wrong?," *Saturday Review,* May 21, 1960, pp. 30–31; "The President Explains," *New Republic,* June 6, 1960, pp. 3–5; "The Whole Truth—Someday," *New Republic,* December 12, 1960, p. 8.

26. Felix Belair, Jr., "President Asserts Secrecy of Soviet Justifies Spying," *New York Times,* May 12, 1960, p. 1.

27. Beschloss, *Mayday,* pp. 56, 123–25; John D. Morris, "Congress United . . . ," *New York Times,* May 11, 1960, p. 1.

28. "Cold-War Candor," *Time,* May 16, 1960, p. 15. *Time* also hailed the

State Department's "manly candor" and applauded the administration as, "In the end, a week of confusion was washed out with one eminently sensible decision: to tell the truth." Ernest K. Lindley, Washington bureau director for *Newsweek,* commended "the President and Secretary Herter for deciding to bring the whole matter of aerial reconnaissance and other forms of intelligence-gathering into the open and examined in honest perspective" (Ernest K. Lindley, "Cheer for Candor," *Newsweek,* May 23, 1960, p. 59). *The New York Times* also defended Eisenhower's and Herter's "honesty" ("Lessons of the U-2," *New York Times,* June 5, 1960, p. 10E).

29. Eisenhower, *Waging Peace,* p. 558; Beschloss, *Mayday,* p. 50.

CHAPTER 2: Managing the News

1. Russell Baker, " 'Kennedy and Press' Seems a Hit; Star Shows Skill as Showman," *New York Times,* January 26, 1961, p. 12.

2. "How a President Makes News: Kennedy Adds Some New Twists," *U.S. News and World Report,* March 13, 1961, pp. 104–5. Wilson's commitment to meeting with the press was short-lived. After World War I began, Presidential Secretary Joseph P. Tumulty took over the duties of briefing the press.

3. Ibid., pp. 105–6.

4. Baker, " 'Kennedy and Press,' " p. 12.

5. "How a President Makes News," p. 106; Theodore C. Sorensen, *Kennedy* (New York: Harper and Row, 1965) pp. 322–23.

6. Jack Gould, "TV: Sensible Innovation," *New York Times,* January 26, 1961, p. 59; "Press Conference on Live TV," *New York Times,* p. 22.

7. Baker, " 'Kennedy and Press,' " p. 12; Arthur Krock, "Presidential Pace," *New York Times,* February 19, 1961, sec. IV, p. 11; "Opinion of the Week: President Evaluated," *New York Times,* January 29, 1961, sec. IV, p. 11; "Kennedy Press Policy Hailed by 2 Democrats," *New York Times,* February 1, 1961, p. 25.

8. Sorensen, *Kennedy,* pp. 322–27; Joseph A. Loftus, "Preparation Key to News Sessions," *New York Times,* March 29, 1962, p. 16; "J.F.K. and Conference," *Time,* March 24, 1961, p. 44; Worth Bingham and Ward Just, "The President and the Press," *Reporter,* February 12, 1962, pp. 20–21; Karl E. Meyer, "JFK's Pressmanship," *New Statesman,* February 23, 1962, p. 253.

9. The luster of both these accomplishments is somewhat diminished if there is truth to the rumor that father Joe's financial involvement was largely responsible for *Why England Slept* and that a ghostwriter had a significant hand in *Profiles in Courage.* See Herbert S. Parmet, *Jack: The Struggles of John F. Kennedy* (New York: Dial, 1980), pp. 68–78, 230–33.

10. William S. White, "Kennedy's Seven Rules for Handling the Press," *Harper's,* April 1961, p. 94.

11. Bingham and Just, "President and Press," p. 19; Parmet, *Jack,* pp. 72, 191.

12. Letter, Joseph C. Alsop to Ted Sorensen, November 10, 1960, General Correspondence, Joseph C. Alsop Papers, folder 1, box 17, Library of Congress; Herbert S. Parmet, *JFK: The Presidency of John F. Kennedy* (New York: Dial, 1983), pp. 2, 23: David Halberstam, *The Powers That Be* (New York: Alfred A. Knopf, 1979), p. 375.

13. Parmet, *Jack,* p. 221; Bingham and Just, "President and Press," p. 19. The *Chattanooga Times* was the profitable newspaper that provided the base for owner and publisher Adoph Ochs's 1896 purchase of the moribund *New York Times.* See Halberstam, *Powers That Be,* pp. 208–11.

14. Parmet, *Jack,* p. 258; Bingham and Just, "President and Press," p. 19; Halberstam, *Powers That Be,* p. 352; Lewis J. Paper, *The Promise and the Performance: The Leadership of John F. Kennedy* (New York: Crown, 1975), pp. 321–22.

15. Halberstam, *Powers That Be,* pp. 352–55.

16. Theodore H. White, *The Making of the President, 1960* (New York: Atheneum, 1961), pp. 336–38; Pierre Salinger, *With Kennedy* (Garden City, N.Y.: Doubleday, 1966), pp. 31–33, 46–47. *"Stuff* the bastards. They're all against Dick anyway" was the succinct and expressive explanation of Nixon's attitude toward the press given to Teddy White by one of the vice-president's advisers in June 1960. Nixon regarded the campaign reporters as "a hostile conspiracy," one that was to be, at best, tolerated. For example, while Kennedy assiduously wooed Henry Luce, Nixon treated the most powerful publisher in the nation almost disdainfully. See White, pp. 335–36.

17. Salinger, *With Kennedy,* p. 299.

18. Ibid., pp. 135–36; "Salinger Pledges Free News Flow," *New York Times,* January 25, 1961, p. 20.

19. "Transcript of the President's News Conference," *New York Times,* January 26, 1961, p. 10.

20. Jack Raymond, "Military Curbed on 'Tough' Talks," *New York Times,* January 28, 1961, p. 1.

21. "Random Notes in Washington: President Finds Secrets Aren't," *New York Times,* May 20, 1961, p. 14; "Lemnitzer Scores Leaks of Secrets," *New York Times,* March 24, 1961, p. 17; Hugh Sidey, *John F. Kennedy, President* (New York: Atheneum, 1964), pp. 100–101.

22. "U.S. to Curb Data About Satellites," *New York Times,* February 12, 1961, p. 21; Jack Raymond, "Administration Tightens Curbs on Publicity from the Pentagon," *New York Times,* April 14, 1961, p. 9.

23. "U.S. Curbs on Missile Test," *New York Times,* April 22, 1961, p. 12; "U.S. Tightens Its Restrictions on Pentagon Intelligence Data," *New York Times,* May 13, 1961, p. 1; "U.S. Moving to Cut Intelligence Leaks," *New York Times,* September 28, 1961, p. 41; "LeMay Interview Is Cleared for TV," *New York Times,* July 23, 1961, p. 44; Jack Raymond, "Pentagon Blocks Articles Written by Generals for Air Force Professional Journal," *New York Times,* October 11, 1961, p. 21; *Government Information Plans and Policies,* report, House Foreign Operations and Government Information Subcommittee, 1963, (Washington, D.C.: Government Printing Office),

pt. 3, p. 297 (Sylvester denied any knowledge of such use of the FBI). Even though the administration focused primarily on what it deemed national-security information, it sought to limit unauthorized disclosures throughout the Executive Branch. In language similar to that used by the 1957 Wright Commission recommendations, which were rejected by Eisenhower amid sharp criticism, the White House in 1961 issued a new code of conduct that prohibited federal employees from releasing *any* "official information." The White House offered no definition of such information, though Salinger denied that it was intended to create "a new information classification." See "Ethics Code Given to Federal Aides," *New York Times,* July 27, 1961, p. 1.

24. "G.O.P. Attacks Salinger and English Language," *New York Times,* January 26, 1961, p. 20; "Goldwater Asks If 'Gag Rule' Is Aim," *New York Times,* January 31, 1961, p. 19; "White House Scored on Its News Policy," *New York Times,* March 23, 1961, p. 15; "G.O.P. Says Salinger Is 'Hiding The Truth,' " *New York Times,* June 24, 1961, p. 8; "G.O.P. Chief Scores Kennedy News Staff," *New York Times,* October 7, 1961, p. 24.

25. "Report to Editors Criticizes Kennedy," *New York Times,* April 19, 1961, p. 6; Sidey, *John F. Kennedy,* p. 99.

26. Bingham and Just, "President and the Press," pp. 18–21.

27. "The Kennedy Image," *U.S. News and World Report,* April 9, 1962, pp. 56–58; Paper, *Promise and Performance,* p. 323; and Fletcher Knebel, "Kennedy vs. the Press," *Look,* August 28, 1962, pp. 17–21.

28. Bingham and Just, "President and Press," pp. 18–21; Henry Brandon, Washington correspondent of the London *Sunday Times,* in Paper, *Promise and Performance,* p. 323; "The Kennedy 'Image'—How It's Built," *U.S. News and World Report,* April 9, 1962, pp. 56–58; Fletcher Knebel, "Kennedy vs. the Press," *Look,* August 28, 1962, pp. 17–21.

29. "Secrecy Issue Raised," *New York Times,* March 8, 1961, p. 12; "Secrecy Held Waning," *New York Times,* April 16, 1961, p. 38; White, "Kennedy's Seven Rules," pp. 95–97; letter, Joseph Alsop to Ted Sorensen, March 7, 1961, folder 4, box 17, General Correspondence, Joseph Alsop Papers, Library of Congress; Schlesinger in Paper, *Promise and Performance,* pp. 250–51.

30. Dwight D. Eisenhower, *Waging Peace, 1956–1961* (Garden City, N.Y.: Doubleday, 1965), pp. 521–27.

31. Ibid., p. 524.

32. Ibid., pp. 524–25.

33. Ibid., pp. 612–14; David Halberstam, *The Best and the Brightest* (New York: Random House, 1972), pp. 66–68; Roger Hilsman, *To Move a Nation: The Politics of Foreign Policy in the Administration of John F. Kennedy* (Garden City, N.Y.: Doubleday, 1967), pp. 30–33.

34. Halberstam, *Best and Brightest,* pp. 66–68; "The Massacre," *Time,* April 28, 1961, pp. 19–23.

35. "Bitter Week," *Time,* April 28, 1961, pp. 11–12; "Text of Address by President to U.S. Editors," *New York Times,* April 20, 1961, p. 2.

36. Bernhard M. Auer, "A Letter from the Publisher," *Time,* April 28, 1961, p. 9.

37. Halberstam, *Powers That Be,* pp. 373–75, 447–48; Gay Talese, *The Kingdom and the Power* (New York: World Publishing Company, 1969), pp. 4–5; Harrison Salisbury, *Without Fear or Favor* (New York: Ballantine, 1980), pp. 137–57.

38. Salisbury, *Without Fear,* p. 158; Halberstam, *Powers That Be,* p. 448.

39. John F. Kennedy, "The President and the Press," speech presented to the American Newspaper Publishers Association, April 27, 1961; reprinted in *Vital Speeches,* May 15, 1961, pp. 450–52.

40. "News Media Wary on Curbing Facts," *New York Times,* April 29, 1961, p. 21; "Press Is Divided on Kennedy Talk," *New York Times,* April 30, 1961, p. 68. See also "The Meaning of Freedom," *Time,* May 5, 1961, p. 38; "News—and Responsibility," *Newsweek,* May 8, 1961, pp. 24–25; "News and National Interest," *Christian Century,* May 17, 1961, pp. 611–12; Francis P. Rourke, "How Much Should the Government Tell?," *Saturday Review,* May 13, 1961, pp. 17–19, 31. There were some dissenting views within the press. For example, the Catholic Journal *America* hailed Kennedy's speech and criticized publishers for continuing to think of "the U.S. press in terms of local or national politics, rather than in terms of the world ideological struggle" ("Press Responsibility," *America,* May 13, 1961, p. 270). James Hagerty, former Eisenhower press secretary who had gone on to become vice-president for news at ABC, also supported Kennedy strongly ("News Media Wary," p. 21).

41. "Kennedy Pledges Free News Access," *New York Times,* May 10, 1961, p. 3; "Whose News?," *Newsweek,* May 22, 1961, p. 88; "No Self Censorship," *Time,* May 19, 1961, p. 48; "Censorship Is Opposed," *New York Times,* May 22, 1961, p. 9.

42. James Reston, "The President and the Press—the Old Dilemma," *New York Times,* May 10, 1961, p. 44.

43. Raymond L. Garthoff, *Reflections on the Cuban Missile Crisis* (Washington, D.C.: Brookings Institution, 1987), p. 5. For a full account of Operation Mongoose see *Alleged Assassination Plots Involving Foreign Leaders,* interim report of Senate Select Committee to Study Governmental Operations with Respect to Intelligence Activities, Senate Report 94-465, 94th Cong., 1st sess., November 20, 1975 (Washington, D.C.: Government Printing Office, 1975).

44. Garthoff, *Reflections,* pp. 6–12.

45. Ibid., p. 14; Elie Abel, *The Missile Crisis* (Philadelphia: J. B. Lippincott, 1966), pp. 12–13. CIA Director John McCone was one of the few senior members of the Kennedy national-security bureaucracy to suspect early that the Soviets were installing ballistic missiles in Cuba.

46. Garthoff, *Reflections,* pp. 16–17; "Press and President," *Time,* September 21, 1962, pp. 48–49.

47. For accounts of the crisis itself see Abel, *Missile Crisis;* Garthoff,

*Reflections;* Sorensen, *Kennedy;* Parmet, *JFK;* Arthur M. Schlesinger, Jr., *A Thousand Days: John F. Kennedy in the White House* (Boston: Houghton, Mifflin, 1965).

48. Schlesinger, *Thousand Days,* pp. 809–10; Abel, *Missile Crisis,* pp. 98–99; Parmet, *JFK,* pp. 290–91; Salisbury, *Without Fear,* p. 161.

49. Salisbury, *Without Fear,* p. 161.

50. James Reston testimony before Subcommittee on Foreign Operations and Government Information, House Government Operations Committee, hearings, 88th Cong., 1st sess., May 19, 1963; printed as *Government Information Plans and Policies, pt. 1: News Media Panel Discussion.* (Washington, D.C.: Government Printing Office, 1963), p. 57; "The Press as a Public Issue," *Reporter,* December 6, 1962, pp. 18–19; "Managing the News," *Commonweal,* December 21, 1962, p. 327.

51. John H. Coburn, "Summary of News Management and Control by Federal Government," reprinted in *Government Information Plans and Policies, pt. 1,* p. 14. Coburn, editor of the *Richmond Times-Dispatch,* was chairman of the ASNE's Freedom of Information Committee.

52. Ibid., pp. 12, 14.

53. E. W. Kenworthy, "President Ending News Curbs; Defends Secrecy During Crisis," *New York Times,* November 21, 1962, p. 1.

54. Testimony of Arthur Sylvester, assistant secretary of defense for public affairs, before Subcommittee on Foreign Operations and Government Information, House Committee on Government Operations, hearings, Subcommittee on Foreign Operations and Government Information, House Government Operations Committee, House of Representatives, 88th Cong., 1st sess., May 27–28, 1963; printed as *Government Information Plans and Policies, pt. 3: Information Procedures in the Defense Department* (Washington, D.C.: Government Printing Office, 1963), pp. 273, 310; statements of Gene Robb and W. J. Coughlin and testimony of Sylvester in *Government Information Plans and Policies,* pt. 1, pp. 7, 34, 144–45.

55. Arthur Sylvester, "Memorandum for Department of Defense Personnel," October 27, 1962, exhibit III in *Government Information Plans and Policies,* pt. 3, p. 355; Robert Manning testimony in *Government Information Plans and Policies,* pt. 1, p. 87. The State Department directive was issued October 31. Manning stated that his department's directive originated internally, the result of four or five months of discussion, and was not sent down from the White House.

56. "White House Memorandum to Editors and Radio and Television News Directors," October 24, 1962, exhibit IV-A in *Government Information Plans and Policies,* pt. 3, p. 356. The specific categories were stated as follows:

(1) Any discussion of plans for employment of strategic or tactical forces of the United States including types of equipment and new or planned locations of command or control centers or detection systems.

(2) Estimates of U.S. capability of destroying targets, including numbers of weapons required, size and character of forces required, ability of these

forces to penetrate defenses, and accuracy or reliability of our forces or weapons systems.

(3) Intelligence estimates concerning targets or target systems, such as numbers, types, and locations of aiming points in the target system, enemy missile and bomber forces, etc.

(4) Intelligence estimates of enemy plans or capabilities, or information which would reveal the level of success of U.S. intelligence efforts or operations with respect to Cuba or the Communist bloc.

(5) Details as to numbers or movements of U.S. forces, including naval units and vessels, aircraft, missile forces or ground forces, ammunition, equipment, etc. Announcement may be made of such unit movements after the movement has been completed.

(6) Degree of alert of military forces.

(7) Location of aircraft or supporting equipment. Presence of aircraft observable in the public domain may be confirmed.

(8) Emergency dispersal plans of aircraft or units including dispersal capabilities, times, schedules or logistical support.

(9) Official estimates of vulnerability to various forms of enemy action, including sabotage, of U.S. Armed Forces and installations.

(10) New data concerning operational missile distribution, numbers, operational readiness. Estimates of effectiveness of strike capability of missile forces.

(11) Details of command and control systems, including new or planned command posts and facilities, estimates of ability to survive enemy attack, security measures, etc. including sea or airborne commend posts.

(12) Details of airlift or sealift capabilities, including size and nature of forces to be lifted, time limits for such lifts, and supply capabilities, with respect to possible specific areas of operation.

57. Kenworthy, "President Ending News Curbs," p. 1; Robert Manning testimony in *Government Information Plans and Policies*, pt. 1, pp. 85, 110; "Salinger Disavows Managing the News but Accuses Editors," *New York Times*, March 23, 1963, p. 1.

58. Partial transcript of tape recording of Sylvester's remarks to United States Air Force public-affairs officers meeting in Las Vegas, Nevada, October 29, 1962, reprinted as exhibit V-B in *Government Information Plans and Policies*, pt. 3, p. 360; Coburn, "Summary," p. 15; "U.S. Aide Defends Lying to Nation," *New York Times*, December 7, 1962, p. 5.

59. "Classic Conflict: The President and the Press," *Time*, December 14, 1962, p. 45. In this and other comments on information issues during the crisis, *Time* downplayed any cause for conflict. "One reason for the perfunctory quality of some of the press criticism is that, during two years in office, Kennedy had committed no serious offenses against press freedom. Even when he buttoned official Washington up tight during the Cuban crisis, the news still flowed." See also "Quarantining the News," *Time*, November 2, 1962, p. 60. It should be pointed out that *Time*'s favorable disposition toward Kennedy information policies could have been inspired at least in part

by the White House's persistent courting of its publisher, Henry Luce, and, especially, its White House correspondent, Hugh Sidey; see Halberstam, *Powers That Be,* pp. 351–63.

60. The phrase "news management" was coined in 1955 by James Reston to describe Eisenhower information policies during the Geneva summit meeting with Khrushchev ("Salinger Disavows"; "How Much Management of the News?," *Newsweek,* April 8, 1963, p. 60).

61. "Managing the News," *New York Times,* October 31, 1962, p. 36; "Managing the News," *Commonweal,* December 21, 1962, pp. 327–28; "The Great Teacher Sylvester," *Nation,* December 22, 1963, pp. 433–34. See also: Arthur Krock, "Mr. Kennedy's Management of the News," *Fortune,* March 1963, p. 82; Richard C. Tobin, "News as a Weapon," *Saturday Review,* December 8, 1962, pp. 61–62; "In Defense of Truth," *Nation,* January 12, 1963, pp. 22–23; Mary McGrory, "Strictly Off the Record, Gentlemen!," *America,* March 16, 1963, p. 356; "How News Is 'Managed' by Officials in Washington," *U.S. News and World Report,* April 15, 1963, pp. 38–42; "Editor Finds Danger in U.S. News Policy," *New York Times,* April 18, 1963, p. 19; Peter Kihss, "U.S. Urged to Ban Slanting of News," *New York Times,* April 25, 1963, p. 17; James Magmer, "News Management Is Still a Live Issue," *Catholic World,* June 1963, pp. 180–86.

62. Letter, Joseph Alsop to John F. Kennedy, November 24, 1962, General Correspondence, Joseph Alsop Papers, folder 5, box 18, Library of Congress.

63. Walter Lippmann, "Managed News," *Newsweek,* April 15, 1963, p. 23; Lester Markel, "The 'Management' of News," *Saturday Review,* February 9, 1963, p. 51; William V. Kennedy, "The Press and National Defense," *America,* November 3, 1962, p. 974, and "Mr. Salinger's 12 Points," *America,* November 17, 1962, p. 1084; James Reston, "How Adam, Miss Eve, 'Managed the News,' " *New York Times,* March 20, 1963, p. 6; Richard Horchler, "Managing the News," *Commonweal,* March 22, 1963, pp. 12, 513; Karl E. Meyer, "Kennedy and the Press," *New Statesman,* April 12, 1963, p. 513; See also "All the News That Manages to Fit," *National Review,* March 12, 1963, pp. 182–83; Hanson W. Baldwin, "Managed News: Our Peacetime Censorship," *Atlantic Monthly,* April 1963, pp. 53–59; Max Ascoli, "A Few Anguished Questions," *Reporter,* April 25, 1963, p. 22; "Don't Swallow Everything," *Time,* March 29, 1963, p. 51.

64. "How Much Management of the News?" *Newsweek,* April 8, 1963, p. 61; See also "Furor over 'Managed' News," *U.S. News and World Report,* April 8, 1963, p. 103. "Nixon Criticizes Kennedy on Cuba," *New York Times,* March 9, 1963, p. 2; Tom Wicker, "Storm Clouds of '64," *New York Times,* March 11, 1963, p. 14.

65. "Rusk Aides Told to Report Talks," *New York Times,* November 2, 1962, p. 15; *Government Information Plans and Policies,* pt. 1, pp. 128, 131–32.

66. The segments of the hearings discussed here are the previously cited *Government Information Plans and Policies,* pts. 1 and 3. The other two sets

of hearings, pts. 2 and 4, dealt with planning for wartime censorship and news coverage of Vietnam, respectively.

67. Meyer, "Kennedy and the Press," p. 513.

68. Tom Wicker, *On Press* (New York: Viking, 1978), pp. 1–19. See also Halberstam, *Powers That Be.*

69. Wicker, *On Press*, pp. 1–19; Salisbury, *Without Fear*, pp. 378–90. *Sullivan v. The New York Times* involved a criminal libel suit filed by local officials in Birmingham, Alabama, against the *Times* and Harrison Salisbury for 1960 coverage of race relations in that city. The ruling, issued on March 9, 1964, established that public officials could not recover damages "for a defamatory falsehood relating to his official conduct unless he proves that the statement was made with 'actual malice,' that is with knowledge that it was false or with reckless disregard of whether it was false or not." Salisbury, Without Fear or Favor, p. 388.

70. Lippmann, "Managed News," p. 23.

71. *Government Information Plans and Policies*, pt. 1, pp. 68, 71–72.

CHAPTER 3: Dramatize the Truth

1. "U.S. Made Target of Vietminh Fete," *New York Times*, January 3, 1955, p. 6; "Vietminh Enters Conformity Era," *New York Times*, January 5, 1955, p. 7. The reporter was probably Tillman Durdin, who was covering the Far East for the *Times* in 1955.

2. Dana Adams Schmidt, "Saigon's Premier Gaining Strength," *New York Times*, January 20, 1955, p. 3.

3. "Demonstration in Hanoi," *New York Times*, January 5, 1955, p. 20; "Hope in Vietnam," *New York Times*, January 24, 1955, p. 14.

4. The definition of "mainstream press" used here is for the most part subjective. It looked to include mass-circulation general-interest news agencies rather than journals of opinion, with national reach and some sort of foreign-news component. In the period under discussion, this came down essentially to the wire services, the *New York Times*, *Time*, *Newsweek*, and *U.S. News and World Report*. *Life* magazine was examined, but not really included in this group, for it was not as devoted to the sort of coverage the other magazines provided. The television networks were excluded for two reasons. First, there simply is no record of television news broadcasts until 1965. Second, the evening news broadcasts, the backbone of television journalism, were extremely modest operations until the 1960s. The average temperature in Saigon ranges between eighty-five degrees Fahrenheit in summer and seventy-eight degrees Fahrenheit in winter, according to the 1988 edition of *Collier's Encyclopedia*.

5. George C. Herring, *America's Longest War, 1950–1975*, 2nd ed. (New York: Alfred A. Knopf, 1986), pp. 11–20; Ronald H. Spector, *Advice and Support: The Early Years, 1941–1960* (Washington, D.C.: Center for Military History, 1983), pp. 115–16.

6. Herring, *America's Longest War*, pp. 28–41; Spector, *Advice and Support*, pp. 182–214; Stanley Karnow, *Vietnam: A History* (New York: Viking, 1983), pp. 188–205.

7. Peggy Durdin, "Uncle Ho's Disciplined Joy," *New Yorker*, December 17, 1955, p. 140; Tillman Durdin memo to *Times Talk*, internal newsletter of *The New York Times*, February 1951, reprinted in Ruth Adler, ed., *The Working Press: Special to the New York Times* (New York: Putnam's 1966), pp. 96–97.

8. Durdin in Adler, ed., *Working Press*, p. 97.

9. William M. Hammond, *Public Affairs: The Military and the Media, 1962–1968* (Washington, D.C.: Center for Military History, 1988), p. 7.

10. Otto Friedrich, "How to Be a War Correspondent," *Yale Review*, March 1959, pp. 474–80.

11. For example, in May 1954, *Time* had fourteen foreign bureaus staffed by twenty-eight correspondents. In the same month, *Newsweek* had five foreign bureaus staffed by eight reporters, while *U.S. News* had six bureaus essentially staffed by five "regional editors." The *Times* listed twenty-eight foreign "offices," a number of which were more business offices than full-fledged news bureaus. See Edwin Emery and Michael Emery, *An Interpretative History of the Mass Media*, 6th ed. (New York: Prentice-Hall, 1988); David Halberstam, *The Powers That Be* (New York: Alfred A. Knopf, 1979); and Eric Barnouw, *The Tube of Plenty: The Evolution of American Television* (New York: Oxford University Press, 1975).

12. Friedrich, "War Correspondent," pp. 478–79.

13. *Time*'s man in Saigon, John Mecklin, would later gain a degree of notoriety as the chief public-information officer for the United States in South Vietnam in 1962–63.

14. Friedrich, "War Correspondent," pp. 474–75.

15. Ibid., pp. 475–79.

16. Ibid., pp. 478–79.

17. Herring, *America's Longest War*, pp. 44–45; Karnow, *Vietnam*, p. 224; Spector, *Advice and Support*, pp. 228–29.

18. Herring, *America's Longest War*, pp. 57, 60–61; Spector, *Advice and Support*, pp. 229–30, 250, 254; "The Beleaguered Man," *Time*, April 4, 1955, pp. 22–25.

19. Spector, *Advice and Support*, pp. 229–30, 250, 254; "The Beleaguered Man," *Time*, April 4, 1955, pp. 22–25; Herring, *America's Longest War*, pp. 57, 60–61.

20. Dana Adams Schmidt, "Saigon's Premier Gaining Strength," *New York Times*, January 29, 1955, p. 3; C. L. Sulzberger, "Trying to Build Stability in Vietnam," *New York Times*, March 12, 1955, p. 18; "Crisis in Vietnam," *New York Times*, March 28, 1955, p. 26.

21. C. L. Sulzberger, "Diem Opposes Allied Policy in Vietnam," *New York Times*, June 8, 1955, p. 28; "What We're Doing in Indochina," *U.S. News and World Report*, March 4, 1955, p. 82; Joseph Alsop, "Quemoy-Poland," *Washington Post and Times Herald*, April 11, 1955, p. 9.

22. Karnow, *Vietnam,* pp. 218–19; "Night of Despair," p. 33.

23. "Beleaguered Man," pp. 22–25; Karnow, *Vietnam,* pp. 213–18; Herring, *America's Longest War,* pp. 48–49.

24. "Tremors from Washington," *Time,* May 2, 1955, p. 34.

25. "Beleaguered Man," p. 22; "U.S. in Middle of a Gang War," *U.S. News and World Report,* May 13, 1955, p. 40; "Civil War: Invitation to the Reds," *Newsweek,* May 9, 1955, p. 36.

26. Herring, *America's Longest War,* pp. 52–53.

27. A. M. Rosenthal, "Saigon Is Swept by Civil War; Big Area Is Afire," *New York Times,* April 29, 1955, p. 1; A. M. Rosenthal, "Vietnam Premier Clings to Power As Rival Flees; Given Bao Dai New Chance," *New York Times,* May 2, 1955, p. 1; "The Revolt That Failed," *Time,* May 9, 1955, pp. 24–25; Herring, *America's Longest War,* p. 54.

28. Rosenthal, "Saigon Is Swept"; Rosenthal, "Vietnam Premier"; "The Revolt That Failed," p. 24; "Civil War," pp. 36–37; "Milder Message Is Sent by Bao Dai," *New York Times,* May 2, 1955, p. 7; Herring, *America's Longest War,* p. 43; "Agreement of a Sort," *Time,* May 23, 1955, p. 39; Henry Lieberman, "Diem Wins Poll in South Vietnam, Ousting Bao Dai," *New York Times,* October 24, 1955, p. 1; "The Red or the Green," *Time,* October 17, 1955, p. 40.

29. Schmidt, "Saigon's Premier," p. 3; "Hope in Vietnam," p. 14. See also "Hopeful Outlook for Free Vietnam Reported Offered by General Collins," *New York Times,* January 28, 1955, p. 1; "New Gains for Vietnam," *New York Times,* February 15, 1955, p. 26; "Struggle Weird in South Vietnam," *New York Times,* April 29, 1955, p. 3; "Crisis in Vietnam," p. 26; Sulzberger, "Trying to Build Stability," p. 18; Rosenthal, "Saigon Is Swept," p. 1; "Tragedy in Saigon," *New York Times,* April 30, 1955, p. 16.

30. Joseph Alsop, "The Rooted and the Rootless," *Washington Post and Times Herald,* April 1, 1955, p. 35; Joseph Alsop, "The Major Casualty," *Washington Post and Times Herald,* April 4, 1955, p. 9.

31. "What We're Doing in Indochina," *U.S. News and World Report,* March 4, 1955, p. 32; "British Get Jump in Red Trade," *U.S. News and World Report,* April 8, 1955, p. 32; "U.S. in Middle of a Gang War," p. 39; "Beleaguered Man," p. 22; "Decision and Indecision," p. 34; "Tremors from Washington," *Time,* May 2, 1955, p. 34.

32. "Sparks of Rebellion," *Newsweek,* April 11, 1955, p. 44; "Beleaguered," p. 42; "Decline—and Fall?" *Newsweek,* May 2, 1955, p. 34.

33. "Madness in Vietnam," *New York Times,* February 24, 1955, p. 8E; Foster Hailey, "South Vietnam Head Escapes as Gunman Fires at Him at Fair," *New York Times,* February 23, 1957, p. 1; Foster Hailey, "Man from Vietnam," *New York Times Magazine,* May 5, 1957, p. 25; "An Asian Liberator," *New York Times,* May 10, 1957, p. 13; "Country at Peace," *Time,* February 11, 1957, p. 30; "Foreign Aid Repaid," *Time,* May 20, 1957, p. 25; Ernest K. Lindley, "A Friend Named Diem," *Newsweek,* May 20, 1957, p. 40; "Indo-China: Another Place Where Reds Are Losing," *U.S. News and World Report,* March 1, 1957, p. 83. The tributes to South Viet-

nam's success and Diem's leadership continued in the following years. See Greg MacGregor, "Vietnam Assists in Making Farms," *New York Times,* February 22, 1958, p. 2; Tillman Durdin, "Saigon Planning Big Export Gains," *New York Times,* July 3, 1958, p. 3; "South Vietnam Is Still Free," *New York Times,* October 30, 1958, p. 30; "Vietnam: Stability," *Newsweek,* February 17, 1958, p. 48; Tillman Durdin, "Vietnam Plateau Is Being Settled," *New York Times,* April 4, 1959, p. 10; "The Threat to Vietnam," *New York Times,* October 24, 1959, p. 20; "South Vietnam Wins Specialists' Praise," *New York Times,* October 24, 1959, p. 22; Joseph Alsop, "The Asian Thunderclouds," *Washington Post and Times Herald,* April 27, 1960, p. A17.

34. E. W. Kenworthy, "3 Top Officials Deny 'Scandal' in Aid from U.S. to Vietnam," *New York Times,* July 31, 1959, p. 4; E. W. Kenworthy, "Steel Bid Is Cited at Inquiry on Aid," *New York Times,* August 1, 1959, p. 4; E. W. Kenworthy, "Correspondent Disputes Charge U.S. Aid in Vietnam Is 'Fiasco,' " *New York Times,* August 12, 1959, p. 2; "Vietnam Aid Charge Is Called Unproved," *New York Times,* August 15, 1959, p. 2.

35. Tillman Durdin, "Red Activities Up in South Vietnam," *New York Times,* April 13, 1959, p. 3; "Two U.S. Soldiers Slain in Vietnam," *New York Times,* July 10, 1959, p. 1; "Vietnam Troops Rout Communist Guerrillas," *New York Times,* October 31, 1959, p. 2; Herring, *America's Longest War,* pp. 69–70; "Vietnamese Reds Step Up Killings," *New York Times,* April 17, 1960, p. 27; "Vietnamese Troops Attacked," *New York Times,* February 3, 1960, p. 9; Tillman Durdin, "Peasants Shifted by South Vietnam," *New York Times,* April 29, 1960, p. 3; Tillman Durdin, "Reds Push Drive in South Vietnam," *New York Times,* May 2, 1960, p. 13; "Saigon Force Kills 26 Reds," *New York Times,* October 30, 1960, p. 25; "Vietnam-Red Battle Reported," *New York Times,* November 3, 1960, p. 5; "Reds in Vietnam Kill U.S. Aide in Ambush," *New York Times,* November 1, 1960, p. 1; Jacques Nevard, "Aggression Laid to Vietnam Reds," *New York Times,* November 9, 1960, p. 37. See also "Where Reds Are Trying to Grab Another Country," *U.S. News and World Report,* May 2, 1960, p. 44.

36. Tillman Durdin, "Dictatorial Rule In Saigon Charged," *New York Times,* May 1, 1960, p. 1; "New Party's Attack Ignored," *New York Times,* May 2, 1960, p. 13; Tillman Durdin, "Criticism Rising in South Vietnam," *New York Times,* May 27, 1960, p. 4; Robert P. Martin, "Where Danger Threatens Another U.S.-Backed Country," *U.S. News and World Report,* May 16, 1960, p. 120.

37. "Regime in Saigon Is Overthrown, Rebel Units Say," *New York Times,* November 11, 1960, p. 1; "Washington Hears of Ouster," *New York Times,* November 11, 1960, p. 8; "Ngo's Firm Rule Irritated Many," *New York Times,* November 11, 1960, p. 8; "Upheavals in Vietnam and Laos Have Roots in Indochina War," *New York Times,* November 12, 1960, p. 2; "Southeast Asia Stirs," *New York Times,* November 13, 1960, sec. IV, p. 1; Tillman Durdin, "Southeast Asia Unrest Grows," *New York Times,* November 13, 1960, sec. IV, p. 8; "Failure of a Coup," *New York Times,* November 13, 1960, sec. IV, p. 10; "Revolt at Dawn," *Time,* November 21,

1960, p. 27; "Costly Victory in Vietnam," *Life,* November 28, 1960, p. 30; "Stand at Saigon," *Newsweek,* November 21, 1960, p. 44.

38. For example, in April 1955 national police held and beat United Press correspondent Louis Gilbert ("Saigon Arrest Scored," *New York Times,* April 20, 1955, p. 15). Later that year, Lucien Bodard, longtime Vietnam correspondent for *France-Soir,* was expelled, as was Max Clos of *Le Monde* ("Saigon Ousts Writer," *New York Times,* November 18, 1955, p. 7).

39. Douglass Cater and Walter Pincus, "The Foreign Legion of U.S. Public Relations," *Reporter,* December 12, 1960, p. 20.

40. "U.S. Backers Form Group," *New York Times,* December 2, 1955, p. 3. Sanders, who had been friends with Diem since 1952, was a member of the Friends' executive committee while covering the country for various publications. When Diem visited the United States in May 1957, most of his speeches were written by either Sanders or Joseph Buttinger. (Francis Faulkner, "Bao Chi: The American News Media in Vietnam, 1960–1975," unpublished Ph.D. dissertation, University of Massachusetts, 1981, pp. 15–18.)

41. "Origins of the Insurgency in South Vietnam, 1954–1960," *The Pentagon Papers* (Senator Gravel ed.) (Boston: Beacon Press, 1971), vol. I, p. 267.

42. Ibid., pp. 252, 266–67.

43. Cater and Pincus, "Foreign Legion," pp. 18–19; "Whose News?," *New Republic,* November 25, 1957, p. 5; Adrian Jaffe and Milton C. Taylor, "A Crumbling Bastion," *New Republic,* June 10, 1961, p. 20; Alsop, "Major Casualty," p. 9.

44. Stanley Karnow, "Diem Defeats His Own Best Troops," *Reporter,* January 19, 1961, pp. 24–29; Herring, *America's Longest War,* pp. 76–76; *Pentagon Papers* (Gravel), vol. II, pp. 1, 20, 633–35.

45. *Pentagon Papers* (Gravel), vol. II, pp. 18, 73: Karnow, *Vietnam,* p. 248.

46. "Laos: At the Brink," *Newsweek,* April 3, 1961, p. 21; Herring, *America's Longest War,* p. 77.

47. Rostow to McGeorge Bundy, January 30, 1961, John F. Kennedy Papers, National Security File, box 193, JFK Library; *Pentagon Papers* (Gravel), vol. II, pp. 19, 50, 59–60, 63; Herring, *America's Longest War,* pp. 77–79; Karnow, *Vietnam,* p. 250.

48. *Pentagon Papers* (Gravel), vol. II, pp. 51, 60, 63, 68–71.

49. Ibid., pp. 26, 54–55, 59; Rostow to M. Bundy, January 30, 1961, Kennedy Papers, National Security File, box 193; Herring, *America's Longest War,* pp. 78–80; Karnow, *Vietnam,* p. 250.

50. *Pentagon Papers* (Gravel), vol. II, p. 18. See also a series of Joseph Alsop columns, all from the *Washington Post,* including "The Crunch," March 6, 1961, p. A13; "Where Is the Line?," March 10, 1961, p. A17; "The Pickle We're In," April 10, 1961, p. A11; "The Hollow Conference," May 22, 1961, p. A17.

51. "A Program of Action to Prevent Communist Domination of South Vietnam," Report of the Vietnam Task Force, April 26, 1961, Kennedy Papers, National Security File, box 193.

52. Durbrow to Rusk, April 12, 1961, Kennedy Papers, National Security

File, box 193; Joseph Alsop, "Colonel Thao's War," *Washington Post,* April 12, 1961, p. A17; Joseph Alsop, "Warnings Aplenty," *Washington Post,* April 11, 1961, p. A17; "Poor Neighbor," *Time,* March 31, 1961, p. 16; Joseph Alsop, "The Double Standard," *Washington Post,* April 19, 1961, p. A17; Joseph Alsop "Cloud over Southeast Asia," *Washington Post,* October 6, 1961, p. A17; Joseph Alsop, "Gen. Giap and Gen. Taylor," *Washington Post,* October 23, 1961, p. A17; Joseph Alsop, "Solid Proof of 'Aggression,' " *Washington Post,* October 21, 1961, p. A19; Joseph Alsop, "The Pseudo-Taylor Report," *Washington Post,* October 27, 1961, p. 33; Robert P. Martin, "If GI's Go to Vietnam—the Way It Looks Out There," *U.S. News and World Report,* November 6, 1961, p. 39; Jack Raymond, "Washington Due to Press for Reform in Vietnam," *New York Times,* November 5, 1961, p. 1.

53. "A Program of Action"; Durbrow to Rusk, March 11, 1961, Kennedy Papers, National Security File, box 193.

54. Nolting to Rusk for Vice President Johnson, May 31, 1961, Kennedy Papers, National Security File, box 193.

55. Rusk to Nolting, October 2, 1961, Kennedy Papers, National Security File, box 194; Anspacher to USIA, October 27, 1961, Kennedy Papers, National Security File, box 194. United States Information Service was the name of the overseas operations of the United States Information Agency.

56. "Richer Prize," *Time,* April 14, 1961, p. 31; "Little Man Who Stands Tall . . . in Vietnam," *Newsweek,* May 22, 1961, p. 36.

57. "The Face of the Enemy," *Time,* December 15, 1961, p. 29; Robert S. Elegant, "Report from Vietnam," *Newsweek,* November 6, 1961, p. 46; Robert Trumbull, "Search in Cambodia Finds No Red Bases," *New York Times,* November 22, 1961, p. 1; "U.S. May Recall Envoy in Saigon," *New York Times,* December 1, 1961, p. 4.

58. Karnow, "Diem Defeats His Own Best Troops," p. 24; Jerry A. Rose, "The Fading Strength of Vietnam," *New Republic,* November 13, 1961, p. 7; Sol Sanders to Joseph Alsop, March 22, 1961, Alsop Papers.

59. Takashi Oka to Joseph G. Harrison, November 2, 1961, Kennedy Papers, National Security File, box 194.

60. *Pentagon Papers* (Gravel), vol. II, p. 59.


CHAPTER 4: In Country


1. Joseph Alsop, "The Helicopters," *Washington Post,* April 30, 1962, p. A17.

2. Homer Bigart to Emmanuel Freedman, April 12, 1962, Turner Catledge Papers, New York Times Archives.

3. Joseph Alsop, "The Focus of Alarm," *Washington Post,* May 4, 1962, p. A15; Homer Bigart, "Vietnam Victory Remote Despite U.S. Aid to Diem," *New York Times,* July 25, 1962, p. 1.

4. *The Pentagon Papers* (Senator Gravel ed.) (Boston: Beacon Press, 1971), vol. II, pp. 73–77, 80.

5. Stanley Karnow, *Vietnam: A History,* (New York: Viking, 1983), p. 251; George C. Herring, *America's Longest War, 1950–1975,* 2nd ed. (New York: Alfred A. Knopf, 1986), p. 80; *Pentagon Papers* (Gravel), vol. II, pp. 85–98; Joseph Alsop, "The Pseudo-Taylor Report," *Washington Post,* October 27, 1961, p. A19.

6. *Pentagon Papers* (Gravel), vol. II, pp. 90, 93, 98–99.

7. Herring, *America's Longest War,* p. 83; *Pentagon Papers* (Gravel), vol. II, p. 79; Karnow, *Vietnam,* p. 253.

8. E. W. Kenworthy, "Pentagon Sets Up Vietnam Command Under a General," *New York Times,* February 9, 1962, p. 1; "Buildup," *Newsweek,* October 27, 1961, p. 40.

9. Robert P. Martin, "About U.S. Troops for Vietnam—Report from the Scene," *U.S. News and World Report,* October 27, 1961, p. 65.

10. Herbert J. Gans, *Deciding What's News: A Study of CBS Evening News, NBC Nightly News, Newsweek, and Time* (New York: Pantheon, 1979), pp. 42–43.

11. Francis Faulkner, "Bao Chi: The American News Media in Vietnam, 1960–1975," unpublished Ph.D. dissertation, University of Massachusetts, 1981, p. 41; William M. Hammond, *Public Affairs: The Military and the Media, 1962–1968* (Washington, D.C.: Center for Military History, 1988), p. 9. See also lists of correspondents in the mastheads of *Time, Newsweek,* and *U.S. News and World Report* for 1962.

12. Karnow, *Vietnam,* p. 718; David Halberstam, *The Making of a Quagmire,* (New York: Harper and Row, 1965), p. 135. By "American press corps" I mean both American journalists and third-country nationals, such as Faas and Peter Arnett of AP and Sully of *Newsweek,* working for American news organizations.

13. Halberstam, *Making of a Quagmire,* pp. 126–28; Robert Shaplen, *The Lost Revolution* (New York: Harper and Row, 1965), p. 161; "The Firing Line," *Time,* August 4, 1961, p. 27.

14. Halberstam, *Making of a Quagmire,* p. 124.

15. Keyes Beech, *Not Without the Americans* (Garden City, N.Y.: Doubleday, 1971), pp. 260–62; Halberstam, *Making of a Quagmire,* pp. 124, 131–33; Malcolm Browne, *The New Face of War* (Indianapolis: Bobbs-Merrill, 1965), p. 264; Halberstam in Ruth Adler, ed., *The Working Press: Special to the New York Times* (New York: Putnam's, 1966), p. 101; Richard Tregaskis, *Vietnam Diary* (New York: Holt, Rinehart and Winston, 1963), pp. 7–8.

16. Ibid., p. 125.

17. Halberstam, *Making of a Quagmire,* p. 125; Robert P. Martin, "Where War Is Hot and Getting Hotter," *U.S. News and World Report,* February 19, 1962, p. 37. For example, during May 1962, the *New York Times* reported combat action on twenty days. *Time* reported combat action during both of its May articles on South Vietnam; *U.S. News* did the same in its one May article on Vietnam, as did *Newsweek* in its three May Vietnam pieces.

18. Browne, *New Face of War*, pp. 1–8.

19. Neil Sheehan, *A Bright Shining Lie: John Paul Vann and American in Vietnam* (New York: Random House, 1988), pp. 197–99.

20. Sheehan, *A Bright Shining Lie*, pp. 197–98.

21. Halberstam, *Making of a Quagmire*, pp. 82–94.

22. Browne, *New Face of War*, pp. xi–xii; Halberstam, *Making of a Quagmire*, pp. 60–61; Faulkner, "Bao Chi," p. 34.

23. Karnow, *Vietnam*, pp. 253–54; Herring, *America's Longest War*, pp. 86–87; "Buildup," p. 40; Robert P. Martin, "Where War Is Hot and Getting Hotter," *U.S. News and World Report*, February 19, 1962, p. 35; Homer Bigart, "U.S. Is Expanding Role in Vietnam," *New York Times*, February 10, 1962, p. 3; Halberstam, *Making of a Quagmire*, pp. 127–28.

24. François Sully, "Drawing the Line," *Newsweek*, February 19, 1962, p. 37.

25. "Buildup," p. 40; Bigart, "U.S. Is Expanding Role"; Sully, "Drawing the Line," p. 37; Martin, "Where War Is Hot"; Howard Sochurek, "Far Off War We Have Decided to Win," *Life*, March 16, 1962, p. 36; Halberstam, *Making of a Quagmire*, pp. 87, 129–30.

26. Robert Trumbull, "Still 'Paris of the East,' " *New York Times*, June 3, 1961, p. 3; Halberstam, *Making of a Quagmire*, pp. 85, 94; Browne, *New Face of War*, pp. 1–8.

27. James Reston in Adler, ed., *Working Press*, pp. 101–4.

28. Braestrup, pp. 29–33, 39–43.

29. Joseph Alsop, "Col. Thao's War," *Washington Post*, April 14, 1961, p. A15; Joseph Alsop, "Warnings Aplenty," *Washington Post*, April 17, 1961, p. A13; Joseph Alsop, "The Double Standard," *Washington Post*, April 19, 1961, p. A17; Durbrow to Rusk, April 12, 1961, Kennedy Papers, National Security File, box 193.

30. *Pentagon Papers* (Gravel), vol. II, p. 103; Hammond, *Military and the Media*, pp. 12–13; Roger Hilsman, *To Move a Nation: The Politics of Foreign Policy in the Administration of John F. Kennedy* (Garden City, N.Y.: Doubleday, 1967), pp. 134–35; Pierre Salinger, *With Kennedy* (Garden City, N.Y.: Doubleday, 1966), p. 134; John Mecklin, *Mission in Torment: An Intimate Account of the U.S. Role in Vietnam* (Garden City, N.Y.: Doubleday, 1965), p. 110.

31. "Transcript of the President's News Conference on Foreign and Domestic Affairs," *New York Times*, February 15, 1962, p. 14.

32. Mecklin, *Mission in Torment*, pp. 168–70.

33. Rusk to Nolting, November 28, 1961, Kennedy Papers, National Security File, box 195; "U.S. 'Copter Crashes in Combat in Vietnam," *New York Times*, February 7, 1962, p. 3; "Transcript of Kennedy's News Conference on Foreign and Domestic Affairs," *New York Times*, February 8, 1962, p. 14.

34. Rusk to Nolting, February 20, 1962, Kennedy Papers, National Security File, box 195.

35. Felt to Joint Chiefs of Staff, March 29, 1962, Kennedy Papers, Na-

tional Security File, box 196; Ball to Rusk, March 26, 1962, Kennedy Papers, National Security File, box 196; Sylvester to CINCSTRIKE et al., March 1962, Kennedy Papers, National Security File, box 196.

36. Harriman to Nolting, April 4, 1962, Kennedy Papers, National Security File, box 196; L. D. Battle to M. Bundy, April 18, 1962, Kennedy Papers, National Security File, box 202; Karnow, *Vietnam,* pp. 253–54.

37. "Transcript of Kennedy's News Conference," p. 14.

38. Halberstam, *Making of a Quagmire,* p. 80.

39. Ibid., pp. 106–7. See also Sheehan, *Bright, Shining Lie,* pp. 58–60; Browne, *New Face of War,* pp. 262–74.

40. "Buildup," p. 40; Bigart, "U.S. Is Expanding Role"; Sully, "Drawing the Line," p. 37; Martin, "Where War Is Hot"; Homer Bigart, "Saigon Americans Adding Amenities," *New York Times,* June 21, 1962, p. 3. See also Tillman Durdin, "U.S. Role in Vietnam Holds Many Risks," *New York Times,* April 22, 1962, sec. IV, p. 4; Homer Bigart, "Denial of Purple Heart to G.I. Angers 'Copter Men in Vietnam," *New York Times,* April 24, 1962, p. 10 (Kennedy, realizing that a public-relations bomb had just blown up in his face, issued an Executive Order that the decoration be awarded); David Halberstam, "U.S. Deeply Involved in the Uncertain Struggle for Vietnam," *New York Times,* October 21, 1962, sec. IV, p. 3; Robert Trumbull, "U.S. Heavily Committed in Struggle to Save South Vietnam," *New York Times,* July 22, 1967, sec. IV. p. 3.

41. "War in Vietnam: Means and Ends," *Newsweek,* April 2, 1962, p. 31; Robert P. Martin, "New Tactics—or Endless War," *U.S. News and World Report,* July 30, 1962, p. 62; "Long Trail Awinding," *Newsweek,* July 9, 1962, p. 33; Halberstam, "U.S. Deeply Involved"; Halberstam, *Making of a Quagmire,* pp. 51–52.

42. "War in Vietnam: Means and Ends"; Martin, "New Tactics"; Bigart, "Vietnam Victory Remote"; Francois Sully, "Vietnam: Two Views, Official . . . and Unofficial," *Newsweek,* September 24, 1962, p. 30; Halberstam, "U.S. Deeply Involved."

43. Jacques Nevard, "Americans Voice Doubt on Vietnam," *New York Times,* July 29, 1962, p. 13; Halberstam, "U.S. Deeply Involved"; Sully, "Vietnam: Two Views"; Bigart, "Vietnam Victory Remote"; Martin, "New Tactics."

44. Halberstam, *Making of a Quagmire,* p. 131; "Saigon Impeding Western Press," *New York Times,* March 24, 1962, p. 6; Bigart, "M'Namara Terms Saigon Aid Ample," *New York Times,* May 12, 1962, p. 1; Bigart, "Delays in Saigon Harass Newsmen," *New York Times,* May 7, 1962, p. 7; "Saigon Acts to Oust Newsweek Reporter," *New York Times,* September 5, 1962, p. 5; Francois Sully, "Vietnam: The Unpleasant Truth," *Newsweek,* September 17, 1962, p. 68; Hammond, *Military and the Media,* pp. 24–29; Mecklin, *Mission in Torment,* pp. 132–38; Ball to Nolting, March 23, 1962, Kennedy Papers, National Security File, box 196.

45. Jack Foisie, "News Gap in South Vietnam," *Nation,* July 14, 1962, p. 12; Nolting to Rusk, November 16, 1961, Kennedy Papers, National Security

File, box 195; Nolting to Rusk, November 13, 1961, Kennedy Papers, National Security File, box 195; Sylvester to M. Bundy, April 7, 1962, Kennedy Papers, President's Office File, box 128A; Bigart, "Vietcong Troops Elude Pursuers," *New York Times,* June 18, 1962, p. 5.

46. Rusk to Nolting, November 24, 1961, Kennedy Papers, National Security File, box 195; Tregaskis to Salinger, January 4, 1963, Kennedy Papers, White House Central File, box 74; Nolting to Susan Mary Alsop, January 23, 1962, Alsop Papers, General Correspondence, box 17; Alsop, "The Focus of Alarm," *Washington Post,* May 4, 1962, p. A15; Alsop, "The Helicopters," p. A17.

CHAPTER 5: "Let Them Burn"

1. Halberstam, *The Making of a Quagmire* (New York: Harper and Row, 1965), pp. 210–11; Stanley Karnow, *Vietnam: A History* (New York: Viking, 1983), p. 281.

2. Homer Bigart, "Flights Halted by U.S.," *New York Times,* February 15, 1962, p. 1.

3. Homer Bigart, "M'Namara Terms Saigon Aid Ample," *New York Times,* May 12, 1962, p. 1; Halberstam, *Making of a Quagmire,* p. 76.

4. Halberstam, *Making of a Quagmire,* pp. 24, 72, 76–77; Halberstam, "U.S. Deeply Involved in the Uncertain Struggle for Vietnam," *New York Times,* October 21, 1962, sec. IV, p. 3.

5. Bigart to Freedman, March 25, 1962, Turner Catledge Papers, New York Times Archives; Bigart in Ruth Adler, ed., *The Working Press: Special to the New York Times* (New York: Putnam's, 1966), p. 184.

Robert Trumbull was chief of the *Times'* Far Eastern correspondents and a twenty-five-year veteran of covering Vietnam. He complained to *Times* military-affairs specialist Hanson Baldwin that, "Offensive as the Pentagon's policy of concealment is, I do not object so much to that as I do to the artistic affront of having a bad policy handled by incompetent men." Official information ran far behind what the correspondents had found out on their own. The daily communiqué issued by the South Vietnamese "is all but disregarded," Trumbull said. "On every communiqué, the correspondents have to check their files to be sure they haven't already sent the information days before." (Catledge to Dryfoos, March 23, 1962, Turner Catledge Papers, New York Times Archives; Trumbull to Baldwin, July 30, 1962, Hanson W. Baldwin Papers, box 12, Yale University Library; Trumbull to Baldwin, August 18, 1962, Baldwin Papers, box 12; Trumbull to Baldwin, July 20, 1962, Baldwin Papers, box 12.)

6. "The Non-War," *Newsweek,* July 2, 1962, p. 74; Robert P. Martin, "Where War Is Hot and Getting Hotter," *U.S. News and World Report,* February 19, 1962, p. 35; Jack Foisie, "News Gap in South Vietnam," *Nation,* July 14, 1962, p. 12; "Saigon Impeding Western Press," *New York Times,* March 24, 1962, p. 6.

7. Francis Faulkner, "Bao Chi: The American News Media in Vietnam, 1960–1975," unpublished Ph.D. dissertation, University of Massachusetts, 1981, p. 42; Homer Bigart, "G.I.'s in Vietnam Lied as Ordered," *New York Times,* May 5, 1962, p. 8; Felt to Joint Chiefs of Staff, April 9, 1962, Kennedy Papers, National Security File, box 196.

8. Faulkner, "Bao Chi," pp. 42–44; Bigart, "G.I.'s in Vietnam"; Homer Bigart, "Delays in Saigon Harass Newsmen," *New York Times,* May 7, 1962, p. 7.

9. François Sully, "Vietnam: The Unpleasant Truth," *Newsweek,* August 20, 1962, p. 40; "The Unpleasant Truth," *Newsweek,* September 17, 1962, p. 68; "Saigon Acts to Oust Newsweek Reporter," *New York Times,* September 5, 1962, p. 5; John Mecklin, *Mission in Torment: An Intimate Account of the U.S. Role in Vietnam* (Garden City, N.Y.: Doubleday, 1965), pp. 134–36; William P. Hammond, *Public Affairs: The Military and the Media, 1962–1968* (Washington, D.C.: Center for Military History, 1988), pp. 26–27; Faulkner, "Bao Chi," pp. 44–46.

10. Hammond, *Military and the Media,* pp. 29–30; Mecklin, *Mission in Torment,* pp. 138–40; Halberstam, "Vietnam Attacks a Red Sanctuary," *New York Times,* November 21, 1962, p. 7; Halberstam, "Curbs in Vietnam Irk U.S. Officers," *New York Times,* November 22, 1962, p. 6.

11. Mecklin, *Mission in Torment,* pp. 139–40; Halberstam, "Curbs in Vietnam"; Faulkner, "Bao Chi," pp. 47–48; Hammond, *Military and the Media,* pp. 29–30.

12. "Mrs. Nhu Criticizes Americans in Saigon," *New York Times,* November 28, 1962, p. 19; Mecklin, *Mission in Torment,* p. 125.

13. Mecklin, *Mission in Torment,* p. 126; Halberstam, *Making of a Quagmire,* pp. 28–32; Halberstam to Freedman, Foreign Desk Papers, New York Times Archives.

14. Mecklin, *Mission in Torment,* pp. 114–17, 148; Neil Sheehan, *A Bright Shining Lie: John Paul Vann and America in Vietnam* (New York: Random House, 1988), pp. 350–51; Felt to Sylvester, November 26, 1962, Kennedy Papers, National Security File, box 197.

15. Sheehan, *Bright Shining Lie,* p. 39.

16. Ibid., pp. 42–43.

17. Ibid., pp. 55–56, 75, 78–79, 92–95.

18. Ibid., pp. 79–89.

19. Ibid., pp. 270–71.

20. Ibid., pp. 203–8.

21. For a detailed description of the battle itself, see ibid., pp. 211–64.

22. Ibid., pp. 270–77.

23. David Halberstam, "Vietcong Downs Five U.S. Helicopters, Hits Nine Others," *New York Times,* January 3, 1963, p. 1; David Halberstam, "Vietnamese Reds Win Major Clash," *New York Times,* January 4, 1963, p. 2; David Halberstam, "Motley U.S. Force Blocks Vietcong," *New York Times,* January 5, 1963, p. 2; David Halberstam, "Vietnam Defeat Shocks U.S. Aides," January 7, 1963, p. 2; David Halberstam, "Harkins Praises

Vietnam Troops," *New York Times,* January 11, 1963, p. 3 (because of the New York City newspaper strike, all of the preceding citations are from the *Times'* Western edition). Others at the *Times* picked up on Halberstam's reporting. See, for example, "Setback in Vietnam," a January 5 editorial that blamed the politicization of the ARVN for the defeat, and Hanson Baldwin's column of the same day, which criticized excessive dependence on American technology to win the war. See also "The Helicopter War Runs into Trouble," *Time,* January 11, 1963, p. 29; "A Bloody Nose," *Newsweek,* January 14, 1963, p. 34; "Year of the Man," *Newsweek,* January 21, 1963, p. 46; Sol W. Sanders, "Close-up of Guerrilla War," *U.S. News and World Report,* January 21, 1963, p. 48; "The 'Hot' War U.S. Seems to Be Losing," *U.S. News and World Report,* January 21, 1963, p. 46.

24. Sheehan, *Bright, Shining Lie,* pp. 277–78; Joint Chiefs to Kennedy, January 3, 1963, Kennedy Papers, National Security File, box 197; Harkins to Dodge, January 3, 1963, Kennedy Papers, National Security File, box 197.

25. "Report of Visit by Joint Chiefs of Staff," n.d. (sometime between January 20 and 31, 1963), Kennedy Papers, National Security File, box 197; Felt to Rusk, January 11, 1963, Kennedy Papers, National Security File, box 197.

26. A few weeks later, Saigon USIS chief John Mecklin had been ordered to write a memo critical of the press corps, and ordered to write it again when the first draft was not sufficiently tough. Portions of the paper were leaked, including passages describing some Saigon reporting as "irresponsible, sensationalized, and anatagonistc." Reporters started calling him "Meck the Knife." Soon after, Mecklin left South Vietnam temporarily for major surgery. Upon hearing the news, one reporter was heard to say, "I hope the s.o.b. dies." Sheehan, *Bright, Shining Lie,* p. 314; Halberstam, *Making of a Quagmire,"* p. 147; Hammond, *Military and the Media,* p. 37; Mecklin, *Mission in Torment,* pp. 147–48.

27. Sheehan, *Bright Shining Lie,* pp. 315, 321–22; Halberstam, *Making of a Quagmire,* pp. 167–68.

28. Sheehan, *Bright, Shining Lie,* pp. 332–33; Halberstam, *Making of a Quagmire,* pp. 177–78.

29. Sheehan, *Bright Shining Lie,* p. 334; Halberstam, *Making of a Quagmire,* pp. 197–98.

30. Halberstam, *Making of a Quagmire,* pp. 199, 207.

31. Halbertam, *Making of a Quagmire,* pp. 205–7; Karnow, *Vietnam,* pp. 279–80; Marguerite Higgins, *Our Vietnam Nightmare* (New York: Harper and Row, 1965), pp. 18–19.

32. Karnow, *Vietnam,* p. 281; Halberstam, *Making of a Quagmire,* p. 211.

33. Halberstam, *Making of a Quagmire,* pp. 211–14; Karnow, *Vietnam,* pp. 217–18, 281; George C. Herring, *America's Longest War: 1950–1975,* 2nd ed. (New York: Alfred A. Knopf, 1986), p. 95; *The Pentaagon Papers* (Senator Gravel edition) (Boston: Beacon Press, 1971), vol. II, p. 228; Sheehan, *Bright Shining Lie,* p. 335.

CHAPTER 6: "Get on the Team"

1. John Mecklin, *Mission in Torment: An Intimate Account of the U.S. Role in Vietnam* (Garden City, N.Y.: Doubleday, 1965), pp. 184–86; David Halberstam, *The Making of a Quagmire* (New York: Harper and Row, 1965), pp. 234–40; Stanley Karnow, *Vietnam: A History* (New York: Viking, 1983), p. 285; George C. Herring, *America's Longest War: 1950–1975*, 2nd ed. (New York: Alfred A. Knopf, 1986), p. 97; Neil Sheehan, *A Bright Shining Lie: John Paul Vann and America in Vietnam* (New York: Random House, 1988), pp. 356–57.

2. Halberstam, *Making of a Quagmire*, p. 231; Sheehan, *Bright Shining Lie*, pp. 354–56; *The Pentagon Papers* (Senator Gravel edition) (Boston: Beacon Press, 1971), vol. II, pp. 232–33; Karnow, *Vietnam*, p. 285; Herring, *America's Longest War*, p. 97.

3. Herring, *America's Longest War*, pp. 92–97; *Pentagon Papers* (Gravel), vol. II, pp. 233, 241.

4. Halberstam, *Making of a Quagmire*, pp. 194–95.

5. Ibid., pp. 205–6, 215; Sheehan, *Bright Shining Lie*, p. 351.

6. Halberstam, *Making of a Quagmire*, pp. 226–28.

7. Even pro-Diem *Time* painted a grim picture of the viciousness with which the police attacked the protesters and lamented that "All these discontents need not have erupted if government troops had not stupidly and brutally gunned down nine Buddhist demonstrators at a rally in Hue. . . ." Halberstam, *Making of a Quagmire*, p. 207; David Halberstam, "Anti-U.S. Feeling Rises in Vietnam as Unrest Grows," *New York Times*, August 24, 1963, p. 1; David Halberstam, "Failure to Solve Political Proglems May Erode Will of People to Press War," *New York Times*, October 6, 1963; "The Buddhist Crisis," *Time*, July 26, 1963, p. 24; Robert P. Martin, "Collision Course in Vietnam—U.S. vs. an Unruly Ally," *U.S. News and World Report*, September 16, 1963, p. 36; "Vietnam: Getting to Know the Nhus," *Newsweek*, September 9, 1963, p. 33.

8. Karnow, *Vietnam*, p. 281; David Halberstam, "Police in Saigon Jostle Newsmen," *New York Times*, July 8, 1963, p. 3; "Envoy to Saigon Meets Kennedy," *New York Times*, July 9, 1963, p. 5; Halberstam, *Making of a Quagmire*, p. 240; Sheehan, *Bright, Shining Lie*, pp. 352–53, 356–57.

9. Reporters found clever ways to beat the censorship. "All our attempts to slip out the news that Vu Van Mau, the Foreign Minister, had resigned were caught except Mal Browne's," Halberstam remembered. "Mal got it through by typing the news onto the caption of a photo of soldiers and sending it out by wirephoto." William M. Hammond, *Public Affairs: The Military and the Media, 1962–1968* (Washington, D.C.: Center for Military History, 1988), p. 56, Halberstam, *Making of a Quagmire*, p. 229–43; Hightower to AP General Desk, August 27, 1963, Turner Catledge Papers, New York Times Archives.

10. Halberstam, *Making of a Quagmire,* pp. 229–43; Halberstam, "Plan Said to Be Nhu's," *New York Times,* August 23, 1963, p. 1; Tad Szulc, "Kennedy Weight Policy," *New York Times,* August 23, 1963, p. 1.

11. Marguerite Higgins, *Our Vietnam Nightmare* (New York: Harper and Row, 1965), p. 108.

12. Ibid., pp. 108, 122, 165.

13. Ibid., pp. x, 107, 128.

14. Joseph Alsop, "The Command Post," *Washington Post,* September 16, 1963, p. A15; Joseph Alsop, "The Crusaders," *Washington Post,* September 23, 1963, p. A17.

15. Halberstam, *Making of a Quagmire,* p. 269.

16. Ibid., pp. 270–74; "The Queen Bee," *Time,* August 9, 1963, p. 21; "The View from Saigon," *Time,* September 20, 1963, p. 62.

17. Halberstam, *Making of a Quagmire,* pp. 273–74.

18. Sheehan, *Bright Shining Lie,* pp. 348–50; Halberstam, *Making of a Quagmire,* p. 268.

19. Halberstam, *Making of a Quagmire,* p. 193; Halberstam, "G.I.'s Told Not to Criticize Vietnam," *New York Times,* June 24, 1963, p. 11.

20. To be sure, there was still conflict. Some American officials in Saigon were still close-mouthed and antagonistic, and some still put a premium on glossing over negative developments. Beginning in May 1963, Americans assigned to South Vietnam were reminded that, no matter what their rank, they were "American spokesmen," and that when questioned by the press they should, "as song writer Johnny Mercer put it, 'accentuate the positive and eliminate the negative.' " Individual stories still inspired official anger and dismay. An August 15 story by Halberstam, based largely on guidance from Vann, warned that, despite the massive American buildup, "South Vietnam's military situation in the vital Mekong Delta has deteriorated in the past year." The article was attacked specifically in public by senior officials such as Dean Rusk after it had been privately analyzed and picked apart. A week and a half later, on the Monday after the pagoda raids, a meeting in a tension-filled Oval Office dealt with the American response. Kennedy was particularly upset about the tough message to Diem that Hilsman, Averill Harriman, and Michael Forrestal had drafted and sent, with the vacationing president's cursory approval, the previous Saturday. Kennedy opened the meeting by demanding to be convinced that "we were not being influenced by the *New York Times;* specifically the Halberstam article. He said that Halberstam was a 28-year-old kid and he wanted assurance that we were not giving his sources consideration in our decision; that this reminded him of Matthews on Cuba." Hilsman, who was the focus of the president's anger that day, quickly—and not completely truthfully—told Kennedy "that in all cases Halberstam was inaccurate and incorrect and that our decision was not based on any information or opinion in the *New York Times.*" And the administration was, as Halberstam learned from a friend in the State Department, vigorously trying to find ways to discredit him. "It was a damn good thing you never belonged to any leftwing groups or anything like that,"

his friend told him, "because they were really looking for stuff like that." (Hammond, *Military and the Media*, p. 45; Halberstam, *Making of a Quagmire*, pp. 190–92; Felt to Joint Chiefs of Staff, August 17, 1963, Kennedy Papers, National Security File, boxes 198–99; memorandum of conversation, White House Meetings, August 26, 1963, Roger Hilsman Papers, box 4, John F. Kennedy Presidential Library; Herring, *America's Longest War*, pp. 98–99; Karnow, *Vietnam*, pp. 286–88; *Pentagon Papers* (Gravel) vol. II, pp. 234–38.

21. House Committee on Government Operations, Subcommittee on Foreign Operations and Government Information, hearings, May 24, 1963, in *Government Information Policies and Plans*, pt. 4: *Vietnam News Coverage* (Washington, D.C.: Government Printing Office, 1963). See also pt. 1: *News Media Panel Discussion* and *Department of State-Department of Defense*, March 19 and 25, 1963; pt. 3: *Information Procedures in the Department of Defense*, May 27–28, 1963.

22. Trueheart to Rusk, July 7, 1963, Kennedy Papers, National Security File, boxes 198–99; Ball to Trueheart, July 12, 1963, Kennedy Papers, National Security File, boxes 198–99; Hammond, *Military and the Media*, p. 41.

23. Memorandum for the record, March 19, 1962, Roger Hilsman Papers, box 3; Mecklin to Nolting, November 27, 1962, Kennedy Papers, National Security File, box 200.

24. Mecklin, *Mission in Torment*, pp. 149–51; Kennedy to Harkins and Nolting, May 3, 1963, Kennedy Papers, National Security File, box 197; Bail to Nolting, May 21, 1963, Kennedy Papers, National Security File, box 197.

25. Halberstam, *Making of a Quagmire*, pp. 208, 219–20; Sheehaan, *Bright Shining Lie*, p. 358.

26. Herring, *America's Longest War*, pp. 99–105; *Pentagon Papers* (Gravel) vol. II, pp. 232–62; Karnow, *Vietnam*, pp. 289–96; memorandum of conversation, August 26, 1963, Hilsman Papers, box 4; Felt to Rusk, August 31, 1963, Kennedy Papers, National Security File, boxes 198–99.

27. Sheehan, *Bright Shining Lie*, pp. 358–61; Halberstam, *Making of a Quagmire*, pp. 247–49.

28. Ball to Lodge, August 21, 1963, Kennedy Papers, National Security File, boxes 198–99; Trueheart to Rusk, August 21, 1963, Kennedy Papers, National Security File, boxes 198–99; Lodge to Rusk, October 5, 1963, Kennedy Papers, National Security File, box 200; Lodge to Rusk, October 11, 1963, Kennedy Papers, National Security File, box 200; Hightower to AP General Desk, August 27, 1963, Turner Catledge Papers, New York Times Archives; Sheehan, *Bright Shining Lie*, pp. 356–57; Halberstam, *Making of a Quagmire*, p. 240; Mecklin, *Mission in Torment*, pp. 184–86.

29. Halberstam, *Making of a Quagmire*, pp. 300–301.

CHAPTER 7: "I Don't Know"

1. Jack Langguth, "The War in Vietnam Can Be Won, but—," *New York Times Magazine*, September 19, 1965, p. 30.

2. *The Pentagon Papers* (Senator Gravel edition) (Boston: Beacon Press, 1971), vol. II, p. 117.

3. George C. Herring, *America's Longest War: 1950–1975,* 2nd ed. (New York: Alfred A. Knopf, 1986), pp. 108–17; Stanley Karnow, *Vietnam: A History* (New York: Viking, 1983), pp. 323, 345–46, 357–58.

4. Herring, *America's Longest War,* pp. 110, 118–19; *Pentagon Papers* (Gravel), vol. II, pp. 311–26.

5. *Pentagon Papers* (Gravel), vol. II, pp. 311–13; Herring, *America's Longest War,* p. 119.

6. Karnow, *Vietnam,* pp. 364–70; Herring, *America's Longest War,* pp. 119–20.

7. Karnow, *Vietnam,* pp. 374–76; Herring, *America's Longest War,* pp. 122–23; "Editorial Reaction to Asian Conflict," *New York Times,* August 7, 1964, p. 8.

8. Herring, *America's Longest War,* pp. 126, 146–47; Karnow, *Vietnam,* pp. 421–26.

9. Herring, *America's Longest War,* pp. 137–45, 167; Karnow, *Vietnam,* pp. 421–26.

10. Peter Braestrup, *Big Story* (Boulder: Westview Press, 1977), p. 6; Jack Raymond, "U.S. Spurs Flow of Vietnam News," *New York Times,* July 23, 1964, p. 3; "The Viet Beat," *Newsweek,* September 7, 1964, p. 76. See also mastheads of August 17, 1964, issues of *Time, U.S. News and World Report,* and *Newsweek.*

11. Braestrup, *Big Story,* p. 7.

12. "Correspondents In-Country," Robert Shaplen Papers, December 24, 1965, box 9. Mass Communications History Collection, Wisconsin State Historical Society.

13. Peter Grose to Emmanuel Freedman, February 29, 1964, Foreign Desk Papers, New York Times Archives; Grose to Freedman, April 25, 1964, Foreign Desk Papers, New York Times Archives.

14. James Reston in Ruth Adler, ed., *The Working Press: Special to the New York Times* (New York: Putnam's, 1966), pp. 102–4; Charles Mohr to Clifton Daniel et al., September 1965, Daniel Papers, New York Times Archives; Reston to Daniel, August 25, 1965, Daniel Papers, New York Times Archives.

15. R. W. Apple to Seymour Topping, November 7, 1966, Foreign Desk Papers, New York Times Archives; Apple to Topping, November 14, 1966, Foreign Desk Papers, New York Times Archives.

16. The technicalities of dispatching film, and their effect on television coverage of the war, will be explored in greater depth later in this chapter.

17. "The Pundit and the Prole," *Newsweek,* September 6, 1965, p. 49; Grose to Freedman, April 25, 1964, Foreign Desk Papers, New York Times Archives; J. I. Henry to Freedman, November 10, 1964, Foreign Desk Papers, New York Times Archives.

18. Apple to Topping, February 21, 1967, Foreign Desk Papers, New York Times Archives; Apple to Topping, November 2, 1967, Foreign Desk

Papers, New York Times Archives; Topping to Apple, November 2, 1967, Foreign Desk Papers, New York Times Archives.

19. David Halberstam, *The Making of a Quagmire* (New York: Harper and Row, 1965), p. 243; Grose to Freedman, February 29, 1964, Foreign Desk Papers, New York Times Archives; Mohr to Freedman, August 7, 1964, Foreign Desk Papers, New York Times Archives; Apple to Daniel, n.d., Daniel Papers, New York Times Archives.

20. Reston to Daniel, August 25, 1965, Daniel Papers, New York Times Archives; Topping to Apple, November 2, 1967, Foreign Desk Papers, New York Times Archives.

21. Mohr to Catledge et al., September 1965, Daniel Papers, New York Times Archives; Reston in Adler, ed., *Working Press,* p. 103.

22. Mohr to Catledge et al., September 1965, Daniel Papers, New York Times Archives; "Crud, Fret, and Jeers," *Time,* June 10, 1966, p. 53; Jack Raymond, "It's a Dirty War for Correspondents, Too," *New York Times Magazine,* February 23, 1966, p. 32; "The Viet Beat," *Newsweek,* September 7, 1964; Braestrup to Baldwin, December 6, 1966, Baldwin Papers, box 11.

23. "The Press: Room for Improvement," *Newsweek,* July 10, 1967, p. 76; Clarence R. Wyatt, " 'Truth from the Snares of Crisis': The American Press and the Vietnam War," unpublished M.A. thesis, University of Kentucky, 1984; Braestrup, *Big Story,* p. 30; Braestrup to Baldwin, December 6, 1966, Baldwin Papers; Baldwin to Daniel, January 7, 1966, Daniel Papers, New York Times Archives; Raymond, "It's a Dirty War," p. 92; Francis Faulkner, "Bao Chi: The American News Media in Vietnam, 1960–1975," unpublished Ph.D. dissertation, University of Massachusetts, 1981, pp. 158–59.

24. "The Viet Beat," p. 76; "The Press: Room for Improvement," p. 76.

25. "The Press: Room for Improvement," p. 76; Westmoreland to Wheeler, November 9, 1967, William C. Westmoreland Papers, box 20, Washington National Records Center; Raymond, "It's a Dirty War," p. 92.

26. Wheeler to Westmoreland, April 20, 1967, Westmoreland Papers, box 20; Wheeler to Westmoreland, April 19, 1967, Westmoreland Papers, box 20; Wheeler to Westmoreland, August 2, 1967, Westmoreland Papers, box 20.

27. Mohr to Catledge et al., September 1965, Daniel Papers, New York Times Archives.

28. Ibid.

29. Ibid.

30. Ibid.

31. Topping to Daniel, February 6, 1966, Foreign Desk Papers, New York Times Archives; Apple to Topping, February 27, 1967, Foreign Desk Papers, New York Times Archives; Topping to Apple, February 27, 1967, Foreign Desk Papers, New York Times Archives; Topping to Apple, September 23, 1967, Foreign Desk Papers, New York Times Archives; Rosenthal to Daniel, November 22, 1967, Daniel Papers, New York Times Archives.

32. Military Assistance Command–Vietnam, Office of Information, Correspondent Accreditation Files, boxes 15–22, RG 334-74-593, Adjutant Gen-

eral's Office, Department of the Army, Washington National Records Center; Braestrup, *Big Story,* pp. 10–11; "Memorandum for the Press," Office of the Assistant Secretary of Defense for Public Affairs, October 4, 1966, Daniel Papers, New York Times Archives; "The Press: Room for Improvement," pp. 76–78.

33. Correspondent Accreditation Files, boxes 15–22; Braestrup, *Big Story,* pp. 10–13.

34. Correspondent Accreditation Files, boxes 15–22, Braestrup, *Big Story,* pp. 10–13.

35. David Halberstam, *The Powers That Be* (New York: Alfred A. Knopf, 1979), pp. 407–17; "Correspondents In-Country," December 24, 1965, Shaplen Papers, box 9.

36. "TV's First War," *Newsweek,* August 30, 1965, p. 32; "Burning of Village Described," *New York Times,* August 4, 1965, p. 2.

37. William M. Hammond, *Public Affairs: The Military and the Media, 1962–1968* (Washington, D.C.: Center for Military History, 1988), pp. 188–90.

38. Halberstam, *Powers That Be,* p. 490; "Memorandum of Discussion on Meeting in Mr. Moyers' Office," August 10, 1965, Lyndon B. Johnson Papers, NSF, boxes 196–97, Lyndon B. Johnson Presidential Library; Hammond, *Military and the Media,* pp. 190–93.

39. "TV's First War," p. 32.

40. Braestrup, *Big Story,* p. 34.

41. Ibid., pp. 36–38; "The Most Intimate Medium," *Time,* October 14, 1966, p. 56; Edward J. Epstein, *News From Nowhere: Television and the News* (New York: Random House, 1973), p. 33; "TV's First War," p. 32; "The Press: Room for Improvement," p. 76; Daniel C. Hallin, *The "Uncensored War": The Media and Vietnam* (Berkeley: University of California Press, 1989), p. 133; Jack Gould, "How Is TV Covering Vietnam?," *New York Times,* December 26, 1965, sec. II, p. 15; "Mortars at Martini Time," *Time,* December 1, 1967, p. 86.

42. James C. Hagerty, "TV: Exposing the False Glory of War," *New York Times,* December 25, 1966, sec. II, p. 18; "Mortars at Martini Time," p. 86; "T.R.B. From Washington," *New Republic,* June 1967, p. 1; Hallin, *"Uncensored War,"* pp. 3–12; Wyatt, " 'Truth from the Snares of Crisis,' " pp. 93–98; George Gent, "A Psychiatrist and a TV Aide Dispute Vietnam Coverage," *New York Times,* October 8, 1966, p. 63.

43. "TV's First War," *Newsweek,* August 30, 1965, p. 32.

44. Robert S. Elegant, "How to Lose a War," *Encounter,* August 1981, pp. 73–90; "TV's First War," p. 32; Gould, "How Is TV Covering Vietnam?," sec. II, p. 2; Robert E. Dallon, "TV Editors Face Problem on War," *New York Times,* May 29, 1967, p. 51; "The Press: Room for Improvement," p. 76; "How Bloody Can It Be?," *Newsweek,* December 25, 1967, p. 75; George A. Bailey, "Television War: Trends in Network Coverage of Vietnam, 1965–1970," *Journal of Broadcasting,* Spring 1976, pp. 147–58; Lawrence W. Lichty, "The Night at the End of the Tunnel," *Film Comment,*

July–August 1975, pp. 32–35; Lawrence W. Lichty, "The War We Watched on Television," *AFI Report,* Winter 1973, pp. 29–37; Lawrence W. Lichty, "Video Versus Print," *Wilson Quarterly,* vol. VI, no. 5 (1982), pp. 48–57.

45. Brock Brown, "Worthy Try at Covering a Big Story," *Life,* January 21, 1966, p. 15.


CHAPTER 8: "Fighting in the Open"


1. "Other Side of the Hill," *Newsweek,* May 4, 1964, p. 32.

2. Greenfield to M. Bundy, n.d., Lyndon Johnson Papers, NSF, Aides File—M. Bundy; George C. Herring, *America's Longest War: 1950–1975,* 2nd ed. (New York: Alfred A. Knopf, 1986), p. 130; Wheeler to Sharp, June 6, 1966, Westmoreland Papers, box 26; Sylvester to Westmoreland, June 29, 1966, Westmoreland Papers, box 2; William M. Hammond, *Public Affairs: The Military and the Media, 1962–1968* Washington, D.C.: Center for Military History, 1988), pp. 271–74.

3. Jack Langguth, "160 U.S. and Saigon Planes Bomb 2 Bases in North in Record Raid: Continuing Strikes Are Expected," *New York Times,* March 3, 1965, p. 1; Sieverts to Greenfield, April 30, 1965, James Thomson Papers, box 25, John F. Kennedy Presidential Library.

4. David Halberstam, "Raid Fears Cited in North Vietnam," *New York Times,* March 2, 1965, p. 3; "Hanoi Is Pictured as Upset by Raids," *New York Times,* May 25, 1965, p. 2; James Cameron, "From Hanoi: U.S. Bombings Bring Mood of Siege," *New York Times,* December 7, 1965, p. 1; "AFP's Man in Hanoi," *Newsweek,* August 15, 1966, p. 54.

5. Harrison E. Salisbury, *Behind the Lines—Hanoi* (New York: New York Times Company, 1967), pp. 404–07; Hammond, *Military and the Media,* pp. 274–79; Harrison E. Salisbury, "Visitor to Hanoi Inspects Damage Attributed to American Raids," *New York Times,* December 26, 1966, p. 1.

6. Salisbury, "U.S. Raids Batter 2 Towns; Supply Route Is Little Hurt," *New York Times,* December 27, 1966, p. 1; Salisbury, "No Military Targets, Namdinh Insists," *New York Times,* December 31, 1966, p. 3.

7. Hammond, *Military and the Media,* pp. 276–79; E. W. Kenworthy, "Eisenhower Says U.S. Aims Only at Military Targets," *New York Times,* December 28, 1966, p. 1.

8. Neil Sheehan, "Washington Concedes Bombs Hit Civilian Areas in North Vietnam," *New York Times,* December 28, 1966, p. 1; Phil Goulding, *Confirm or Deny: Informing the People on National Security* (New York: Harper and Row, 1970), pp. 52–92; Wheeler to Westmoreland, February 4, 1967, Westmoreland Papers, box 20; Wheeler to Westmoreland, March 2, 1967, Westmoreland Papers, box 20; Westmoreland to Wheeler, March 4, 1967, Westmoreland Papers, box 20; "Behind Enemy Lines," *Newsweek,* January 9, 1967, pp. 61–62.

9. David Halberstam, *The Powers That Be* (New York: Alfred A. Knopf,

1979), p. 534; Howard K. Smith, "Credibility and the *Times*," *National Review*, January 24, 1967, pp. 73–74; "Sorry 'bout That," *New Republic*, January 7, 1967, pp. 7–9.

10. Baldwin to Daniel, December 27, 1966, Baldwin Papers, box 11; Hanson Baldwin, "Bombing of the North," *New York Times*, December 30, 1966, p. 1; "The Tragedy of Vietnam," *New York Times*, January 2, 1967, p. 18; Daniel to Gerstenzang, January 16, 1967, Daniel Papers, New York Times Archives.

11. "Behind Enemy Lines," p. 61; Harry S. Ashmore and William C. Baggs, *Mission to Hanoi* (New York: G. P. Putnam's Sons, 1968); Halberstam, *Powers That Be*, p. 314.

12. "Top of the Week," *Newsweek*, January 18, 1965, p. 7.

13. "Memorandum of Discussion," August 10, 1965, Johnson Papers, NSF, LBJ Library, boxes 196–97.

14. Greenfield, "Memorandum for Discussion," December 8, 1964, Thomson Papers, JFK Library, box 24.

15. Hammond, *Military and the Media*, pp. 80–85; Barry Zorthian Interview, Oral History Collection, LBJ Library; "The Viet Beat," *Newsweek*, September 7, 1964, pp. 76–77; Jack Raymond, "U.S. Spurs Flow of Vietnam News," *New York Times*, July 23, 1964, p. 3.

16. Hammond, *Military and the Media*, pp. 140, 160–61; Greenfield and Jorden to Moyers, August 13, 1965, Johnson Papers, NSF, boxes 196–97; "War Censorship Discussed by U.S." *New York Times*, August 16, 1965, p. 3.

17. "Memorandum for Correspondents: Rules Governing Public Release of Military Information in Vietnam," October 31, 1966, Disaccreditation File, MACV Office of Information, box 14, RG 334-74-593, Adjutant General's Office, Department of the Army, Washington National Records Center.

18. Arthur Krock, "Information Lid on Latest Tonkin Incident," *New York Times*, September 24, 1964, p. 40; Jack Raymond, "U.S. Names Ships in Tonkin Clash," *New York Times*, October 2, 1964, p. 1; "Bureaucratic Censorship," *New York Times*, October 3, 1964, p. 28; "Tonkin Gulf: Round II," *Nation*, October 5, 1964, p. 177; " 'Yep, We Were There,' " *Time*, October 9, 1964, p. 28; Jack Raymond, "M'Namara Warns on A-Bomb Spread," *New York Times*, October 7, 1964, p. 1.

19. "News Curb Considered," *New York Times*, March 13, 1965, p. 3; "Restrictions Are Imposed on Press at Danang Base," *New York Times*, March 17, 1965, p. 3; "Newsmen Report U.S. Imposes Curbs on Coverage in Vietnam," *New York Times*, March 18, 1965, p. 4; "News Restrictions Disavowed By U.S.," *New York Times*, March 19, 1967, p. 3.

20. "Newsmen Report"; "Restrictions Are Imposed"; Jack Langguth, "U.S. Easing Curbs on Vietnam News," *New York Times*, March 28, 1965, p. 3; "Curbs on Newsmen Eased at U.S. Base," *New York Times*, April 24, 1965, p. 15; "U.S. Reporters in Danang Cautioned on New Curbs," *New York Times*, April 27, 1965, p. 25; Emerson Chapin, "Newsmen Assail Danang Facilities," *New York Times*, May 2, 1965, p. 8.

21. Herring, *America's Longest War,* pp. 150–51; "Memorandum for Correspondents"; Charles Mohr, "The Changing War," *New York Times,* October 29, 1965, p. 2; Charles Mohr, "War and Misinformation," *New York Times,* November 26, 1965, p. 2; Hanson Baldwin, "The Information War in Saigon," *Reporter,* February 24, 1966, p. 30; transcript of "Warfront/'68," *NET Journal,* January 8, 1968, p. 5; Wheeler to Westmoreland, December 21, 1966, Westmoreland Papers, box 26; Wheeler to Westmoreland, March 4, 1967, Westmoreland Papers, box 20; Westmoreland to Wheeler, March 10, 1967, Westmoreland Papers, box 20; Wheeler to Westmoreland, March 11, 1967, Westmoreland Papers, box 20; Abrams to Westmoreland, August 20, 1967, Westmoreland Papers, box 20; Carver to Goulding, October 13, 1967, Westmoreland Papers, box 16; Sidle to Henkin, n.d., Westmoreland Papers, box 16; Rusk to Bunker, November 27, 1967, Westmoreland Papers, box 3; Westmoreland to Sharp, December 4, 1967, Westmoreland Papers, box 20.

22. "M'Namara, Lodge Arrive in Vietnam," *New York Times,* July 16, 1965, p. 1; "Memorandum for Correspondents"; James Reston, "The Casualty Controversy," *New York Times,* November 26, 1965, p. 36; "U.S. Toll Figures Held Misleading," *New York Times,* December 8, 1965, p. 15; "Casualty Figures," *Newsweek,* March 20, 1967, p. 41.

23. Sieverts to Greenfield, April 30, 1965, James Thomson Papers, box 25, John F. Kennedy Presidential Library.

24. "The Press: Room for Improvement," p. 76; David C. Hallin, *The "Uncensored War": The Media and Vietnam* (Berkeley: University of California Press, 1989), pp. 3–12; Clarence R. Wyatt, " 'Truth from the Snares of Crisis': The American Press and the Vietnam War," unpublished M.A. thesis, University of Kentucky, 1984, pp. 93–98.

25. "Crud, Fret, and Jeers," *Time,* June 10, 1966, p. 53.

CHAPTER 9: "Buddha Will Understand"

1. Don Oberdorfer, *Tet!* (New York: Da Capo Press, 1984), pp. 161–71; Peter Braestrup, *Big Story* (Boulder, Co.: Westview Press, 1977) pp. 347–48; Shana Alexander, "What Is the Truth of the Picture?," *Life,* March 1, 1968, pp. 18–19; photographs, *New York Times,* February 2, 1968, pp. 1, 12.

2. Braestrup, p. 347; Oberdorfer, *Tet!,* pp. 166–70; Alexander, "What Is the Truth," p. 18.

3. Stanley Karnow, *Vietnam: A History* (New York: Viking, 1983), p. 523; "Hanoi Attack," *Newsweek,* February 12, 1968, p. 23; "The General's Gamble," *Time,* February 9, 1968, pp. 22–24; Oberdorfer, *Tet!,* p. xii; George C. Herring, *American's Longest War: 1950–1975,* 2nd ed. (New York: Alfred A. Knopf, 1986), p. 187; Alexander, 'What Is the Truth," p. 18.

4. William C. Westmoreland, *A Soldier Reports* (New York: Dell, 1980), pp. 553–58; Robert S. Elegant, "How to Lose a War," *Encounter,* August 1981, pp. 73–90.

5. Oberdorfer, *Tet!,* p. 158; "More Than a Diversion," *New York Times,*

February 2, 1968, p. 34; "More of the Same Won't Do," *Newsweek*, March 18, 1968, p. 25; "A Showdown In Vietnam?," *U.S. News and World Report*, February 19, 1968, p. 35.

6. Doris Kearns, *Lyndon Johnson and the American Dream*, (New York: Harper and Row, 1976), p. 50.

7. Kathleen J. Turner, *Lyndon Johnson's Dual War: Vietnam and the Press* (Chicago: University of Chicago Press, 1985), p. 46; "Mismanaging the News," *Saturday Evening Post*, March 7, 1964, p. 80.

8. Turner, *Lyndon Johnson's Dual War*, pp. 62–67; James Deakin, "I've Got a Secret," *New Republic*, January 30, 1965, p. 13; Arthur Krock, "The President as News Source," *New York Times*, April 4, 1966, sec. IV, p. 11; "Johnson and the Press—What the Grumbling Is About," *U.S. News and World Report*, March 22, 1965, p. 49; Richard B. Stolley, "The Widening No Man's Land: President vs. The Press," *Life*, May 7, 1965, p. 34; James Reston, "Hocus-Pocus at the White House," *New York Times*, January 7, 1966, p. 28; "What's Happened to the LBJ Image?," *U.S. News and World Report*, January 17, 1966, p. 39; "News Manipulation by U.S. Is Charged," *New York Times*, September 28, 1966, p. 14; "Newsmen Ascribe an Air of Secrecy to Administration," *New York Times*, November 1, 1966, p. 25; James Deakin, "Deeper and Deeper into the Credibility Gap," *New Republic*, January 14, 1967, p. 10.

9. Kearns, *Lyndon Johnson and the American Dream*, 166, 251–53; Turner, *Lyndon Johnson's Dual War*, p. 72. Herring, *America's Longest War*, pp. 320–21; Larry D. Berman, *Planning a Tragedy* (New York: W. W. Norton, 1982), pp. 56–58.

10. Turner, *Lyndon Johnson's Dual War*, pp. 4–6; Jorden to Cooper, August 28, 1965, James Thomson Papers, box 21; Redmon to Moyers, December 27, 1965, Moyers Office Files, box 11, LBJ Library; Moyers to LBJ, May 3, 1966, Moyers Office Files, box 12; Redmon to Moyers, June 9, 1966, Moyers Office Files; Redmon to Moyers, September 27, 1966, Moyers Office Files, box 12; Donnelley to Christian, May 5, 1967, Christian Office Files, box 2; Katzenbach to LBJ, October 2, 1967, Johnson Papers, NSF, box 96; "The Viet Beat," *Newsweek*, September 7, 1964; "Inventory: Department of State's Public Affairs Activities on Viet-Nam," August 13, 1965, Johnson Papers, NSF, boxes 196–97.

11. Nathan to Komer, April 5, 1967, Christian Office Files, box 2, LBJ Library; Moose to Rostow, November 23, 1967, Johnson Papers, NSF, box 99; Ricci to Ricci to Carter, n.d., Moyers Office Files, box 11; "Inventory: Department of State's Public Affairs Activities on Viet-Nam," p. 2; "U.S. Will Send Out More Aides to Talk on Vietnam Policy," *New York Times*, April 24, 1965, p. 2; Donald Janson, "U.S. 'Truth Team' Debates in Iowa," *New York Times*, May 6, 1965, p. 13; Donald Janson, "Campus Tour Encourages Vietnam 'Truth' Team," *New York Times*, May 8, 1965, p. 4.

12. "Memorandum for the Record," August 4, 1965, Johnson Papers, NSF, boxes 196–97; "Financial Support to the American Friends of Vietnam," September 10, 1965, Johnson Papers, NSF, box 22; "August 3 Dinner

Meeting on the Information Problem," August 4, 1965, Johnson Papers, NSF, boxes 196–97.

13. C. P. Trussell, "G.O.P. Says Role of U.S. in War Is Concealed by Administration," *New York Times*, April 22, 1964, p. 1; Charles Mohr, "Goldwater Asks Vietnam Report," *New York Times*, August 30, 1964, p. 1; Charles Mohr, "Initial Campaign Buoys Goldwater," *New York Times*, September 13, 1964, p. 65; Charles Mohr, "Goldwater Scores McNamara on Vietnam War," *New York Times*, October 1, 1964, p. 24; Moyers to LBJ, October 3, 1964, Moyers Office Files, box 10.

14. Herring, *America's Longest War*, p. 133.

15. Ibid., pp. 139–43; Kearns, *Lyndon Johnson and the American Dream*, pp. 293–95; Turner, *Lyndon Johnson's Dual War*, p. 149.

16. Kearns, *Lyndon Johnson and the American Dream*, p. 282; "Foreign Policy: LBJ's Test," *Newsweek*, February 10, 1964, p. 19. See also James Reston, "A Mystifying Clarification from McNamara," *New York Times*, January 29, 1964, p. 32; James Reston, "Blabbermouth Approach to Vietnam." *New York Times*, March 1, 1964, sec. IV, p. 8.

17. "What Price Vietnam?" *New York Times*, February 10, 1965, p. 4; "Opinion: At Home and Abroad," *New York Times*, March 14, 1965, sec. IV, p. 11; Russell Baker, "Befuddled in Asia," *New York Times*, March 2, 1965, p. 34.

18. "Information for What?" *New York Times*, April 30, 1965, p. 34; "Opinion: At Home and Abroad," *New York Times*, June 20, 1965, section IV, p. 11; "Vietnam: The Problem of Candor," *Newsweek*, January 24, 1966, p. 24.

19. E. W. Kenworthy, "Fulbright Plans Hearing on U.S. Policy in Thailand," *New York Times*, September 1, 1966, p. 1; " 'Managed News' from Vietnam? Here's What the Pentagon Says," *U.S. News and World Report*, September 12, 1966, p. 104; "Editors Criticize Johnson News Policy but Back War Decisions," *New York Times*, April 21, 1967, p. 22; "Candor, Credibility, Confidence," *Nation*, December 6, 1966, p. 424.

20. "Information for What?," *New York Times*, April 30, 1965, p. 34; "Opinion: At Home and Abroad," *New York Times*, June 20, 1965, sec. IV, p. 11; "Vietnam: The Problem of Candor," *Newsweek*, January 24, 1966, p. 24; E. W. Kenworthy, "Fulbright Plans Hearing on U.S. Policy in Thailand," *New York Times*, September 1, 1966, p. 1; " 'Managed News' from Vietnam? Here's What The Pentagon Says," *U.S. News and World Report*, September 12, 1966, p. 104; "Editors Criticize Johnson News Policy but Back War Decisions," *New York Times*, April 21, 1967, p. 22.

21. "Candor, Credibility, Confidence," *Nation*, December 6, 1965, p. 424.

22. "Significant Rumblings," *Newsweek*, January 18, 1966, p. 34.

23. Redmon to Moyers, June 9, 1966, Moyers Office Files, box 12; Moyers to LBJ, June 9, 1966, Moyers Office Files, box 12.

24. Moyers to LBJ, September 13, 1966, Moyers Office Files, box 12; Sharp to Wheeler, December 24, 1966, Westmoreland Papers, box 26.

25. Wheeler to Sharp, February 17, 1967, Westmoreland Papers, box 20; Wheeler to Sharp, March 6, 1967, Westmoreland Papers, box 20; "Text of Westmoreland's Address at A.P. Meeting and of His Replies to Questions," *New York Times,* April 25, 1967, p. 14; "Transcript of Westmoreland Speech," *New York Times,* April 29, 1967, p. 10; William M. Hammond, *Public Affairs: The Military and the Media, 1962–1968* (Washington, D.C.: Center for Military History, 1988), pp. 287–90.

26. "Editors Criticize Johnson News Policy"; "The Truth About War in Vietnam," *U.S. News and World Report,* July 31, 1967, p. 40; "A Nation at Odds," *Newsweek,* July 10, 1967, p. 16.

27. David Halberstam, *The Powers That Be* (New York: Alfred A. Knopf, 1979), pp. 507–10.

28. Ibid., pp. 475–84; Oberdorfer, *Tet!,* pp. 86–92; Hedley Donovan, "Vietnam: Slow, Tough, but Coming Along," *Life,* June 2, 1967, p. 68; "Thunder from a Distant Hill," *Time,* October 6, 1967, p. 26.

29. Herring, *America's Longest War,* p. 188.

30. Kaplan to Rostow, October 9, 1967, Johnson Papers, NSF, box 99.

31. Locke to LBJ, "Measurements of Progress in South Vietnam," October 7, 1967, Johnson Papers, NSF, box 99; Zorthian to Hays, December 12, 1967, Johnson Papers, NSF, box 11; Moose to Rostow, November 27, 1967, Johnson Papers, NSF, box 99; Lodge to Rostow, October 18, 1967, Johnson Papers, NSF, box 99; Lodge to Rostow, October 10, 1967, Johnson Papers, NSF, box 99; Jorden to Rostow, October 12, 1967, Johnson Papers, NSF, box 99; Rostow to LBJ, October 9, 1967, Johnson Papers, NSF, box 99; Moose to Rostow, December 11, 1967, Johnson Papers, NSF, box 100; Rostow to LBJ, January 16, 1968, Johnson Papers, NSF, box 100; Wright to Rostow, January 22, 1968, Johnson Papers, NSF, box 100; Westmoreland to Palmer et al., November 9, 1967, Westmoreland Papers, box 3; Habib to Kaplan, September 26, 1967, Johnson Papers, NSF, box 99; Wheeler to Sharp, November 9, 1967, Westmoreland Papers, box 20; Herring, *America's Longest War,* p. 182.

32. Hammond, *Military and the Media,* p. 287; Westmoreland to Wheeler, Johnson, and Sharp, August 2, 1967, Westmoreland Papers, box 20; R. W. Apple, "Vietnam: The Signs of Stalemate," *New York Times,* August 7, 1967, p. 1; Wheeler to Westmoreland, August 8, 1967, Westmoreland Papers, box 20; Westmoreland to Wheeler and Sharp, August 12, 1967, Westmoreland Papers, box 20.

33. Braestrup, pp. 49–54; Herring, *America's Longest War,* p. 183; Hedrick Smith, "Westmoreland Says rank of Vietcong Thin Steadily," *New York Times,* November 22, 1967, p. 1; Hammond, *Military and the Media,* pp. 333–38; Karnow, *Vietnam,* pp. 512–14; Oberdorfer, *Tet!,* pp. 98–106; "Vietnam: War Tide Turning to U.S.," *U.S. News and World Report,* November 27, 1967, p. 50; Howard Handleman, "The Coin Has Flipped Over to Our Side," *U.S. News and World Report,* November 27, 1967, p. 52.

34. Hedrick Smith, "Optimists vs. Skeptics," *New York Times,* Novem-

ber 24, 1967, p. 2; James Reston, "Communique from the Home Front," *New York Times*, November 17, 1967, p. 46; David Halberstam, "Return to Vietnam," *Harper's*, December 1967, p. 47; "Whose Benefit? Whose Doubt?," *Newsweek*, November 17, 1967, p. 68.

35. "Top of the Week," *Newsweek*, January 18, 1965, p. 7.

36. Oberdorfer, *Tet!*, p. 70; Herring, *America's Longest War*, pp. 188–89; Robert Pisor, *The End of the Line: The Siege of Khe Sanh* (New York: W. W. Norton, 1982), pp. 77–80; Karnow, *Vietnam*, p. 542.

37. Oberdorfer, *Tet!*, pp. 124, 139–56; Herring, *America's Longest War*, p. 190; Pisor, *End of the Line*, pp. 242–46.

38. Quoted in Herring, *America's Longest War*, p. 187.

39. Karnow, *Vietnam*, pp. 498–502, 545–46; George Christian, "The Night Lyndon Quit," *Texas Monthly*, April 1988, p. 109.

40. Braestrup, *Big Story*, pp. 505–6.

41. Ibid., p. 32.

42. Ibid., pp. 92, 536; Oberdorfer, *Tet!*, p. 168.

43. Braestrup, *Big Story*, p. 75; Oberdorfer, *Tet!*, pp. 2–33.

44. Braestrup, *Big Story*, pp. 77–177; Oberdorfer, *Tet!*, pp. 30–31.

45. Oberdorfer, *Tet!*, pp. 5–6, 180; Braestrup, *Big Story*, pp. 241, 337–38.

46. Braestrup, *Big Story*, p. 118.

47. Ibid., pp. 218–20.

48. Ibid., pp. 249–53; "Americal Division Daily Summary," March 17, 1968, RG 338, Records of United States Army Commands, 1942–, United States Army Vietnam, 23rd Infantry Division, 1967–71, Public Information Office.

49. Wheeler to Westmoreland and Sharp, January 31, 1968, Westmoreland Papers, box 3; Braestrup, *Big Story*, p. 278.

50. Sharp to Westmoreland, February 25, 1968, Westmoreland Papers, box 23; "Memorandum for the Record: Denial of Intelligence Information to the Enemy," February 26, 1968, Johnson Papers, NSF, box 98; "U.S. Tightens Curbs on Battle Reports That Would Aid Foe," *New York Times*, February 27, 1968, p. 2; Westmoreland to Clifford, March 4, 1968, Johnson Papers, NSF, box 98.

51. Hammond, *Military and the Media*, p. 367; "American Forces Leaving Khe Sanh For Nearby Posts," *New York Times*, June 27, 1968, p. 1; Bernard Weinraub, "War Correspondent Is Barred 6 Months by U.S. Command," July 28, 1968, p. 10; "U.S. Eases Curb on War Reporter," *New York Times*, July 31, 1968, p. 3.

52. "More Than a Diversion," p. 34; "Double Trouble," *Time*, February 9, 1968, p. 15; "Needed: The Courage to Face the Truth," *Newsweek*, March 18, 1968, p. 39; "Misled, in Every Sense," *New Republic*, February 17, 1968, p. 7; "Shifting on the War," *Newsweek*, March 25, 1968, p. 54; "Escalating Opinion," *Newsweek*, March 25, 1968, p. 97; "Cronkite Takes a Stand," *Newsweek*, March 11, 1968, p. 108.

53. "Shifting on the War," p. 54.

CHAPTER 10: No More Bodies

1. Transcript, "CBS Evening News with Walter Cronkite," July 7, 1970, Shaplen Papers, box 1.

2. Stanley Karnow, *Vietnam: A History* (New York: Viking, 1983), pp. 581–83; George C. Herring, *America's Longest War: 1950–1975*, 2nd ed. (New York: Alfred A. Knopf, 1986), pp. 222–25.

3. Herring, *America's Longest War*, pp. 222–23.

4. Karnow, *Vietnam*, p. 502; Herring, *America's Longest War*, p. 229.

5. "Betting on 'the Silent Majority,' " *Newsweek*, November 17, 1969, p. 35; Herring, *America's Longest War*, p. 229; Karnow, *Vietnam*, p. 600.

6. "Even Split Found in Views on War," *New York Times*, March 15, 1970; Herring, *America's Longest War*, p. 239.

7. Gladwin Hill, "Environment May Eclipse Vietnam as College Issue," *New York Times*, November 30, 1969, p. 1; "Nixon's Plea to End the Killing," *Newsweek*, October 19, 1970, p. 15.

8. "Assessing the Laos Invasion," *Newsweek*, April 5, 1971, p. 25.

9. Stanley Cloud, "The Anguish of a Yankee Gentleman," *Time*, September 13, 1971, p. 12.

10. "Viet Nam: The New, Underground Optimism," *Time*, December 12, 1969, p. 14.

11. "The Proxy War," *Newsweek*, January 25, 1971, p. 49; Terence Smith, "U.S. Vietnam Policy: An Assessment," *New York Times*, June 3, 1970, p. 1; Maynard Parker, "Vietnamization Is Not Peace," *Newsweek*, November 23, 1970, p. 63.

12. Iver Peterson, "Saigon's Armed Forces Improving, but Big Test Is Still Ahead," *New York Times*, January 26, 1971, p. 2.

13. Herring, *America's Longest War*, pp. 240–41.

14. Ibid.

15. "The Last Big Push—or a Wider War?," *Newsweek*, February 15, 1971, p. 21; "Indochina: Tough Days on the Trail," *Time*, March 8, 1971, p. 20.

16. "Assessing the Laos Invasion," p. 25; "What It Means for Vietnamization," *Time*, April 5, 1971, p. 26; Iver Peterson, "Americans in South Vietnam Attribute the Setback in Laos to Faulty Planning and Intelligence," *New York Times*, March 30, 1971, p. 15.

17. "What It Means for Vietnamization," p. 26; "Vietnamization: The Reality and the Myth," *Newsweek*, August 2, 1971, p. 39.

18. "The War That Won't Go Away," *Newsweek*, April 17, 1972, p. 16; "Nixon at the Brink over Viet Nam," *Time*, May 22, 1972, p. 11.

19. "Meanwhile, in Viet Nam," *Time*, November 13, 1972, p. 19.

20. "Finally Their Own Way Out?," *Newsweek*, February 9, 1970, p. 38; "No Decent Exit from Viet Nam for the U.S.," *Time*, September 13, 1971, p. 11.

21. Fox Butterfield, "Saigon Restricts Its Press on War," *New York Times,* April 4, 1972, p. 9; Malcolm W. Browne, "14 Saigon Papers Close, Muffling Opposition Press," *New York Times,* September 16, 1972, p. 3; Fox Butterfield, "Small Saigon Newspaper Sole Key to Thieu Views," *New York Times,* January 16, 1973, p. 3; Herring, *America's Longest War,* pp. 214, 251–53.

22. "U.S. Command Finds Nothing for a Report," *New York Times,* January 10, 1971, p. 2.

23. "Newsweek and Reuters Given Warning by Saigon on Reports," *New York Times,* June 24, 1969, p. 5; Tad Szulc, "Saigon Curbs on U.S. Press Disturbs Pentagon," *New York Times,* February 1, 1970, p. 3.

24. "Briefings: The Ritual of Noncommunication," *Time,* October 10, 1969, p. 42; Craig R. Whitney, "News Policy for Vietnam War: As Little as Possible," *New York Times,* December 23, 1971, p. 5.

25. "Saigon 'Newsmen' Were U.S. Agents," *New York Times,* January 29, 1970, p. 12; "4 U.S. Agents Posed as Saigon Newsmen," *New York Times,* January 30, 1970, p. 7; "U.S. Denies Agents Posed as Newsmen to Spy on the Press," *New York Times,* January 31, 1970, p. 5; "The Unreal MACOI," *Time,* February 9, 1970, p. 52; "Cover Story," *Newsweek,* February 9, 1970, p. 63.

26. "U.S. Barring Newsmen from Cambodian Battle," *New York Times,* April 30, 1970, p. 4.

27. "Beyond the Checkpoint," *Newsweek,* June 15, 1970, p. 56; Robert S. Anson, "Between the Lines: Report from Phnom-Penh," *Time,* May 4, 1970, p. 79.

28. Henry Kamm, "Newsmen Lead Perilous Existence in Cambodia," *New York Times,* June 7, 1970, sec. IV, p. 3.

29. Arthur Higbee, UPI cable, December 17, 1971, Shaplen Papers, box 30.

30. "U.S. Silent on Speculation About an Invasion of Laos," *New York Times,* January 31, 1971, p. 1; Ralph Blumenthal, "Security Termed Blackout Reason," *New York Times,* February 2, 1971, p. 9.

31. Blumenthal, "Security Termed"; "Japanese Report Invasion On," *New York Times,* February 3, 1971, p. 14; Ralph Blumenthal, "Embargo Still On; Newsmen Told to Keep Even Its Existence Secret," *New York Times,* February 5, 1971, p. 14.

32. Craig R. Whitney, "Big Gap at the Briefings on Laos," *New York Times,* February 13, 1971, p. 4; "4 Photographers Missing As Copter Is Downed in Laos," *New York Times,* February 11, 1971, p. 1; "U.S. Copters Will Carry Correspondents to Laos," *New York Times,* February 25, 1972, p. 3; Craig R. Whitney, "Newsmen Going into Laos by Helicopter Will Be Without U.S. Military Escort," *New York Times,* February 25, 1971, p. 11; Gloria Emerson, "Saigon's Copter Pilots Are Criticized," *New York Times,* March 5, 1971, p. 1.

33. Whitney, "Big Gap."

34. Ralph Blumenthal, "Casualty Reports by U.S. Again Raise Skepti-

cism," *New York Times,* February 16, 1971, p. 8; Gloria Emerson, "A 'Mist' Hangs over the Laotian Campaign," *New York Times,* February 21, 1971, sec. IV, p. 1; "Pipeline an Old One, Pentagon Discloses," *New York Times,* March 4, 1971, p. 3; "Again, the Credibility Gap?," *Time,* April 5, 1971, p. 13.

35. Craig R. Whitney, "The High Price of Trying to Tell What's Happening," *New York Times,* February 28, 1971, sec. IV, p. 1.
36. "Kennedy Assails Vietnamization," *New York Times,* February 18, 1971, p. 13; "Again, the Credibility Gap?," p. 13.
37. Whitney, "News Policy for Vietnam War," p. 5; "Reports, Then Denial, Befog Vietnam News," *New York Times,* January 30, 1972, p. 5.
38. "Saigon Will Tighten Its Rules on Press Coverage of War," *New York Times,* July 22, 1971, p. 5; "Rules on War News Tightened by Saigon," *New York Times,* December 1, 1971, p. 9.
39. "Saigon Is Imposing Tough Restraints on News Coverage," *New York Times,* April 16, 1972, p. 2; Sydney Schanberg, "Foreign Newsmen Warned in Saigon," *New York Times,* June 22, 1972, p. 8; Sydney Schanberg, "South Vietnamese Launch Push to Retake Quangtri," *New York Times,* June 29, 1972, p. 1; Joseph B. Treaster, "Saigon Reports 3 Hour Battle Northeast of Quangtri," *New York Times,* July 15, 1972, p. 6.
40. Malcolm W. Browne, "Saigon Officers' Hostility to Foreign Newsmen at Peak," *New York Times,* July 13, 1972, p. 2; "Viet Nam: New Dangers Covering an Old Story," *Time,* August 14, 1972, p. 66.
41. Schanberg, "Foreign Newsmen Warned"; "Penalties Are Stiff in Thieu's Decree," *New York Times,* July 18, 1972, p. 4.
42. "Viet Nam: New Dangers."
43. "The My Lai Massacre," *Time,* November 28, 1969, p. 15; Seymour Hersh, *My Lai 4: A Report on the Massacre and Its Aftermath* (New York: Random House, 1970), pp. 102–50; William R. Peers, *The My Lai Inquiry* (New York: W. W. Norton, 1979), pp. 165–209; William Beecher, "Army Inquiry Charges 14 Officers in Suppression of Songmy Facts; West Point's Head Accused, Quits," *New York Times,* March 18, 1970, p. 1.
44. William Wilson, "I Had Prayed to God That This Thing Was Fiction . . . ," *American Heritage,* February 1990, p. 46; Hersh, *My Lai 4,* pp. 102–50; Peers, *My Lai Inquiry,* pp. 165–209.
45. "Hip-Pocket AP," *Newsweek,* December 8, 1969, p. 83; Rosenthal to Sulzberger, December 3, 1969, Daniel Papers, New York Times Archives.
46. William Shawcross, *Sideshow: Kissinger, Nixon, and the Destruction of Cambodia* (New York: Simon and Schuster, 1979), pp. 26–35; Herring, *America's Longest War,* p. 225; Karnow, *Vietnam,* pp. 591–92; Henry A. Kissinger, *White House Years* (Boston: Little Brown, 1979), pp. 242–54.
47. Seymour M. Hersh, "General Bombed in North Before President's Order," *New York Times,* June 11, 1972, p. 1; "The Private War of General Lavelle," *Newsweek,* June 26, 1972, p. 17; "Lavelle's Private War," *Time,* June 26, 1972, p. 14; "The Lavelle Case," *Time,* September 25, 1972, p. 20; Craig R. Whitney, "Behind the Lavelle Incident, Weak Links in the Chain of the Command," *New York Times,* June 14, 1972, p. 21.

48. Harrison E. Salisbury, *Without Fear or Favor* (New York: Ballantine, 1980), pp. 60–63; "Man with the Monkey Wrench," *Time,* June 28, 1972, p. 18; "The Suspect: A Hawk Who Turned Dove," *Newsweek,* June 28, 1971, p. 16.

49. Salisbury, *Without Fear,* pp. 331–34; "A Great Sense of Elation," *Newsweek,* June 28, 1971, p. 25.

50. Shawcross, *Sideshow,* pp. 34–35, 157–59.

51. Salisbury, *Without Fear,* pp. 334–35; "Victory for the Press," *Newsweek,* July 12, 1971, p. 16; "The Nuances of a Great Case," *Newsweek,* July 17, 1971, p. 18.

52. Salisbury, p. 339–43.

53. "A Great Sense of Elation."

54. "Press List," February 1969, Shaplen Papers, box 9; "Press List of MACV Accredited News Correspondents, November 1972," Shaplen Papers, box 9; "Press List of Accredited Correspondents, September 1, 1973," Shaplen Papers, box 9.

55. "Government Delegates Balk at Saigon Procedure and Stay on Plane for Day," *New York Times,* January 29, 1973, p. 3; "Saigon Bars Newsmen from Tan Son Nhut Base," *New York Times,* February 2, 1973, p. 10; "Newsmen Detained at Saigon Air Base," *New York Times,* February 9, 1973, p. 11; Fox Butterfield, "Vietcong Guests Blocked in Saigon," *New York Times,* February 15, 1973; p. 13; "Saigon Tells Newsmen M.P.'s Shoot Intruders," *New York Times,* February 18, 1973, p. 2.

56. "South Vietnam to Expel an American Newsman," *New York Times,* February 25, 1973, p. 13; Sylvan Fox, "Saigon Expelling a U.P.I. Newsman," *New York Times,* March 8, 1973, p. 13; "Detained Newsmen Released," *New York Times,* May 1, 1973, p. 9; "Saigon Detains 4 from A.B.C., Holds film of Vietcong," *New York Times,* January 1, 1974, p. 4; "Times Bureau Chief Is Freed by Saigon," *New York Times,* January 30, 1974, p. 6; "Passport of Wife of Newsman Lifted After Trip to Hanoi," *New York Times,* July 8, 1973, p. 13.

57. David K. Shipler, "Saigon Police Attack During a Censorship Protest," *New York Times,* October 11, 1974, p. 4; James M. Markham, "Saigon Police Kill French Newsman," *New York Times,* March 16, 1975, p. 1; David Butler, *The Fall of Saigon: Scenes from the Sudden End of a Long War* (New York: Simon and Schuster, 1985), pp. 435–37.

58. "No Truce in Saigon," *Time,* March 25, 1974, p. 52; "U.S. Envoy in Saigon Charges Times Article Was Inaccurate," *New York Times,* March 9, 1974, p. 3.

59. "Reunion in Retreat," *Time,* March 31, 1975, p. 63; "Saigon Curbs Reports on Troop Movements," *New York Times,* March 23, 1975, p. 3.

60. "They Stayed," *Time,* May 13, 1975, p. 49.

61. Butler, *Fall of Saigon,* pp. 336–43, 402–3.

62. "They Stayed," p. 49.

# Bibliography

SPECIAL COLLECTIONS

Joseph C. Alsop Papers, Library of Congress
Hanson W. Baldwin Papers, Yale University Library
Turner Catledge Papers, New York Times Archives
Richard Critchfield Papers, Mass Communications History Collection, Wisconsin State Historical Society
Clifton Daniel Papers, New York Times Archives
Richard Dudman Papers, Library of Congress
Foreign Desk Papers, New York Times Archives
Gilbert Harrison Papers, Library of Congress
Roger Hilsman Papers, John F. Kennedy Presidential Library
Lyndon B. Johnson Papers, Lyndon B. Johnson Presidential Library
John F. Kennedy Papers, John F. Kennedy Presidential Library
Records of the Military Assistance Command–Vietnam Office of Information, Washington National Records Center.
Oral History Collection, Lyndon B. Johnson Library
Oral History Collection, U.S. Army Center for Military History
Robert Shaplen Papers, Mass Communications History Collection, Wisconsin State Historical Society
James Thomson Papers, John F. Kennedy Presidential Library
Records of the United States Army Commands, 1942–, United States Army Vietnam, 23rd Infantry Division, 1967–71, Public Information Office, Washington National Records Center
William C. Westmoreland Papers, Washington National Records Center

BOOKS, DISSERTATIONS, AND THESES

Abel, Elie. *The Missile Crisis*. Philadelphia: J. B. Lippincott, 1966.

Adler, Ruth, ed. *The Working Press: Special to the New York Times*. New York: Putnam's, 1966.

*Alleged Assassination Plots Involving Foreign Leaders*. Interim report of the Senate Select Committee to Study Governmental Operations with Respect to Intelligence Activities, Senate Report 94-465, 94th Cong., 1st sess., November 20, 1975 (Washington, D.C.: Government Printing Office, 1975).

Ambrose, Stephen E. *Eisenhower*, vol. II: *The President*. New York: Simon and Schuster, 1984.

Aronson, James. *Deadline for the Media*. Indianapolis: Bobbs-Merrill, 1972.

Ashmore, Harry S. and William C. Baggs. *Mission to Hanoi*. New York: G. P. Putnam's Sons, 1968.

Barnouw, Eric. *Tube of Plenty: The Evolution of American Television*. New York: Oxford University Press, 1975.

Beech, Keyes. *Not Without the Americans*. Garden City, N.Y.: Doubleday, 1971.

Berman, Larry D. *Planning a Tragedy*. New York: W. W. Norton, 1982.

Beschloss, Michael R. *Mayday: Eisenhower, Khrushchev, and the U-2 Affair*. New York: Harper and Row, 1986.

Braestrup, Peter. *Big Story*. Boulder, Co.: Westview Press, 1977.

———. *Vietnam as History*. Washington, D.C.: University Press of America, 1984.

———. *Battle Line: Report of the Twentieth Century Fund Task Force on the Military and the Media*. New York: Priority Press, 1985.

Brelis, Dean. *The Face of South Vietnam*. Boston: Houghton Mifflin, 1968.

Browne, Malcolm. *The New Face of War*. Indianapolis: Bobbs-Merrill, 1965.

Butler, David. *The Fall of Saigon: Scenes from the Sudden End of a Long War*. New York: Simon and Schuster, 1985.

Cameron, Allan V., ed. *Viet-Nam Crisis: A Documentary History*, vol. I: *1940–1956*. Ithaca, N.Y.: Cornell University Press, 1971.

Cormier, Frank. *LBJ: The Way He Was*. Garden City, NY: Doubleday, 1977.

Dudman, Richard. *Forty Days with the Enemy*. New York: Liveright, 1971.

Ehrlichman, John. *Witness to Power*. New York: Simon and Schuster, 1982.

Eisenhower, Dwight, D. *Waging Peace, 1956–1961*. Garden City, N.Y.: Doubleday, 1965.

Emerson, Gloria. *Winners and Losers: Battles, Retreats, Gains, Losses and Ruins from the Vietnam War*. New York: Harcourt Brace Jovanovich, 1976.

Emery, Edwin. *The Press and America*. Englewood Cliffs, NJ: Prentice-Hall, 1978.

Epstein, Edward J. *News from Nowhere: Television and the Times.* New York: Random House, 1973.

Fairlie, Henry. *The Kennedy Promise: The Politics of Expectation.* Garden City, N.Y.: Doubleday, 1977.

Faulkner, Francis. "Bao Chi: The American News Media in Vietnam, 1960–1975." Unpublished Ph.D. dissertation, University of Massachusetts, 1981.

Fulbright, J. W. *The Pentagon Propaganda Machine.* New York: Liveright, 1970.

Gans, Herbert J. *Deciding What's News: A Study of CBS Evening News, NBC Nightly News, Newsweek, and Time.* New York: Pantheon, 1979.

Garthoff, Raymond L. *Reflections on the Cuban Missile Crisis.* Washington, D.C.: Brookings Institution, 1987.

Geyelin, Philip, and Cater, Douglass. *The American Media: Adequate or Not?* Washington, D.C.: American Enterprise Institute, 1970.

Goldman, Eric F. *The Tragedy of Lyndon B. Johnson.* New York: Alfred A. Knopf, 1969.

Goulden, Joseph. *Truth Is the First Casualty.* New York: Rand McNally, 1969.

Goulding, Phil. *Confirm or Deny: Informing the People on National Security.* New York: Harper and Row, 1970.

*Government Information Plans and Policies, Parts 1–4.* Report, House Foreign Operations and Government Information Subcommittee, 1963.

Halberstam, David. *The Making of a Quagmire.* New York: Harper and Row, 1965.

———. *The Best and the Brightest.* New York: Random House, 1972.

———. *The Powers That Be.* New York: Alfred A. Knopf, 1979.

Hallin, Daniel C. *The "Uncensored War": The Media and Vietnam.* Berkeley: University of California Press, 1989.

Hammond, William M. *Public Affairs: The Military and the Media, 1962–1968.* Washington, D.C.: Center for Military History, 1988.

Herr, Michael. *Dispatches.* New York: Avon, 1978.

Herring, George C. *America's Longest War: 1950–1975.* 2nd ed. New York: Alfred A. Knopf, 1986.

Hersh, Seymour. *My Lai 4: A Report on the Massacre and Its Aftermath.* New York: Random House, 1970.

———. *Cover Up.* New York: Random House, 1972.

Higgins, Marguerite. *Our Vietnam Nightmare.* New York: Harper and Row, 1965.

Hilsman, Roger. *To Move a Nation: The Politics of Foreign Policy in the Administration of John F. Kennedy.* Garden City, N.Y.: Doubleday, 1967.

Hohenberg, John. *Foreign Correspondents: The Great Reporters and Their Times.* New York: Columbia University Press, 1964.

Just, Ward. *To What End.* Boston: Houghton Mifflin, 1968.

Karnow, Stanley. *Vietnam: A History.* New York: Viking, 1983.

Kearns, Doris. *Lyndon Johnson and the American Dream*. New York: Harper and Row, 1976.

Keogh, James. *President Nixon and the Press*. New York: Funk and Wagnalls, 1972.

Kern, Montague; Levering, Patricia; and Levering, Ralph. *The Kennedy Crises: The Press, the Presidency and Foreign Policy*. Chapel Hill: University of North Carolina Press, 1983.

Kissinger, Henry A. *White House Years*. Boston: Little, Brown, 1979.

Klein, Herbert. *Making It Perfectly Clear*. Garden City, N.Y.: Doubleday, 1980.

Knightley, Phillip. *The First Casualty*. New York: Harcourt Brace Jovanovich, 1975.

MacDonald, J. Fred. *Television and the Red Menace: The Video Road to Vietnam*. New York: Praeger, 1985.

Mecklin, John. *Mission in Torment: An Intimate Account of the U.S. Role in Vietnam*. Garden City, N.Y.: Doubleday, 1965.

Minor, Dale. *The Information War*. New York: Hawthorn Books, 1970.

Minow, Newton. *Presidential Television*. New York: Basic Books, 1973.

Oberdorfer, Don. *Tet!* New York: Da Capo Press, 1980.

Paper, Lewis J. *The Promise and the Performance: The Leadership of John F. Kennedy*. New York: Crown, 1975.

Parmet, Herbert S. *Jack: The Struggles of John F. Kennedy*. New York: Dial, 1980.

————. *JFK: The Presidency of John F. Kennedy*. New York: Dial, 1983.

Peers, William R. *The My Lai Inquiry*. New York: W. W. Norton, 1979.

*The Pentagon Papers* (Senator Gravel Edition), Boston: Beacon Press, 1971. Vols. I–IV.

Pisor, Robert. *The End of the Line: The Siege of Khe Sanh*. New York: W. W. Norton, 1982.

Porter, William E. *Assault on the Media: The Nixon Years*. Ann Arbor: University of Michigan Press, 1976.

Pollak, Richard, ed. *Stop the Presses, I Want to Get Off*. New York: Delta Books, 1971.

Rust, William J. *Kennedy in Vietnam*. New York: Charles Scribners' Sons, 1985.

Salinger, Pierre. *With Kennedy*. Garden City, N.Y.: Doubleday, 1966.

Salisbury, Harrison. *Behind the Lines—Hanoi*. New York: New York Times Company, 1967.

————. *Without Fear or Favor*. New York: Ballantine, 1980.

————. *Vietnam Reappraisal: Lessons from a War*. New York: Harper and Row, 1984.

Schandler, Herbert Y. *The Unmaking of a President: Lyndon Johnson and Vietnam*. Princeton, N.J.: Princeton University Press, 1977.

Schlesinger, Arthur M., Jr. *A Thousand Days: John F. Kennedy in the White House*. Boston: Houghton Mifflin, 1965.

Shaplen, Robert. *The Lost Revolution*. New York: Harper and Row, 1965.

————. *The Road from War*. New York: Harper and Row, 1970.

Shawcross, William. *Sideshow: Kissinger, Nixon, and the Destruction of Cambodia*. New York: Simon and Schuster, 1979.

Sheehan, Neil. *A Bright Shining Lie: John Paul Vann and America in Vietnam*. New York: Random House, 1988.

Sidey, Hugh. *John F. Kennedy, President*. New York: Atheneum, 1964.

Sims, Robert B. *The Pentagon Reporters*. Washington, D.C.: National Defense University Press, 1983.

Sorensen, Theodore C. *Kennedy*. New York: Harper and Row, 1965.

Spector, Ronald H. *Advice and Support: The Early Years, 1941–1960*. Washington, D.C.: Center for Military History, 1983.

Stevenson, Charles A. *The End of Nowhere: American Policy Toward Laos Since 1954*. Boston: Beacon Press, 1973.

Talese, Gay. *The Kingdom and the Power*. New York: World Publishing Company, 1969.

Tebbel, John, and Watts, Sarah Miles. *The Press and the Presidency: From George Washington to Ronald Reagan*. New York: Oxford University Press, 1986.

Tregaskis, Richard. *Vietnam Diary*. New York: Holt, Rinehart and Winston, 1963.

Thompson, Kenneth, ed. *The Kennedy Presidency: Seventeen Intimate Perspectives of John F. Kennedy*. Lanham, Md.: University Press of America, 1985.

Truman, Harry S. *Memoirs*, vol. 2: *Years of Trial and Hope*. Garden City, N.Y.: Doubleday, 1956.

Turner, Kathleen J. *Lyndon Johnson's Dual War: Vietnam and the Press*. Chicago: University of Chicago Press, 1985.

Ungar, Sanford. *The Papers and the Papers*. New York: E. P. Dutton, 1972.

Walt, Lew. *Strange War, Strange Strategy*. New York: Award Books, 1970.

Westmoreland, William C. *A Soldier Reports*. New York: Dell, 1980.

White, Theodore H. *The Making of the President, 1960*. New York: Atheneum, 1961.

Wicker, Tom. *On Press*. New York: Viking, 1978.

Wyatt, Clarence R. " 'Truth from the Snares of Crisis': The American Press and the Vietnam War." Unpublished M.A. thesis, University of Kentucky, 1984.

Yergin, Daniel. *Shattered Peace: The Origin of the Cold War and the National Security State*. Boston: Houghton Mifflin, 1977.

ARTICLES

The book made extensive use of hundreds of periodical articles, primarily from *The New York Times*, the *Washington Post, Time, Newsweek,* and *U.S. News and World Report,* for the years 1955 through 1975. Please see notes after each chapter for specific references.

# Index